DINÉJÍ NA`NITIN

DINÉJÍ NA`NITIN

Navajo Traditional Teachings and History

Robert S. McPherson

UNIVERSITY PRESS OF COLORADO
Boulder

Published by the University Press of Colorado
5589 Arapahoe Avenue, Suite 206C
Boulder, Colorado 80303

The University Press of Colorado is a proud member of

The Association of American University Presses.

The University Press of Colorado is a cooperative publishing enterprise supported, in part, by Adams State University, Colorado State University, Fort Lewis College, Metropolitan State University of Denver, Regis University, University of Colorado, University of Northern Colorado, Utah State University, and Western State Colorado University.

Manufactured in the United States of America
Cover design by Charles Yanito (artist)

ISBN: 978-1-60732-216-0 (paper)
ISBN: 978-1-60732-217-7 (e-book)

Library of Congress Cataloging-in-Publication Data

McPherson, Robert S., 1947-
Dinéjí Na'nitin : Navajo traditional teachings and history / Robert S. McPherson.
p. cm.
Includes bibliographical references and index.
ISBN 978-1-60732-216-0 (hardcover : alk. paper) — ISBN 978-1-60732-217-7 (ebook)
1. Navajo Indians—History. 2. Navajo philosophy. 3. Navajo Indians—Social life and customs. I. Title.
E99.N3M33 2012
979.1004'9726—dc23

2012035285

To those elders who cared to share

CONTENTS

ACKNOWLEDGMENTS

No book is written in a vacuum, and this one is no exception—especially when one considers the large number of Navajo elders who have contributed their understanding to it. I have tried to listen carefully to their thoughts and express them in such a way that future generations can benefit from their knowledge. Their consistent concern that cultural beliefs be passed on has been the motivation for this work.

Along the way, I have been assisted by good friends whose influence should be recognized. Of the younger set there is Marilyn Holiday, Baxter Benally, Karen Toledo, Carla Phillips, Don Mose, Clayton Long, and John Fahey. Each of them has helped identify people, places, and ideas that are part of the story that unfolds here. Those who are older include John Holiday, Jim Dandy, and Harry Walters, all of whom are steeped in traditional lore and understanding. Both young and old have shared valuable insight on Navajo traditional teaching and history. In their company, I am comfortable that what is found between the covers of this book is both sensitive to cultural concerns and accurate in their portrayal. If there are errors of fact or interpretation, I accept full responsibility.

Two organizations deserve special recognition. The first is the Utah Humanities Council, whose unflinching support of examining diversity and providing financial assistance for projects over the years has made much of my work possible. I have never worked with a finer organization that knows how to get things done while thriftily providing necessary resources. The second, the Utah Historical Society, has published some of these chapters while encouraging research and opportunities for public presentation. It has also provided photographs of important people and places. I am grateful for the many good friends I have in this organization and the assistance they have provided. Others who have helped in various aspects of this work are the San Juan County Historical Commission, the Navajo Nation Museum, photographer Kay Shumway, acquisitions editor Michael Spooner, and the staff at the University Press of Colorado.

Finally, I wish to express my appreciation to family members who have provided "release time" to allow me to work on this project. Foremost is my wife, Betsy, who encourages and supports my traveling and writing at the expense of vacation time and Saturday afternoons. I hope this work brings as much pleasure to her and our children as it does to the people for whom it is written.

DINÉJÍ NA'NITIN

Introduction

Entering the Táchééh

As I completed this manuscript in mid-July 2011, two seemingly unrelated items to most people came to my attention. The first was the containment of Arizona's largest fire in the history of the state, recently burning in the White Mountains of the Bear Wallow Wilderness. The blaze eventually dipped into part of western New Mexico—scorching over 538,000 acres total, destroying seventy-two buildings, and at one point causing the evacuation of 10,000 people.[1] Started on May 29 by an abandoned campfire, the conflagration eventually required 1,700 firefighters to suppress the blaze, burning 841 square miles of rugged territory, primarily in eastern Arizona. By July 3, 95 percent of the fire was contained, with mop-up crews extinguishing remnants in isolated pockets. A related concern was the damage summer rains could bring as they washed over the charred areas.

The second occurrence was not nearly so dramatic. I received a copy of *Bitter Water: Diné Oral Histories of the Navajo-Hopi Land Dispute* compiled by Malcolm D. Benally.[2] The editor of the *Western Historical Quarterly* invited me to review this monograph, which I happily agreed to do. Once I opened the book, I encountered interviews with four Navajo matrons who had no desire to comply with the federal mandate that removed them from Hopi Partitioned Lands (HPL). After years of litigation that involved the best minds of both tribes as well as the federal government, the expenses to relocate Hopis and Navajos had mushroomed from the initial estimate of $30 million to today's $400 million.[3] Still, the Navajos living in the HPL area had no desire to move; in their minds

DOI: 10.7330/9781607322177.c00

the entire issue boiled down to Washington's insensitivity to traditional Navajo practices. The voices of four angry elders rang loud and clear.

In both the instance of the wildfire and the relocation, something more caught my attention. It was not the events but their interpretation. Looking first at the fire, one finds that although the flames never touched the Navajo Reservation, the *Navajo Times* featured its spread and eventual control on the front page for three weeks running. Of particular interest was the June 23 issue with its banner headline "Unnatural Disaster—Disasters Signal Imbalance in the Natural World." The two previous issues (June 9 and 16) discussed primarily the fire's physical spread, where crews were operating, and the logistical support necessary to contain it. A short section in the second issue entitled "Praying for Dził Ligai [White Mountain]" told how Apache prayers for their sacred mountain tempered the destruction and kept the fire away from important cultural sites.

In "Unnatural Disaster," it was the Navajos' turn to interpret the event. As the tribal newspaper, it not surprisingly expressed views far different than those filed by other press agencies. The thoughts of "traditional medicine people" opened the article, which then focused on the comments of "a traditional Navajo practitioner and faculty member at Diné College, Avery Denny." The article warned that Mother Nature was upset, and this was her way of making necessary corrections. Here, Mother Nature was not figurative but literal. Denny stated that the exploitation of resources and contemporary Navajo lifestyles were angering the orb and that the four sacred elements of fire, air, water, and earth controlled by holy people (Diyin Dine'é) were providing this and other lessons. Fires, tornados, tsunamis, earthquakes, droughts, blizzards, extreme temperatures—the list goes on—were physical manifestations of the spiritual sickness now pervading the earth and plaguing its people.

Avery commented, "As humans, we do not look at what we are doing to the natural world. We share this world with other beings," specifying plants and animals that were the first holy beings to live on the earth.[4] Ramon Riley, cultural resource director for the White Mountain Apache Tribe, chimed in: "Even our children are going crazy—they are not who they are. Their identities are going away. We used to massage our mountains with our ceremonies. Every day we did that."[5] Denny later added that there was no ceremony to cleanse a person feeling the effects of a manmade fire. This was obviously a different situation than the one full-blooded Navajo Larry Garcia had encountered a month before in Joplin, Missouri. A devastating tornado that demolished two-thirds of the town was heading toward Larry and his wife, Rachel's, home. Two miles away, the "Big Wind" veered in another direction, according to Larry, because of the traditional house blessing he performs every year before tornado season: "We do it the old way with sage and tobacco. I think it saved us."[6] To readers unfamiliar with traditional Navajo beliefs, the connection with fires, tornados, holy people, massaging mountains, existent and nonexistent ceremonies leaves one wondering. Further, what does this have to do with how children act?

One of the criteria I used when reviewing *Bitter Water* was its ability to communicate beyond cultural boundaries. In some instances the book generated more heat than light if one were looking for some type of resolution that allowed Navajo elders to stay on Hopi Partitioned Lands. But one of the work's strengths is the thinking and metaphorical language so familiar to those who have worked with and studied the Navajo. For those unfamiliar, however, a lot was left unclear. How is one to understand these quotes given by various elders: "The mountains were placed here so we could travel."[7] "The fireplace has stories that can be told. I mentioned some. I can tell you the sun does not walk on this ground. The moon does not walk here on this land."[8] "Hantavirus happened because of the government, because of politics."[9] "We carry a Mountain Soil bundle and an arrowhead. These are the tools you have so you can herd sheep, ride horses, and herd cattle."[10] There are others, but this group suffices to make the point that learning a traditional Navajo worldview takes time and explanation. The speakers who gave these quotes assumed the listener understood, so no further explanation seemed necessary.

The purpose of this book is to share some of the insight I have gained over thirty-plus years as I worked and conversed with Navajo elders. Their teachings are perceptive, opening up the world to a very different set of understandings and assumptions not found in the dominant society. They are all connected and framed in a rational network of ideas that, when taken in their entirety, not only make sense but serve as a guide for daily life from birth to death. When heard in isolation, as with the earlier quotes, they are difficult to interpret and in some instances appear to have no connection with concrete, physical reality. Therein lies part of the problem. Where Anglos understand the world in a very physical sense based on the laws of science and other academic disciplines, the world for the Navajo is framed in a religious context that explains how and why certain things happen. It is just as rational as Western thought but is based on different premises, which will be explored in these pages.

As with science, the foundation of this belief system hearkens back to operative principles set in motion at the time of creation. Just as rules of biology, geology, physics, and chemistry explain what occurred eons ago, so do the rules and actions of the holy people who formed the earth spiritually. These gods clearly defined principles and practices as they planned and then prepared the world to be inhabited by the earth surface, or five-fingered, people. Water, plants, insects, and animals—everything found in this world today, as well as in previous worlds beneath this one—were part of the plan. Holy people such as First Man, First Woman, Talking God, House God, Black God, First Boy, First Girl, and many animals in human form met in the *táchééh* (sweat lodge) and later the first hogan to voice their thoughts about the future and how things should operate. They created everything spiritually before it was made physically; for everything the Navajo people were to encounter, there would be an answer, a place for it to fit in the divine scheme as they lived on this earth. Each disease would have its cure; each problem its answer; every plant and animal its place, power, and teaching; and each its own prayers and songs for communication. All was harmonious as long as every creature abided by the rules established by the holy people. As they thought, prayed, sang, and planned, the physical world with its inhabitants began to take shape.

Only the holy people, as they sat in that first sweat lodge and hogan, could manage the complexity of the creation of the worlds discussed in Navajo mythology. That mythology provides a blueprint that outlines how people should act, based on divine rules and principles. No individual will ever have all the knowledge of the holy people, but individuals will have enough to know the general guidelines for life with the help of specialists—medicine people—who control supernatural powers and know how to apply them. Thus knowledge is power, thought opens the door to knowledge, and once it has been gained, knowledge is shared through teachings. This understanding frames the context for that which follows—the different applications of some of those teachings in daily life.

The unifying theme that runs throughout this work is the role of traditional Navajo thought in daily life, its pervasive interpretation, and incidents that fostered its change. The topic is impossibly broad to cover completely, since Navajo life centers around thinking and reasoning in accordance with traditional teachings. Many academicians have provided excellent, though partial, insight into different aspects of this thought—Washington Matthews and his initial recognition of mythology and its connection to those teachings; Gladys Reichard, with her encyclopedic knowledge of Navajo religion; Father Berard Haile, who had a vast understanding of traditional practices and beliefs; the Franciscan Fathers, who tied culture with language in their dictionary; Clyde Kluckhohn, with a broad understanding of Navajo culture along with specialized topics such as witchcraft; and Charlotte Frisbie and David P. McAllester, who showed how traditional teachings are lived by a medicine man.[11] The list goes on, with dozens of other significant contributors in the field of Navajo studies. Also apparent is that most of those mentioned did their work long ago and would be considered by some to be "dated."

Two more contemporary anthropologists have made important additions to understanding aspects of traditional teachings. The first, John R. Farella, wrote *The Main Stalk: A Synthesis of Navajo Philosophy,* published in 1984.[12] This book explores the meaning of "*Są'a naghái bik'e hózhǫ́*," which has been glossed any number of ways but which generally refers to the concept of long life and happiness as an empowering force in one's life that harmonizes with elements of the universe. Farella's work moves deeply into aspects of Navajo teachings and uses the voices of medicine people to clarify a series of complex thoughts. Maureen Trudelle Schwarz, author of *Molded in the Image of Changing Woman, Navajo Lifeways,* and *Blood and Voice,* also depends heavily on interpretation of events or situations as seen through the eyes of the elders.[13] She uses the ethnographic present to bring the reader into contemporary Navajo culture while explaining why the elders feel as they do. The texts are heavily laced with direct quotes embedded in anthropological analysis.

Missing from this recognition are the names of Navajo cultural or historical specialists who have published on their own in this field. Times are changing. The Navajo Nation actively conducts research and the collection of traditional information that is preserved at tribal headquarters in Window Rock, Arizona. There are Navajo elders anxious to share their knowledge out of concern for its loss and for the benefit of the younger generation. Some of these men and women have either written or coauthored writings about traditional teachings.[14] There has also been a resurgence of historical crafts, such as weaving rugs, making baskets, and producing high-quality silver products—the beginnings of which hearken back to an earlier time but that are now created with ever-increasing sophistication. All of this stimulates discussion about what it was like in the old days, which in turn evokes teachings from that past.

A sub-corollary to this book's main theme is the impact the loss of these teachings is having in contemporary Navajo culture. The reader will find a mix of both historical and modern examples of cultural change—sometimes short and violent, other times long and imperceptible—that has shifted traditional views and practices. It is hoped that these examples will give younger generations cause to reflect on what has been lost as well as what is now available. Paul G. Zolbrod, author of *Diné bahane': The Navajo Creation Story* and a longtime student of Navajo teachings, said it succinctly in a personal communication: "The threat to traditional Navajo lifeways functions as a microcosmic index to what is happening in the macro cultural arena of cultural attrition where ethnic and regional enclaves are similarly undergoing the loss of teachings that help maintain a distinct identity. This is a significant point to make at a time of drastic cultural leveling everywhere, even in the mainstream, where the loss of embedded traditions is deeply felt but not always articulated."[15] Perhaps what is contained within these pages will serve as an "articulation" that will be helpful in the preservation of what is still present.

The genesis of this book occurred in the mid-1970s but continues through today. As a teacher in southeastern Utah who has worked with Navajo people for many years, I quickly embraced their fascinating history and culture as they opened their homes and minds to my desire to learn. The late 1980s and early 1990s proved particularly rich in working with them, but many of these people have since died. History mixed with culture as I wrote about the people in the Four Corners area. Elders asked that I assist them in recording their life stories, three of which have been published with a fourth under way. A county history for Utah's centennial celebration provided another reason for me to find out what the Utah Navajo experience was like from their perspective. The fact that I teach

Navajo students became another reason to understand the people sitting in front of me.

Motivation for those who shared their lives and culture came from a growing concern that the younger generation was losing its understanding of what their grandmothers and grandfathers, and to a lesser extent their mothers and fathers, believed and experienced from the past. The people I befriended and others I simply interviewed expressed intense anguish at having the traditional teachings and history lost. To them, it seemed the youth were buried in a contemporary blizzard of activities sponsored by white culture that made the old ways seem arcane, outdated, and impractical. This is not to suggest that members of the younger generation did not respect their elders but only that, from a perspective of navigating through daily life, it was difficult to use much of what the old ones taught and believed. In the elders' terms, the youth had been "captured" by white society. The difficulty of understanding and practicing beliefs such as those expressed previously by the women of the HPL became an increasing concern. Science, geography, and algebra seemed to make more sense as the two worldviews battled each other in the minds of children and youth educated in the white man's world.

What the reader encounters within these pages is a return to the thoughts, practices, and beliefs of today's elders raised during the first third of the twentieth century, when livestock and agriculture provided a satisfyingly cohesive way of life. This time period serves as the baseline for the elders who shared their understanding of the world. While each person's life is different, it is not surprising to see how similar many of their experiences were; although the heart of the oral testimony here comes from the people of southeastern Utah, the same teachings and historical events are shared by many throughout the reservation. This does not mean, however, that one size fits all. Specific teachings for a geographic site, a community's condition, or a family's experience are unique to that situation; but the principles and beliefs underlying them are generally held in common.

I have not tried to tackle a large philosophical concept, as did Farella. After listening to the elders, I felt comfortable sharing their words about specific topics that continually surfaced. The unifying theme that unites the diversity found within the various chapters is that of Navajo traditional teachings (Dinéjí na'nitin) and history as seen through their eyes. The first chapter looks at different forms of divination, how they work, and what the practitioners see and feel. Hand trembling and crystal gazing are the most common, both crucial in specifying what ails a person and which ceremony to use to correct it. The second chapter examines a historic incident—the 1918–1919 Influenza Epidemic—from a cross-cultural perspective. For the Navajo, this pandemic was one illness for which the holy people had not prescribed a specific cure. The results were devastating. Chapter 3 covers witchcraft from the perspective of its being not only on the dark side but also sacred and a necessary part of existence. While knowledge of this practice is seldom revealed in detail and rarely confessed, there were those in history—Ba'álílee from the Aneth area, for example—who used their understanding of it to control local Navajo people and confront the federal government. It was also eventually Ba'álílee's undoing.

The next four chapters discuss different aspects of Navajo thought and language. The first takes a lengthy look at traditional metaphors. The Navajo language is replete with ways of describing everyday objects and events that are tied to the culture and that teach important values. The following chapter is about Father H. Baxter Liebler, Episcopalian missionary to the Navajos in southeastern Utah who understood this principle and adopted the symbols of their religion to express values from his own. He did this with respect and was accepted by many of the people he taught, yet this undertaking was not without surprises. Next is the history of the Pectol shields that were eventually repatriated through NAGPRA (Native American Graves Protection and Repatriation Act [1990]) because of the knowledge of a Navajo medicine man. More than ever, an increasing respect and value is placed on Native American oral tradition, as proven by the Navajo Nation's ability to provide sufficient evidence that these hotly contested items should be repatriated to their tribe. The fourth chapter in this series returns to examine older Navajo metaphors, looking at how they operate within the culture. Today, however, different ones are replacing them. As traditional teachings provide a diminishing base for metaphorical expression, a new type—still dependent on keen observation and wit—is becoming common. The final chapter concludes with the elders' beliefs about the end of the world. While many cultures have such teachings, the Navajo, because of their view of historical cycles, discern a pattern of what happened in the past that explains what will occur in the future. There are well-acknowledged signposts along the way that warn the people today that the time is soon approaching when a "changeover" will take place, destroying this world just as the worlds beneath this one were obliterated for indiscretion.

A final word about words. This book is about words and thoughts, and so I offer an explanation as to why I have chosen certain terms. Scholars often work with well-defined vocabularies specific to their field. I have chosen to use some expressions that have been discussed by scholars yet found wanting in meeting particular criteria. I have elected to adopt the vocabulary I hear the Navajo people speak—many of whom are well-educated, holding higher education degrees. There were also those immersed primarily in the learning of traditional ways who likewise used these words. For instance, the word *hataałi* has been translated as healer, chanter, singer, medicine person, and ceremonial practitioner. When I listen to Navajo people speak, they use the words *medicine man* or *medicine woman*; that is what I have used here. The same is true with *Ancestral Puebloan*, which is preferred by those of puebloan descent, but the Navajo use their term *Anaasází*. While no offense is intended, I have chosen to use the latter for ease of discourse, general recognition, and because that is what the Navajo say. The same is true with the words *Diné* and *Navajo*, which I use interchangeably. While the People often refer to themselves as Diné in formal discussion, the term *Navajo* is still the one most often spoken and written. Official titles such as the Navajo Nation, the *Navajo Times*, and Miss Navajo indicate that there is no problem in still using that word.

Other terms are a little more problematic because of the cultural baggage attached to them. While I have already defined "traditional" as those teachings and life ways practiced in full force during the first third of the twentieth century that continue today through the elders, it seems appropriate to recognize that the term is on a slippery scale. What is called traditional here would probably have been considered radically new by a person born in the 1860s. Navajo people who use this term now have a clear understanding in their minds of how a traditional person dresses, talks, and thinks.

Less clearly defined are the terms *myth* and *supernatural,* although I find both words used by Navajo people in conversation and written in the *Navajo Times*. The term *myth* is particularly problematic because in English discourse it can be used to mean something untrue, a fable or

Courtesy, Utah State Historical Society.

The Navajo sweat lodge (táchééh) is a place of thought, planning, and action and has been since the time of creation. Earth surface people use the lodge for cleansing and prayer and to teach important aspects of life.

fictional story, or an outright lie. Nothing could be further from the position taken here. When used in this text, it refers to a sacred explanation as to how the holy people created an object, ceremony, and so on for the benefit of the People. The teachings derived from these explanations are driving forces within the culture that provide stability and coherence in an otherwise chaotic world. If one wants to learn what makes Navajo culture unique and vibrant, then one must eventually turn to the myths for those answers. The holy people who set all of this in motion have "supernatural" powers, in other words, an ability beyond what is considered normal human capacity. Again, no slight is intended by using either of these terms, and since I hear informed Navajo people use them, I am comfortable doing so, too.

At this point in most introductions, the author makes a disclaimer assuming full responsibility for errors of fact or interpretation in what the reader is about to encounter. I will not break with that tradition, especially since I am writing about another people. I would like to add in my defense that I have a very strong respect for the Navajo people and their traditional teachings and history. Over the years I have tried to listen carefully to what they say and have transmitted what I have heard through the words they spoke. Extensive quoting throughout the text does not remove my responsibility for maintaining correctness of presentation or interpretation. It is hoped that all readers, regardless of ethnicity, will find pleasure and accuracy in the teachings presented.

As at the time of creation, our discussion begins in a cultural "sweat lodge" or "hogan" of the mind. Before a ceremony starts, the hogan is prepared by hanging a blanket in the doorway, serving as a signal to the holy people. They see it and say, "Let us go down. There is a ceremony of our children."[16] The medicine man cautions, "Don't you dare be leaning up against the wall. Move forward. All of you. Move forward because the holy people are going to walk behind you and take their place with us." That is why the Navajo word for a ceremonial sand painting is *iikááh*, meaning "the coming in of the holy people." So as one turns this page, drop the blanket of the mind over the door and let the holy people enter.

NOTES

1. "Latest Update Wallow Fire," http://www.kvoa.com/full-coverage/wallow-fire/23fcanchor; http://en.wikipedia.org/wiki/Wallow_Fire.
2. Malcolm D. Benally, *Bitter Water: Diné Histories of the Navajo-Hopi Land Dispute* (Tucson: University of Arizona Press, 2011).
3. Ibid., xiii.
4. Alistair Lee Bitsoi, "Unnatural Disaster—Disasters Signal Imbalance in the Natural World," *Navajo Times,* June 23, 2011, A-1.
5. Ibid.
6. Cindy Yurth, "Mo. Tornado Spares Diné Man's Home," *Navajo Times*, June 2, 2011, A-3.
7. Benally, *Bitter Water*.

8. Ibid., 51.
9. Ibid., 52.
10. Ibid., 75.
11. All of these authors have lists of publications too lengthy to outline here. One book by each author is provided as a brief reference as to which I feel is most significant, given the topic of this book: Washington Matthews, *Navaho Legends* (Salt Lake City: University of Utah Press, 1994 [1897]); Gladys A. Reichard, *Navaho Religion: A Study of Symbolism* (Princeton: Princeton University Press, 1950); Father Berard Haile, *Upward Moving and Emergence Way: The Gishin Biye' Version* (Lincoln: University of Nebraska Press, 1981); Franciscan Fathers, *An Ethnologic Dictionary of the Navajo Language* (Saint Michaels, AZ: Saint Michaels Press, 1910); Clyde Kluckhohn and Dorothea Leighton, *The Navaho* (Cambridge, MA: Harvard University Press, 1946); Charlotte J. Frisbie and David P. McAllester, eds., *Navajo Blessingway Singer: The Autobiography of Frank Mitchell, 1881–1967* (Tucson: University of Arizona Press, 1978).
12. John R. Farella, *The Main Stalk: A Synthesis of Navajo Philosophy* (Tucson: University of Arizona Press, 1984).
13. Maureen Trudelle Schwarz, *Molded in the Image of Changing Woman: Navajo Views on the Human Body and Personhood* (1997) and *Blood and Voice: Navajo Women Ceremonial Practitioners* (2003) both by (Tucson: University of Arizona Press); also *Navajo Lifeways: Contemporary Issues, Ancient Knowledge* (Norman: University of Oklahoma Press, 2001).
14. Three examples give an idea of the type of writing being pursued to preserve traditional teachings. There is also a growing field of other types of Navajo writing in literature, political activism, and shared contemporary experience. That is left for another time and place. John Holiday, an elderly Navajo medicine man, wished to share his knowledge in *A Navajo Legacy: The Life and Teachings of John Holiday* (Norman: University of Oklahoma Press, 2005) and sought me out to assist him. The result is an autobiography that stresses life in the "old days." Walking Thunder, with editor Bradford Keeney, wrote *Walking Thunder: Diné Medicine Woman* (Philadelphia: Ringing Rocks, 2001). Featuring glossy pages, color pictures, and a CD with prayers, songs, and stories, this book meshes personal contemporary experience with traditional practices and is packaged to sell. Malcolm D. Benally, author of *Bitter Water* (see note 2), has recorded the thoughts of four Navajo elders who protest their eviction from Hopi land. The book is politically motivated to win support for their resistance. The interviews are written in both Navajo and English; the metaphorical expression of thoughts captures the traditional worldview with themes as contemporary as those today.
15. Paul G. Zolbrod, *Diné bahane': The Navajo Creation Story* (Albuquerque: University of New Mexico Press, 1984); personal communication with author, December 15, 2011.
16. Don Mose interview with author, June 7, 2011.

1

Wind, Hand, and Stars

Reading the Past, Finding the Future through Divination

In 1940 French philosopher Antoine de Saint-Exupéry published in the United States his flying adventures and philosophical meanderings in Wind, Sand, and Stars.[1] *His spirit soared as high as the aircraft he flew, his stories as much for the heart as the mind. At one point he wrote, "To grasp the meaning of the world today we use language created to express the world of yesterday. The life of the past seems to us nearer our true natures, but only for the reason that it is nearer our language."*[2] *While his writing and thoughts heralded a new age of technological innovation in the flight industry, his statement could be no more true for the Navajos living in the Four Corners area of the United States, practicing traditions handed down from generation to generation.*

One of those traditions—that of divination—depended on the workings of the wind, hand, and stars as explained through

DOI: 10.7330/9781607322177.c01

the myths and teachings that unlocked the power to understand the past, present, and future. Rather than through technological innovation, these powers could only be unleashed through the spirit and discipline of those who sought answers otherwise unavailable. Basic to the religious system that permeated Navajo culture, divination provided an entryway to traditional thought and underlying principles of how the world operated. In this chapter, the reader begins a journey with elders who explain exactly how this world of power can assist the five-fingered earth surface beings.

Americans, as with many other cultures, have always had a penchant for figuring out the past and prying into the future. Where facts are lacking, assumptions abound. Even in the most technologically advanced, scientifically based communities where sequential logic reigns supreme, the human element still forecasts, predicts, and investigates to make the future understandable. Take the poor weatherman, who stands in front of his viewing audience and explains that in five days there are going to be thundershowers, yet none appear. Or the business executive who puts data into a computer and then allows the machine to guide his decision-making. Or the detective who has to compile enough convincing evidence to sway a jury's belief that his reconstruction of an event is true, even though a lot of necessary information may never be available. Dozens of other examples exist of "educated guesses"—polls, forecasts, projections, explanations, re-creations—that are accepted each day as a way of reconstructing the past, understanding the present, and preparing for the future; in reality, they may be tentative at best.

Traditional Navajos also have means for arriving at answers to important questions. Unlike the computer-dependent, Madison Avenue business executive, they receive their responses through less tangible, more supernatural means. Called divination by anthropologists, the techniques used by the Diné evoke core beliefs of their religious worldview. There are three major types of divination—listening (íists'ą́ą́'); star (*sǫ' nil'*į́), with its subsidiaries of sun and moon gazing and their affiliate, crystal gazing (*dést'*į́į́*'*, literally, to see, understand); and hand trembling or motion-in-the hand (*ndishiih*)—all of which are related in that they are spiritually based and serve similar functions. The origin myth of hand trembling is different from star gazing and listening, while generally, women may render the former but not the latter. They are used to explore the unknown, to find lost people or objects, to identify a thief or witch, to locate water or other desirable resources, to prevent danger or evil, and—most important—to diagnose the cause of an illness so one can provide a remedy.[3]

Unlike medicine men who heal through chant way ceremonies that last from one to nine days or nights and who have spent hundreds of hours learning the accompanying prayers, songs, and rituals, the diagnostician may spend only a few hours learning the rite, compose some of his own songs and prayers, and require little ceremonial equipment. Chant ways are normally performed by men who have a sacred body of lore based on complex mythology, whereas diviners may be either male or female (often after menopause) who received this gift at birth and had its potential later revealed to them.[4]

Supernatural power plays an important part in identifying future practitioners. For instance, a holder of this power may realize its potential during a ceremony when its latent force is activated. Apprenticeship follows to develop the skill. A person may have a dream to help point the way, or strange supernatural occurrences may hint at the gift's presence. Examples will be given later, but it is important to understand that once the power is used, there are also consequences that come with abuse. Navajos believe tuberculosis, nervousness, paralysis, and mental illness occur when hand trembling rites are misemployed, while problems with sight are associated with star gazing. Every privilege carries both a responsibility and a consequence for its user.[5]

Another characteristic common to all three forms of divination is a general explanation of why it works. The Navajo believe the world is filled with invisible holy people (Diné Diyin) who know what takes place among humans. The gods understand what has happened and what is going to happen, since for them there is no past or future, just one eternal present. Mircea Eliade, in *The Sacred and the Profane*, points out that religious man escapes the limitations of the mundane world and moves through sacred time with no sense of linear progression. Just as a fish makes its way in any direction in the water, so also can the gods move from the past to the present and into the future.[6]

Holy people read thoughts, anticipate needs, provide help, or punish those who transgress their laws. Frank Mitchell, a medicine man, compared their presence to a radio, by which "something may be going on out of your sight, but still you hear it, you hear what is happening . . . you must be very careful . . . They are aware of our actions, whatever we are doing."[7]

WIND LISTENING

Carrying the radio analogy further, one learns that the medium of transmission is *nítch'i*, interpreted variously as Holy Wind, wind, air, breeze, or spirit.[8] *Níyol*, another name for wind, does not carry the same spiritual connotation as nítch'i, which approaches in function the Christian concept of the Holy Ghost as a messenger or comforter of God. Many Navajo myths tell of Holy Wind whispering in the ear of a protagonist in need of assistance, warning of future problems, or helping with protection. Indeed, without this Holy Wind, there would be no life. Myths describe how, at the time of creation, the first people had no wind in them, and so they were weak. Then different-colored winds—black, blue, yellow, and white—came from the four directions and entered the bodies of humans and animals, "giving strength to men ever since for this was nature's first food and it put motion and change into everything, even into the mountains and water."[9] Hair on the head, hair in the skin, swirling patterns of fingerprints and footprints, and the breath of life are proof of this wind's existence. During the fourth month after conception, this Holy Wind enters the body, giving animation to the fetus.

The Holy Wind also brings death. Some of the winds argue over which one will enter the child and be able to claim it as its grandchild. Once the wind enters, it carries with it an expiration date, after which the person will no longer be able to live. Some people say a medicine man can ceremonially replace the old air with new in a patient who has had a heart attack, giving a renewed lease on life.[10]

The nítch'i inside a person communicates with the air outside the body. The winds from the four directions have prayers, songs, precious materials, and qualities associated with their personification. A complex knowledge exists about how they function and interact with humans, but only an overview is provided here to outline their qualities. There are four different-colored Big Winds, similar to tornados, each associated with its own cardinal direction. They warn of bad events that will take place in the future; when one blows through a camp and tosses about possessions, it is a portent of bad luck. As the world becomes increasingly profane and wicked, these Big Winds wait poised, ready to take lives, just as they did with the Anaasází in the past.[11] As long as the Navajos continue to perform the Blessing Way, asking in humility that they not be destroyed, the Big Winds will constrain their power.[12]

Small whirlwinds gather bad gossip and conversation and report it to the holy people. If they spiral in a clockwise direction, they have a good spirit in them; counterclockwise, an evil one. Ghosts travel in the winds and can affect breathing, requiring a ceremonial cure. If a whirlwind takes a person's possession, he should let the object go, offer corn pollen to the wind, and tell it that the item no longer has any value and that if the wind placed a curse on that person, it is no longer in effect. This counters the belief that the wind, by taking sweat and dirt from a victim's body, stole his thinking so he would not know what he was doing.[13]

Myths personify and teach of the wind's character. One of the stories associated with the Wind Chant tells of a whirlwind that approached a man, Older Brother, who unsuccessfully tried to dodge it. He became angry, shot the counterclockwise-moving twister, and watched the dead body of a person materialize. Then he realized he had killed the son of Big Wind and that soon the father would come to reap vengeance. Older Brother built a hogan; covered it with cactus, yucca, and other plants that have sharp protrusions; drew zigzag marks in the path of the approaching cyclone; burned a crescent-shaped design on his breast; then waited. Big Wind approached in the form of a man, but he could not cross the line. He promised to help rather than harm Older Brother if he restored his son. Older Brother ceremonially revived Whirlwind, and, as agreed, Big Wind taught him three sacred songs of protection.[14]

As with people, winds have homes of various sizes and shapes. The rounded basins or pot-like holes found in sandstone are said to be their lodgings. Near Navajo Mountain was a place barren of vegetation and topsoil that made a "thunderous noise" just before violent weather arrived. This used to be one of the wind's homes, but now it is covered with vegetation and thus apparently vacated. Another place is found on the south side of Navajo Mountain in a large hole that goes far down into a rock. One day Joe Manygoats and a friend tossed a stone into the cavern and waited for some time before they heard it hit the bottom. A powerful gust of air arose from the depths, reminding the men that they had failed to calm the wind by calling its sacred name, thus incurring its anger. The men fled.[15]

Holy people should not be taken lightly. They provide warnings and help a person learn. Claus Chee Sonny believes the gods want humans to know the songs and prayers, but this can only be achieved if the "wind people want to communicate them to you."[16] He explains that this is the reason some people fail to learn them even though they try very hard to do so. The gods simply do not want some individuals to have this power.

When treated respectfully, however, winds accurately communicate future events. Talking God, Growling God, and Sun Bearer placed throughout the land many of the holy people "who were to be prophets and teachers of men in the future. The wind acted as messenger between these spirits and the people."[17] Divination, or the receipt of this communication, is based on consulting the wind or animals with acute hearing such as wolves, coyotes, badgers, and members of the cat family.[18] Known as "listening" by the Diné, this form of predicting is the least common of the three types. It is a learned skill that for the talented can be procured in one night. The diagnostician places the dried, powdered eardrum of a badger in his ears, goes outside, and listens for noises that provide a sign of what is being communicated. The listener then interprets what is heard as the cause of the illness or the answer to his question.[19]

W. W. Hill, in *Navaho Warfare*, provides the best description of the use of this technique in the past. Considered the most reliable form of divination by the members of a war party, listening foretold of the group's success or failure. The leader selected two trustworthy men who knew the prayers and understood the symbols to interpret what they heard. He rubbed ear wax from a coyote and a badger on the men's ears so their senses would be heightened, then took them a hundred yards away from camp in the direction of the enemy. There they listened for favorable sounds such as "horses or sheep, the trotting of animals, or visions of horses and sheep, [as] a good omen. Contrarily, if they heard the cry of a crow, screech owl, hoot owl, wolf, coyote, or any other 'man eating' bird or animal; heard footsteps or conversation of the enemy, or heard someone shout as if hurt . . . these were considered bad omens and the party would turn back."[20]

STAR GAZING

Navajos also look beyond the winds to the heavens for divine signs of things about to happen. Like the winds, the sun, moon, and stars are alive and have an ability to interact with man. The sun and moon are the two most prominent celestial orbs. The sun, a fiery disk made of turquoise and other elements, should not be confused with Sun Bearer, the deity who carries the object across the sky on thirty-two trails lying between the solstices. Sun Bearer is a handsome deity, noted for his strength and amorous ability, who figures frequently in the mythology.[21]

Sun Bearer was said to have a turquoise mask and was the giver of life and heat, while Moon Bearer had a white shell mask and controlled female rain, mist, fog, and dew. During late May, Navajos held ceremonies to bless the tender shoots of corn and other plants. This was the only time when the sun and moon communicated with or "saw" each other (one rising, the other setting) to discuss the seed-blessing ceremonies and night prayers offered previously by the Diné. With a good report, the two deities continued to favor man.[22]

The concept of celestial blessings also occurred on an individual, daily basis for the Navajo. If the sun rose in the sky at dawn to find a person still sleeping, it said, "This is not my child." The sleeper was obviously lazy and not fit to receive blessings and riches from the holy people. Metaphorically, sleep is said to be dressed in "torn clothing," and so will be the people who lie in bed with it.[23] The moon also blesses or curses an individual. For example, if a person prays to the moon while holding a fire poker and invokes its warmth for a newborn child, the baby will not get cold easily.[24]

These heavenly bodies may assume a vengeful attitude. Sun Bearer, when speaking of his daily travels across the sky, said, "Every time I make the journey east and west, one of the Earth People shall die. That is my pay." Moon Carrier agreed to the same price. Now, the sun or moon will stop at its zenith if it has not received its compensation, but, fortunately, someone has died every day and so this has not happened. Interestingly, the sun demands the life of a Navajo, while the moon accepts a death from a foreign race. Because the moon is "the sign of the Anglo," there are no formal prayers to it as there are to the sun, the sign for the Navajo.[25]

The most dangerous and prophetic time is during a solar or lunar eclipse. Although Navajos refer to the sun or moon as "dying," they still believe Sun Bearer and Moon Bearer are immortal and that only the "fire" is going out. When the moon is eclipsed, everyone is awakened until it recovers; if it is the sun, then all work or travel ceases, people sit quietly, and only the singers of the Blessing Way are heard chanting. If a pregnant mother looks upon an eclipse, the unborn child will "take on its image." Other ills inflicted during an eclipse occur: if people are eating, they will have stomach troubles; if sleeping, their eyes will not open; and if they look at it, they will become blind.[26]

The solar eclipse that occurred on June 8, 1918, is a good example of the seriousness of what was foretold. Joe Manygoats was herding sheep that day when it happened. His father sent him home, told him to sit quietly, to watch the event indirectly by seeing its reflection in a bowl of water, and to wait until his father returned. The parent sang songs to help the sun come alive, which it did, but from that time on there were intense, red clouds in the morning and evening sky, warning of future troubles.[27]

The holy beings instituted this portent in the beginning of time, when First Man created the symbol of a red-streaked sky. He said, "Whatever I think or say shall be done from these [streaks]. The lower red and gray represents smallpox, whooping cough, and all other diseases. The yellow line above them signifies the passing of these diseases whenever that line appears above the other two."[28] In November 1918 the reservation was convulsed in the throes of an influenza epidemic that did not end until March 1919, after the deaths of thousands of Navajos. The sun had forewarned the people of this catastrophe.

Stars, like the sun and moon, also warn man and guide him into the future. Although accounts vary as to detail, First Man and First Woman are often credited with the placement of constellations and patterns, eight of which are most significant: Ursa Major (Revolving Male) and Cassiopeia (Revolving Female), the Pleiades (seven boys who run and dodge as they practice shooting arrows), Orion (First Slim One), Corvus (Man with Legs Ajar), Scorpius (divided into two parts—First Big One and Rabbit Tracks), and the Milky Way (Sitting for the Dawn). Navajos also recognize individual stars and other small groupings such as Antares (Coyote Star), Hydra (the Horned Rattlesnake), and Polaris (the fire around which Revolving Male and Revolving Female circle).[29] Stars that are not in recognizable patterns or that do not have special significance are there because Coyote, the trickster, impatiently flung star material into the heavens.[30]

The North Star (Polaris), around which Revolving Male and Revolving Female (Big Dipper and Cassiopeia, respectively) rotate, teaches that "only one couple may live by one hogan fire." The holy people also formed other patterns in the stars to provide laws for correct Navajo behavior.

Stars and humans are closely related. Navajos tell how the stars serve as a calendar and clock because of their movements. Many commented, "That is how we know our time from day to day, month to month, season to season, and year to year. These stars follow a special pattern every day of the year."[31] They are named in prayers, each has a Blessing Way song, and each has a special power to benefit people. The holy beings established these powers, saying, "We are creating the stars to help the earth surface people to find their way, so that they can regain their faith and reestablish their balance and their direction."[32]

Navajos tell how the "laws" are written in the stars. First Woman wanted a constant, unchanging reminder of proper behavior for mankind. She could not write it in the water because it always changed, and in the sand it would blow away, but in the stars there was permanence. So she took Rabbit Tracks, whose ends point upward as a sign that in the spring and summer people should not hunt, but in the fall and winter, when the tips point downward, it is appropriate to kill game. Another set of stars, called Horns, shines brighter in the autumn, signaling the time for hunting mountain sheep.

One should not plant crops until the Pleiades disappears around May 15. Once it is over the horizon, the planting starts—seven seeds to a hole, the same number as the stars in the constellation. Man with Legs Ajar assumes a stooping stance because he is carrying a heavy load from the harvest. The brighter his stars shine, the better the crop yield. This reminds the Navajos to work hard during this season so they will have enough food for the winter. The Horned Rattlesnake controls underground water that gives life to springs and streams. Most of the animals are given a star or a constellation to remind them of their responsibilities, whether it is the meadowlark that sings to the sun in the morning or the porcupine that checks the growth of trees in the mountains.[33]

Stars also prescribe important principles in human relations. Just as astrologers use the horoscope in Anglo society today to align stars and planets with the lives of individuals, so do the Navajo have traditions concerning the same heavenly body. For instance, Coyote placed two identical stars (Gemini—Pollux and Castor) in the wrong place, so there is contention and strife on earth as they try to get to their correct positions. Black Star was never "lit" and so wanders about bringing bad luck and painful pricks on the shoulder and back with the little arrows it shoots. Big Star is not to see the Pleiades; they are in-laws and are there to remind people that a husband should never see his mother-in-law. The Milky Way is a trail for the spirits of the deceased, each star a footprint for those who travel between earth and heaven.[34]

Perhaps the strongest connection between man and the heavens comes through star gazing and crystal gazing. Both depend on the power originating from the heavens—in one, a person stares directly at a star or the sun or the moon, and in the other, the light from the star provides an image in a crystal object. First Man initially recognized the power of a crystal, said to belong to males, while females have turquoise. The crystal is a symbol of the mind and clear seeing, so when First Man burned one, the mind awakened. The origin myth of star gazing and wind listening is a lengthy one that goes back to the time when the holy people were not yet empowered to understand the future or unknown occurrences.[35] The story starts with Coyote visiting a man who was a good hunter and had two wives. Through a series of events, the man tricked Coyote, who responded with revenge that made the man sick for four years. No one could determine what ailed him, and so they gathered in a large hogan with five birds—four different types of owls and the whip-poor-will—placed outside to watch and safeguard the proceedings. Finally, Bat came forth and identified four buzzards, each associated with a cardinal direction, as the only ones who knew how to cure the sick and deteriorating man.

Four animals visited the buzzards, but they brought the wrong types of presents. They returned a second time with gifts that pleased the birds, who then prescribed the proper ceremony, which included a sand painting and shooting arrows over the patient from different directions four times to affect a cure. The sick man vomited blood, "Coyote's bad spirit," which was pursued to the north, never to return. The patient began to recuperate. The buzzards instructed the people:

> "From this time on, the people who are going to come on this earth shall use the lenses from the eyes of these five different birds who acted as lookouts for you. Take the lenses out and dry them; take also the water from their eyes and dry it up. Grind all this material to powder, and use it on your eyes when you gaze at the stars. In that way you will be able to find out things that you do not know; you will be able to find out what diseases sick people have. Use it as did the five lookout birds."
>
> The buzzards also told the people how to use the dried and powdered eardrum of the badger in order to hear things while listening.[36]

The animals next held a five-day ceremony so the man could begin his recovery. He returned to his normal good health after having the same ceremony performed four times. Now the holy people knew how to find out what was wrong with the sick and a means to investigate the unknown.

However, it was not until the Twins, Monster Slayer and Born for Water, cleansed the earth of monsters that star gazing and the power of Big Star were used on behalf of the earth surface people to find and kill evil beings. A line from the Great Star Chant tells of Monster Slayer: "Using a rock crystal and a talking prayer stick [*k'eet'áán*], he comes in search for me" to eradicate the monsters. In the sand painting that accompanies part of this ceremony, a "candle-like bar" represents the crystal used for star gazing.[37]

Not everyone can use this power or be a diviner. Unlike hand trembling, where supernatural beings make a person aware that "the ceremony wants you . . . and that you are known," star gazing is a learned rite that may be acquired in as little as a day or two. The individual just quoted was told through star gazing that she should use hand trembling, a form of divination that came more easily to her.[38] Medicine man John Holiday said he performed star gazing for ten years, but it scared him because he used the sun, which hurt his eyes. In his words, however, "This was a natural gift bestowed on me; it was not something I had to learn or ask for. It is totally impossible to look at the sun with the naked eye, but I used to do that." He described the experience as his sight darkening before a "stream of bright light bounced to the earth. The earth, in turn, changed its form to fit the shape of the sun . . . When the white stream descended, it drew an image of the earth and all the things on it . . . showing just a little section of it, magnifying it even more to indicate what the patient was suffering from . . . but I still had to guess."[39] Another person believed the ceremony did not want him, though he knew it worked for others. When asked if Anglos could master this power, he felt they could as long as they learned the songs.[40]

Answers that come as a result of star gazing and crystal gazing take a variety of forms. One woman explained that she hired a diviner and an assistant, who stared at Big Star until a beam of light shone down on the patient. If the ailment was serious, the star appeared to separate, one part turning red and moving downward and the other part remaining stationary. When this woman had the ceremony performed, two practitioners left her inside the hogan and went out to watch. They "saw" her sitting surrounded by a bright light with a black shadow in the form of a porcupine approaching her. The men could not interpret this latter symbol. One saw a great white object in the distance and felt that good awaited her in the future. Five months later a movie outfit from Hollywood employed her and her husband for the next six years as caretakers of its sets and equipment in Monument Valley. Good fortune did indeed lie in her future.[41]

Other people give slightly different explanations. One man believed the diviner looked at the star continuously until a thin strand of light started to vibrate, spread, and then shone directly on the ailment. For instance, if a person were injured internally, the light from Big Star showed on the spot as a red blood vessel. Diagnosis for a remedy followed, with some people visualizing the medicine man who would perform the healing rite.[42]

George Tom tells of an uncle, Spotted Shirt, who with some other men stood atop a hill crystal gazing. A nearby mesa appeared to have a "fire" on top, the glowing spot proving to be the location of a future uranium mine.[43] Harvey Oliver from Aneth describes his grandfather using crystal gazing to view events in World War I in which his son was involved. The grandfather "would tell how it looked underneath the world where his son was fighting the war. He would say, 'our soldiers are going to win again.' It seemed like he could see it clearly."[44]

The amount of paraphernalia needed for star gazing varies. In its simplest form, nothing is required except songs and prayers. As mentioned previously, Holiday merely had to look at the sun until his sight blackened. Out of the darkness a stream of white light bounced to earth and then changed into the form of the earth to fit the shape of the sun. The ailment appeared as if on a screen and remained until he guessed the cause of the sickness. Other medicine men use the help of birds, such as eagles, who see far away. They catch a bird alive, put corn pollen in its eye, then take the resulting "eye water," mix it with finely ground rock crystals, and apply it under the diviner's eyes for "the clearness of the crystal and the far seeing vision of the eagle."[45] Birds, such as herons, turkeys, magpies, quails, roadrunners, and those of the night, also aid with "far-seeing" eye water.[46]

Medicine men most often appeal to the power of Big Star, though any star—referred to as the "main star"—can also be used. One woman told of putting a crystal on the ground and shining a flashlight through it. Two lights appeared, indicating the illness; the diviner recognized the treatment and sucked out a piece of glass from the patient's neck. Selection of the crystal is also arbitrary, ranging from "rock crystal, translucent flint, pieces of bottle glass, colored broken marbles, cut glass, or prisms."[47]

In some instances, a sand painting associated with the Great Star Chant may be used. The sand painting is two feet in diameter and has four points, between each of which rests a colored mountain (mound of sand); the entire painting is surrounded by a zigzag line of lightning. After completing this picture, the diviner extinguishes the light inside the hogan, goes outside, and starts his prayers and songs while those who remain inside concentrate and try to "see." The light from above—white as a favorable sign, red as unfavorable—illuminates the house for those outside. If the hogan is perceived as dark or burning, the patient will die. These findings, and those that others have experienced, are then discussed with the patient to achieve a full understanding.[48] The ceremony must be completed before the main star disappears past the smoke hole, since this and other related stars give life to those portrayed in the sand painting on the floor.[49]

Diviners may also use assistants. Each of them may hold a crystal, or only one may have one, but they all concentrate on what is ailing the patient. They each pick out a star to stare at until they see an indicator, as if on a television screen. "Once you take your eyes off the star, it goes off, leaving a funny feeling in your eyes."[50] Those performing the ceremony say they have a tired, drained feeling at the beginning, and their eyes hurt. By the end, those involved, including the patient, are said to have a happy feeling. As one participant stated, "Your mind searches for all of the possible cures for the patient. Your job is to be an observer of what the star is telling you."[51] Keith Holiday from Navajo Mountain suggests that a white ray from a star provides the answer: "The big stars, these are the ones that are looked at and tell them [diviners] by the stripes that come out of the stars. Some of the stripes are white and some are dark. These [stripes] string in and out among the stars. This is how they find out what it [the illness] is. The diviner is thinking is it this thing that is killing a person. When it [the answer] is found out, it [the stripe] will disappear."[52] Gladys Bitsinnie from Douglas Mesa believes the "star would shine on whatever they were looking for—the whole thing [answer] would get lighted up." If the diagnosis did not at first provide an answer, the process continued until one was found. If the performer does not discover the problem, the patient will not get well. Payment for this service used to be an arrowhead, some food, or a small piece of jewelry; in the 1990s it was around thirty dollars.[53]

In addition to healing the sick, crystal gazing also exposes practitioners of witchcraft and wrongdoing. When theft occurs, the diagnostician may draw a map with terrain features on the floor as he gazes at and explains where the culprit lives. A person who is witched may also bring his car to a diviner, who uses his power to look the vehicle over for supernatural tampering or who may give a general diagnosis through the stars. Witches fear that this power exposes their evil, which may, in turn, lead to their destruction. Just knowing that crystal gazers can see prevents some people from getting involved in witchcraft. One woman told how "a light comes from heaven and shines on that person [witch]. This is what happened to [anonymous]. He was seen through crystal gazing and he died."[54] Sometimes more than one diagnostician is consulted for fear that the first could be in league with the witch.

HAND TREMBLING

Just as "listening" depends on auditory senses and star gazing on sight, hand trembling utilizes touch. During the creation, Gila Monster (Tiníléí; also one of the names used to identify hand trembling) held this power. In one part of the myth, a hunter became lost. The holy people turned to Dark Gila Monster, who "consulted the directions with his hand to learn where he [the hunter] might be found. And he consulted toward the east, the south, the west, the north, upward, and downward."[55] Spotted Gila Monster did likewise, while Magpie and Heron used star gazing, and Wolf Chief, Mountain Lion, and Badger "gave their eardrums" to the Twins to go out and listen. All of them determined the lost hunter was to the south.

The primary origin story of motion-in-the-hand tells of when the holy people were discussing how to learn about the unknown.[56] Big Fly knew that Gila Monster understood how to find out, so he told the group to approach him with a gift of turquoise and corn pollen. This pleased Gila Monster and he offered to assist, saying "I have been all over this earth and know everything about it," then he set his hand in motion.[57] The onlookers learned that there was a wide variety of diseases, but there were an equally large number of medicinal plants to cure them. Gila Monster showed chants and ways to create sickness but also ceremonies to heal. This would be important information for the earth surface people and holy beings to know. He had not learned this skill from someone else or practiced it: "The spirit simply entered him, and that is the way he got it—by way of the spirit."[58] That is also the way it is for hand tremblers who acquire this gift today. The holy people were pleased, declaring, "By motion-in-the-hand they [earth surface people] shall find out the cause of sicknesses, which plants to use, which chants to have, and which medicine men to give them. They shall also find anything lost or stolen in the same way."[59]

Another story tells how Older Brother disobeyed and killed a wood rat for food, even though he knew doing so was forbidden. He became deathly ill and sent Younger Brother to get the Yellow Wind who lived near the San Francisco Peaks. Yellow Wind administered a medicine of

Painting by Charles Yanito.

The holy people control the powers of divination and, when properly summoned, can assist in answering questions about the past, present, and future. Prayer and sacred procedure connect the physical and spiritual worlds, whose separation is slight.

corn pollen that was shaken off of Gila Monster. The patient went into convulsions, was cured, and began to "read thoughts and to have second sight." From this came hand trembling with a prayer that asks the Gila Monster to "come down and help me find the sickness of the patient."[60]

Thus divination is used to diagnose illness caused by supernatural forces or by normal health problems. For instance, a baby's intestines were "seen" to be "twisted like a rope," so the parents took it to a clinic.

A boy was crying and vomiting; hand trembling correctly diagnosed the problem as appendicitis. A man rested his head on a lightning-struck tree, so the diviner correctly identified and prescribed a five-night Shooting Way ceremony. A very sick woman lay in a hogan, her distraught husband anxious to find a cure. He called in a hand trembler who said his wife would be dead in three days. She was.[61]

Witchcraft is also exposed through hand trembling. One diviner switched from hand to hand as he marked the ground, creating a map. When he finished, he knew that a man had witched a small girl, placing some of her hair and sweat in a bundle he had cursed and buried. When relatives confronted the guilty party, the culprit finally confessed to the deed. The trembler also identified the location of the bundle and correctly predicted that the girl would recover.[62] Ted Cly had a hand trembler locate a bead shot into his back by a supernatural power. He explained that the trembler knew who had performed the deed but would not divulge the name. However, the diviner relieved the pain in Cly's back by sucking out the foreign object.[63]

Plants used to cure a sickness can also be seen. The name and location of the plant are revealed to the trembler, as well as how long it will take to affect a cure if administered immediately. When the plant is approached, the medicine man or woman explains who is sick, offers a prayer, and leaves a small present before another member of the same species is picked for the medicine.[64]

Lost or stolen articles are also recovered. A boy was missing fifty dollars and went to his aunt to help him find it. Through hand trembling, she determined that the boy's little nephew had taken the money, spent ten dollars of it, and hidden the rest. The nephew denied knowledge of the deed at first but later confessed and returned the remaining forty dollars. When white men stole some of Left Hand's horses, a trembler told him exactly where to find them.[65]

Five types of ceremonial Gila monsters—black, blue, yellow, white, and spotted—hold this gift, but the black and "spotted" appear to be the most potent. When they received this power, they agreed with Big Star to help mankind, but as two separate entities. One person suggested that the two forces—hand trembling and crystal gazing—were incompatible; if a person had one ability, then the other would not work.[66] Some Navajos credit Gila Monster as the first medicine man, appropriately outfitted in a defensive scaly armor that can also protect a sick patient from harm. His "flint armor" associates him with both protection and healing, as portrayed in the Flint Way ceremony.[67] As he walks about the desert he lifts his forefoot, which sometimes trembles, indicating his divinatory ability. To medicine man John Holiday, "The Gila Monster is like the discipline paddle at the old boarding school," meaning he is powerful and operates under strict enforcement of rules. "Sometimes the hand trembler cannot find the answer or understand the impression, so the sacred spirit will let the hand and fingers grab the diviner's nose or ear, or poke his or her ribs, as if to say, 'Here's the answer, can't you see it? Are you stupid? You can't even guess the answer!'"[68]

This lizard's importance in directing thoughts is found in the prayer to invoke its spirit. The diviner says, "Black Gila Monster, I want you to tell me what is wrong with this patient. Do not hide anything from me. I am giving you a jet bead to tell me what the illness of this patient is."[69] The other colored Gila monsters, with corresponding colored shells or stones, are also addressed; then the procedure is repeated three more times. The Gila monster's spirit shakes the hand and arm and tells what the cause of sickness is, who stole the property, or who is using witchcraft.

Unlike the practice of star gazing, the holy beings select those who will learn hand trembling. One person was sick when the power "came suddenly into me . . . this was how it started." Another believed the gods could bestow this gift on a young child, but he or she may be too young to guess the diagnosis or too unfamiliar with the ceremonies to actually cure: "One would first have to learn all the different symbols that represent illness, such as reptiles, coyotes, dogs, etc. Each one represents an ailment of some kind. Nobody can learn or receive the gift without a cause."[70] People who volunteer to try trembling have the medicine man sprinkle corn pollen on their hands, then sing and pray. Once their hand is "touched," they will be asked to guess the problem and prescribe a treatment.

Navajo Oshley tells how he first learned that he could hand tremble. One day he asked his aunt, a woman well-known for her skill, if she would teach him. She said no, that it was too powerful to learn, but later, when a sick man came for help, she relented. The only time this type of teaching can take place is when someone is being diagnosed. Oshley said:

> She [his aunt] lightly clapped her hand over my hand. She kept urging my hand to move. Then it happened. My hand went out and that is how I learned hand trembling. The man was suffering from spirits of the dead. It felt to me like feathers were standing. She said yes, that is the hand trembling symbol. She said, you will lead your life this way. People will want help from you. She said, "My son, this hand trembling is not for you to get rich on. Only a few dollars is a reward for your service" . . . I said so be it.[71]

When a person attempts to learn if he has this gift, regular corn pollen or "live" corn pollen that has been placed over a Gila monster and then collected is spread on his freshly washed arms and hands. The teacher offers a special prayer to the lizard, confirming whether this person is to be given an opportunity to learn. A song is sung, then the ceremony "decides if it wants you." A diviner told John Holiday he was to be a hand trembler, but when he tried, nothing happened. Another man tried both hands, with no results. The practitioner used hand trembling and "vigorously tore at my hands and arms," but nothing. Finally he said, "You were once bitten by a jackrabbit on this hand and a prairie dog on the other; therefore, it is useless; it will definitely not work for you."[72] If any animal has bitten a hand or an arm, the appendage cannot be used for divining.

Anthropologist Leland C. Wyman and hand trembler Don Mose add detail to these accounts.[73] When pollen is placed on the forearm, either a straight line or a four-point zigzag lightning line will be drawn from the joint down to the wrist before each finger is traced with corn pollen. Mose believes the lightning, or male, design is much more energetic and rough in its signaling compared with the simpler, straight line. The final placement of corn pollen is in the palm of the hand, where either a pinch of pollen followed by four pinches of pollen to outline the points of an arrowhead or a single line of pollen marked with two crossbars to represent the Gila Monster is placed. The lizard's name is mentioned often in the prayers and songs that call upon it to provide divinatory power.

If the hand trembler does not know the songs, others can sing, working as a team. These songs may be specific to the Gila Monster or to other ones used in ceremonies that create a peaceful, spiritual feeling. If the hand starts to tremble before the prayer is finished, it is stopped and the song begun. Wyman identified fifteen or sixteen songs to the

Gila Monster, five of which are often used—although for a hand trembling session that may last about eight minutes, only two or three may be sung.[74] Other sessions may last up to a half hour.

As the involuntary movement of the hand begins—either gently or vigorously, as a tremor or in a wide arc—the hand trembler with eyes closed begins to picture various diseases, their cures, and those who perform the appropriate ceremony. The hand may draw in the sand a picture of the answer that needs to be guessed, and it may tap in agreement or disagreement with the diviner's interpretation. The feelings in the arm and hand are characterized as "'needles in the arm,' 'an electric shock,' 'hitting the crazy-bone,' 'a dash of cold water,' or 'as if the arm were asleep.' One man said that such sensations occur in beginners, who interpret it as 'the spirit going into his [or her] arm' . . . After one has been practicing for a long time the sensations may become painful, especially if one is old or sick."[75] Once the answer has been determined, the hand stops shaking and returns to normal.

Susie Yazzie from Monument Valley, Utah, is a good example of a person who had the "gift" but did not want it. Her detailed account provides an inside view of what the experience meant to her. Often it is older people, who have the maturity to recognize the signals and answers, who receive the power. Susie was young when she had this "strange experience" that seemed as if she were going through a trance: "It's a feeling of anxiety—as if you are in fear of something and you are trying to run from it, but you can't find a safe place. It feels like you levitate off the ground. It is emotionally tiring and a strain. It's like remembering something of your childhood and you become very emotional about it."[76]

The first time she hand trembled, a medicine man sang a song and she started. The power entered her body and moved her from one side of the hogan to the other where her mother sat by the door. She had not yet learned to "think for it" and to control her thoughts to seek answers, so the power took over and "literally threw me around all over the place." The "stream" of power surged throughout her body: "It made my heart seem big and enlarged and moved it around to a point where it weakened me. I was afraid of it and so [I] told the medicine man, Mr. Rock Ridge, to take the special gift away from me for good." He tapped corn pollen on the soles of her feet, the palms of her hands, the top of her head, then all over her body, and the power stopped. For some time after it had been removed, Susie continued to "question" and "think" in that way and felt she could regain the gift if she tried, but there was no desire to do so. She now muses, "It's probably because I gave up that special gift that I am suffering from so many health problems today."[77]

Hand tremblers and crystal gazers, as with any type of doctor trying to diagnose an illness, are not infallible. Rose Mitchell, the wife of Frank Mitchell, a Blessing Way singer, awoke one morning to find her face paralyzed and contorted. There was no apparent cause, so Frank hired a hand trembler to determine what should be done. The Chiricahua Apache Wind Way appeared to be the answer. After having it performed, Rose improved for a short while before the malady returned in full force. A different hand trembler diagnosed that a Navajo Wind Way ceremony was what was needed, but Frank did not concur. He paid for another hand trembler, who agreed that the Navajo Wind Way was necessary. This ceremony also provided only temporary relief. A fourth hand trembler prescribed a Shooting Way ceremony, which also had little impact. The only thing that seemed to make a difference was when Rose gave birth to a baby girl. Then everything returned to normal, but not before a number of large expenses had been incurred because of the ceremonies.[78]

This was not the first time Rose had depended on diviners. When she was a young girl, her family lived at a place called Houses Standing in a Line in the vicinity of Chinle Wash, Arizona. Her father, a medicine man and hand trembler, built a number of hogans and a large stone corral, then settled his family there for a winter camp. At first things went well, but eventually problems plagued the family and one of Rose's older sisters became very ill. Her father, Man Who Shouts, used hand trembling and held some small ceremonies, but to no avail. He called in a star gazer who performed the rite, then determined that the illness and bad luck were caused by the fact that the family's camp was sitting on top of a large Anaasází ruin and that the sister would not live. The father did not believe the diviner and paid for other ceremonies for his daughter, but she died. Soon, two more of Rose's older sisters and an older brother contracted the same illness. Again, the father did hand trembling and had ceremonies performed. Another battery of star gazers and hand tremblers provided diagnoses—all confirming that the presence of the Anaasází spirits was causing the illness. Before long, the two sisters and brother were dead. Finally, the father called his remaining family together and admitted that the star gazers and hand tremblers were correct and that he had seen indications of ruins when he was building the corral. Although he himself was a hand trembler who believed in its power, he had failed to act upon what the other diviners had said. He now agreed, and the family moved to a different location.[79]

Some people with the ability to hand tremble may lose it. In some diviners, old age causes the signals to weaken. In one example, a woman's baby niece crawled out of the house one day, then started to cry uncontrollably. To determine the cause, the woman performed hand trembling using a "natural gift," but she accidentally touched some of the blood from the diagnosed rattlesnake wound. That was the end of her gift. Informants also say that if a person does not take the ceremony seriously, it will "dodge" him, and if the diviner is afraid, its power is not good.[80]

Navajo Oshley told of one time when the power confronted him. His aunt had warned him that if the trembling turned against him, he could rip himself apart. Oshley did not believe her when she said the hand might poke him in the eye or pull at his nose, and he joked that he would just duck his head. However, he was not laughing some time later after he had experienced this phenomenon. When asked why he had painfully twisted his nose, he replied that his hand had done it. He went on to say that hand trembling had "turned against him" because he failed to interpret correctly an obvious signal given in diagnosing the patient's ailment.[81]

Respect for this power is a two-way commitment. When Left Hand, a skeptical Navajo watching a hand trembler, continued to doubt what he saw, the medicine man finished his diagnosis and started patting Left Hand on the knee. Next he started on the face, grabbed his ear and started to twist, then rubbed Left Hand's nose with his finger. Suddenly, his hand dropped and he said, "You didn't believe what I said a while ago, that is why my hand started shaking again . . . That's what the hand-shaking said, that you don't believe. If you don't believe, that is all right with me."[82] Left Hand later learned that everything the medicine man said was true.

Don Mose from Monument Valley shared his views based on a long line of hand tremblers in his family.[83] From his grandfather he learned the male form of hand trembling with the zigzag lightning and the sign of the Gila Monster, a method that is harshly powerful and can be used to detect evil or wrongdoing. His mother taught him a gentler way, with

Courtesy, Oshley family.

Navajo Oshley, an excellent manager of livestock from the Dennehotso–Monument Valley region, was an accomplished hand trembler and assistant in ceremonial gatherings. He learned early that the powers of the Gila Monster were to be taken seriously.

the straight line that ends with the four points of the arrowhead, and a second method that combined crystal gazing with its reproduction of the six sacred mountains blessed with corn pollen and a crystal located in their midst with hand trembling. To Don, the basis for all three ways was spirituality that allowed the diviner to get in tune with the holy people and receive their impressions. The basis for this began when Sun Bearer tested the Twins by switching the places of various mountains and other landforms on the earth to see if the boys could spiritually recognize where they should be. Born for Water, more spiritually in tune and contemplative than Monster Slayer—a holy being of action—proved more skilled in listening to the spirit to learn the answers to the questions. He began pointing out where the mountains were as the two sang the first of five songs entitled "That One over There" (Níléí át'é) in answer to "which one is it," implying "you are going to figure it out or solve the problem." The Twins were successful, received the necessary impressions, identified the proper locations, and eventually returned to earth with what they had sought. These songs are now used with hand trembling by those seeking answers.

Don's mother became aware of her gift when she was twelve years old. She was attending a ceremony when her nose started to bleed incessantly. Her father stopped the ceremony, performed hand trembling, and determined that the holy people present were indicating that her preparation for this responsibility needed to begin: "There's a young special girl that is going to do healing most of her life. Let's prepare her now." From that time throughout her long life of service up until two weeks before her death, she helped many people with this gift. Don received his gift in a different way. As a boy, he had been exposed to its teachings by a medicine man and years later encountered a Gila monster while herding cows with his father and uncle, also a medicine man. After he described what he had seen, the three men returned to the spot, where they encountered a black, foot-long Gila monster to which they made an offering for its power: "There is a purpose that he is there. Come step forward. This young man [Don] will also have the keys to knowing about your ways." Nothing else followed immediately.

When Don was a full-grown man and married, he received other indications that it was time, so he went to his mother and together they visited his grandfather. The elder drew the lightning and Gila Monster, traced the fingers in corn pollen, prayed, and began to sing. The novice "sat there dumbfounded with nothing happening, wondering how grandfather could be singing such complicated songs while motioning with his hand." He opened his eyes, saw his grandson with outstretched hand, then slapped it—"and away my hand went." The hand and arm moved vigorously about for less than a minute, but it was enough to make it feel like it "was about to fall off. I couldn't take it, the power was too great and the only thing I could think of was to have it stop. I couldn't take the pain." The holy people respected that, and his arm dropped.

During this brief event, Don learned two things. The first was that the arm and mind worked together to teach. It seemed that his hand, through his mind, went out the door in a vision-type experience in which he saw some beer and wine he had hidden in the back of his car. His hand waved back and forth, gesturing "no." When the signals stopped, his grandfather knew what the young man had seen: "That's right. Don't ever drink and do this or someday you'll lose the power. You'll misuse it and you will fall badly and lose everything. Wait until the time when you are wise, when your hair turns white. This is when you will use this [power] again." He later experienced exactly what his grandfather had said he would.

When his life finally settled down, Don began to use his gift. Two examples illustrate the practical nature of what he was able to do. The first experience occurred when a mother and daughter visited his mother for help in determining why the young girl was breaking out in hives, had runny eyes, and was lethargic. With his father providing the singing, Don began hand trembling. His hand bounced off the woven rug on a coffee table. He mentally viewed a tree with sheep under it, then the little girl herding the animals before getting up and walking home, then the image of the rug and more sheep. The answer: the girl was allergic to wool, which the weaving of her rug exacerbated. Plants from a medicine person removed the allergy; the now-grown woman is still weaving.

A second instance occurred when Don's brother had not been heard from for a month and his mother became worried. Instead of doing it herself, she asked Don to determine where her other son was and if he would be returning soon. She helped create the four, then six, sacred mountains from clean, sandy soil; sprinkled them with corn pollen; placed a crystal in the middle of the "sand painting"; and began to sing while Don performed hand trembling. He first viewed water, which he perceived was the ocean. Next he saw the head of a bear that appeared to be in a cage, then he saw its mouth and claws before it sat down. The image of his brother appeared standing close by, but it grew smaller as with distance. The hand indicated that he was coming home, and in three days he arrived. Don at first did not want his brother to know he had used hand trembling to determine where he was and what he was doing, but after a while he explained that he had done so and when he did it. The brother laughed and explained that he had been on the West Coast, then he went to California where he had stayed with a girlfriend for a while before returning home. Time and place seemed to fit except for the bear. When asked, the answer came: "We were . . . visiting a zoo and I saw a bear and the bear stood up and looked at me, and it was telling me to go home. So I did." This was at the time when Don was seeing this impression while hand trembling.

Today, some outsiders—both Anglo and Navajo—remain doubtful about these various forms of divination. Anthropologists, doctors, and sociologists try to explain away the mystical side of it, suggest that tremblers have prior knowledge of events, ask questions to arrive at a "general" answer, play on typical Navajo fears, use soothing psychological techniques, or just plain fake it. Wyman, in his investigation of this practice in the 1930s, approached this attitude head-on. In cases where he observed the practice and in one where he had the rite performed for him, there was no prior discussion with either patient or family members: "All my informants insisted that the diagnostician need not know anything about the case before beginning, and that he always goes to work without preliminary gathering of information. They seemed surprised when I suggested such a thing, saying that he 'does not need to' since the information is supposed to come from supernatural means."[84] While Anglo cultists dabble in extrasensory perception (ESP) ranging from crystal balls to tarot cards to palm readers, the clearly defined spiritual aspects that tie into an extensive body of traditional religious beliefs give Navajo practices a very different tone. The surprisingly large number of testimonials by traders who live among the Navajo erases any doubt that divination is based on a fluke chance of "getting it lucky, getting it right."

Perhaps the best-documented and consistent reporting of hand trembling is that of Hastiin Beaal and his work with Franc Newcomb. She and her husband, Arthur, were running the Blue Mesa Trading Post when they started to lose items to theft. One day they could not find three horses, so Franc called on Beaal for help. He laid out a blanket, covered it with fresh sand, went into a trance, pointed, and drew lines with his finger; when the tremors in his body ceased, he gave a clear, blow-by-blow description of where the horses were, who had taken them (without giving names), and how they were winning a race. Later, every detail was substantiated. Arthur was skeptical, Franc a more willing believer, but when some merchandise disappeared from a freight wagon, they again called in the ninety-five-year-old Beaal. He repeated the procedure and arrived at a very detailed explanation of where the stolen saddle and other items could be found. Arthur went to a distant post the next day, found what the diviner said was true, and retrieved the goods.

Beaal became a powerful deterrent to crime in the area. He successfully identified a Navajo who clubbed a trader's wife, helped the police capture two men who decapitated a trader and stole merchandise from his store, pinpointed for the authorities a Mexican who had been stealing sheep, and found $3,000 worth of turquoise and silver pawn taken from a post, as well as a wad of bills accidentally dropped in the sand. He reconstructed each of these incidents verbally in great detail, almost as if he were watching the plot unfold in a movie.[85] The powers of divination were a reality, even to the most skeptical.

What has been presented here is the practitioner's point of view, one that is sincere and valid. Rooted in the teachings of the past and still serving the Navajo today, it is a viable form of religious, social, and cultural power that holds important meaning. To provide explanations of how it works beyond what the diviners say is to attempt to make it appealing or understandable from an outsider's perspective, for one unable to embrace a foreign body of teachings and practices. No system, no matter how modern or technologically advanced, is without flaws and assumptions. To the Navajos, who have used divination to find their answers, these beliefs are as real as the earth, as close as the wind, and as lofty as the heavens.

NOTES

1. Antoine de Saint-Exupéry, *Wind, Sand, and Stars* (New York: Harcourt, Brace, 1940).
2. Ibid., 70.
3. Gladys Reichard, *Navaho Religion: A Study of Symbolism* (Princeton, NJ: Princeton University Press, 1950), 99.

4. Ibid., 99–100; Charlotte J. Frisbie and David P. McAllester, eds., *Navajo Blessingway Singer: The Autobiography of Frank Mitchell, 1881–1967* (Tucson: University of Arizona Press, 1978), 163; William Morgan, "Navaho Treatment of Sickness: Diagnosticians," *American Anthropologist* 33, no. 3 (Summer 1931): 390–392; http://dx.doi.org/10.1525/aa.1931.33.3.02a00050.
5. Reichard, *Navaho Religion*, 100, 122.
6. Mircea Eliade, *The Sacred and the Profane: The Nature of Religion* (New York: Harcourt, Brace and World, 1957), 68–113.
7. Frisbie and McAllester, *Navajo Blessingway Singer*, 100.
8. See James K. McNeley, *Holy Wind in Navajo Philosophy* (Tucson: University of Arizona Press, 1981), for a complete evaluation of the functions of nílch'i.
9. Mary C. Wheelwright, *Myth of Willa-Chee-Ji Degínnh-Keygo Hatrál* (Santa Fe, NM: Museum of Navajo Ceremonial Art, 1958), 1–2.
10. McNeley, *Holy Wind*, 34–35; Ada Black interview with author, October 11, 1991; Shone Holiday interview with Samuel Moon, July 21, 1975, Southeastern Utah Project, Utah State Historical Society and California State University Oral History Program, Fullerton, CA.
11. See Robert S. McPherson, *Sacred Land, Sacred View: Navajo Perception of the Four Corners Region*, Charles Redd Center for Western Studies Monograph 19 (Provo, UT: Brigham Young University Press, 1992), 87–97, for an explanation of how Big Wind, among other elements, destroyed the Anaasází.
12. Joe Manygoats interview with author, December 16, 1991; Ada Black interview with author.
13. Ada Black interview with author; Shone Holiday interview with author, September 10, 1991.
14. Mary C. Wheelwright, *The Myth and Prayers of the Great Star Chant and the Myth of the Coyote Chant* (Santa Fe, NM: Museum of Navajo Ceremonial Art, 1956), 22–23.
15. Manygoats interview with author.
16. Karl Luckert, *A Navajo Bringing-Home Ceremony: The Claus Chee Sonny Version* (Flagstaff: Museum of Northern Arizona Press, 1978), 198.
17. Mary C. Wheelwright, *Myth of Natóhe Bakáji Hatrál* (Santa Fe, NM: Museum of Navajo Ceremonial Art, 1958), 15.
18. Franciscan Fathers, *An Ethnologic Dictionary of the Navajo Language* (Saint Michaels, AZ: Saint Michaels Press, 1910), 365.
19. Leland C. Wyman, "Navaho Diagnosticians," *American Anthropologist* 38, no. 2 (April–June 1936): 245; http://dx.doi.org/10.1525/aa.1936.38.2.02a00050.
20. W. W. Hill, *Navaho Warfare*, Yale University Publications in Anthropology 5 (New Haven, CT: Yale University Press, 1936), 13.
21. Franciscan Fathers, *Ethnologic Dictionary*, 37, 354; Reichard, *Navaho Religion*, 470–475.
22. Franc Johnson Newcomb, *Navaho Neighbors* (Norman: University of Oklahoma Press, 1966), 165.
23. Buck Navajo interview with author, December 16, 1991.
24. Ibid.; Cecil Parrish interview with author, October 10, 1991.
25. Berard Haile, *Upward Moving and Emergence Way: The Gishin Biye' Version* (Lincoln: University of Nebraska Press, 1981), 140; Franciscan Fathers, *Ethnologic*

Dictionary, 41; Washington Matthews, "A Part of the Navajos' Mythology," *American Antiquarian* 5 (1883): 207–224 (Chicago), Special Collections, Harold B. Lee Library, Brigham Young University, Provo, UT; Ada Black interview with Bertha Parrish, June 18, 1987, San Juan County Historical Society, Blanding, UT.

26. Haile, *Upward Moving*, 140; Navajo interview with author; Ernest L. Bulow, *Navajo Taboos* (Gallup, NM: Southwesterner Books, 1982), 1.
27. Manygoats interview with author.
28. Ibid.; Haile, *Upward Moving*, 140.
29. Trudy Griffin-Pierce, "Power through Order: Ethnoastronomy in Navajo Sandpaintings of the Heavens," PhD dissertation, University of Arizona, Tucson, 1987, 124–126; Mary C. Wheelwright, ed., *Navajo Creation Myth: The Story of the Emergence* by Hasteen Klah (Santa Fe, NM: Museum of Navajo Ceremonial Art, 1942), 66; Linda Hadley, *Hózhǫ́ǫ́jí Hane' (Blessingway)* (Rough Rock, AZ: Rough Rock Demonstration School, 1986), 20.
30. Matthews, *Navajo Legends,* 7–8.
31. John Holiday interview with author, September 9, 1991.
32. Ibid.; Parrish interview with author; medicine man cited in Griffin-Pierce, "Power through Order," 138.
33. Franc Johnson Newcomb, *Navaho Folk Tales* (Albuquerque: University of New Mexico Press, 1967), 83–88; Guy Cly interview with author, August 7, 1991.
34. Newcomb, *Navaho Folk Tales*, 85–88; Navajo interview with author; Ada Black interview with author.
35. Leland C. Wyman, "Origin Legends of Navaho Divinatory Rites," *Journal of American Folklore* 49, no. 191/192 (January–June 1936): 134–142; http://dx.doi.org/10.2307/535487.
36. Ibid., 142.
37. Aileen O'Bryan, *The Diné: Origin Myths of the Navaho Indians*, Bureau of American Ethnology Bulletin 163 (Washington, DC: Smithsonian Institution, 1956), 2; Ada Black interview with author; Wheelwright, *Star Chant*, 57, 115.
38. Ada Black interview with author.
39. Ibid.
40. Navajo interview with author.
41. Suzie Yazzie interview with author, August 6, 1991.
42. Cly interview with author; Ella Sakizzie interview with author, May 14, 1991; Ada Black interview with author.
43. George Tom interview with author, August 7, 1991.
44. Harvey Oliver interview with author, May 14, 1991.
45. John Holiday interview with author; Jenny Francis interview with author, March 23, 1993; LaVerne Harrell Clark, *They Sang for Horses: The Impact of the Horse on Navajo and Apache Folklore* (Tucson: University of Arizona Press, 1966), 105–106.
46. Haile, *Upward Moving*, 79, 83.
47. Ibid., 38; Wheelwright, *Great Star*, 115; Emma Chief interview with Samuel Moon, August 7, 1975, Southeastern Utah Project, Utah State Historical Society and California State University Oral History Program, Fullerton, CA.
48. Wyman, "Navaho Diagnosticians," 244–245.
49. Franc Johnson Newcomb, Stanley Fishler, and Mary C. Wheelwright, *A Study of Navajo Symbolism*, Papers of the Peabody Museum 32, no. 3 (Cambridge, MA:

Harvard University Press, 1956), 25–26; see also Berard Haile, *Starlore among the Navaho* (Santa Fe, NM: Museum of Navajo Ceremonial Art, 1947), 38–40, for a slightly different version of this ceremony.

50. Bud Haycock interview with author, October 10, 1991.
51. Fred Yazzie interview with author, August 6, 1991.
52. Keith Holiday interview with author, April 9, 1992.
53. Ibid.
54. Ted Cly interview with Samuel Moon, September 28, 1973, Southeastern Utah Project, Utah State Historical Society and California State University Oral History Program, Fullerton, CA, 7–8; Charlie Blueyes interview with author, August 28, 1988; Mary Blueyes interview with author, July 25, 1988.
55. Haile, *Upward Moving*, 69–70, 83.
56. Wyman, "Origin Legends," 135–136.
57. Ibid., 135.
58. Ibid., 136.
59. Ibid.
60. Ibid.
61. John Holiday interview with author; Frisbie and McAllester, *Navajo Blessingway Singer*, 146; Walter Dyk and Ruth Dyk, *Left Handed: A Navajo Autobiography* (New York: Columbia University Press, 1980), 104–106.
62. Clyde Kluckhohn, *Navaho Witchcraft* (Boston: Beacon, 1944), 200–202.
63. Ted Cly, cited in Samuel Moon, *Tall Sheep: Harry Goulding, Monument Valley Trader* (Norman: University of Oklahoma Press, 1992), 126.
64. Ada Black interview with author.
65. John Holiday interview with author; Dyk and Dyk, *Left Handed,* 402–403.
66. Wyman, "Navaho Diagnosticians," 239; Ada Black interview with author; Navajo interview with author.
67. Gerald Hausman, *The Gift of the Gila Monster: Navajo Ceremonial Tales* (New York: Touchstone Book, 1993), 57–58.
68. John Holiday and Robert S. McPherson, *A Navajo Legacy: The Life and Teachings of John Holiday* (Norman: University of Oklahoma Press, 2005), 290–291.
69. Clyde Kluckhohn and Dorothea Leighton, *The Navaho* (Cambridge, MA: Harvard University Press, 1946), 210–212.
70. Ada Black interview with author; John Holiday interview with author.
71. Navajo Oshley interview with Winston Hurst and Wesley Oshley, January 5, 1978.
72. John Norton interview with author, January 16, 1991; Parrish interview with author; John Holiday interview with author.
73. Wyman, "Navaho Diagnosticians," 238–240; Don Mose interview with author, June 7, 2011.
74. Wyman, "Navaho Diagnosticians," 240.
75. Ibid., 239, 242.
76. Susie Yazzie interview with author, November 10, 2000.
77. Ibid.
78. Rose Mitchell with Charlotte J. Frisbie, ed., *Tall Woman: The Life Story of Rose Mitchell, a Navajo Woman, ca. 1874–1977* (Albuquerque: University of New Mexico Press, 2001), 183–184.

79. Ibid., 99–106.
80. Oshley interview with Hurst and Oshley; John Holiday interview with author; Navajo interview with author.
81. Oshley interview with Hurst and Oshley.
82. Dyk and Dyk, *Left Handed,* 486–488.
83. Mose interview with author.
84. Wyman, "Navaho Diagnosticians," 238.
85. Newcomb, *Navajo Neighbors*, 183–198.

2

The 1918–1919 Influenza Epidemic

A Cultural Response

Divination, as discussed in the previous chapter, forewarns and forearms the Navajo for what lies ahead. Unfortunately, the 1918 Influenza Epidemic may have been foretold, but nothing in Navajo teaching and practice could stop this totally unfamiliar disease. No ceremonially prescribed cure existed. Not since the creation of the earth had the People faced such devastating consequences. Even First Man, who is credited with emplacing both sicknesses and their cures, could not have foreseen the effect this illness would have on the People. Today, it is still difficult to determine just how wide-ranging its impact was.

What follows is a comparative study of how three different cultures—Anglo, Navajo, and Ute-Paiute—dealt with a sickness no one could control. Best practices seemed to favor the

DOI: 10.7330/9781607322177.c02

> *Anglos' modern medicine, with its germ theory of disease, but even then there were no guarantees; over a half million people in the United States permanently succumbed to its effects. For the Navajo, who stressed a religious approach, it appeared that the holy people were equally befuddled. Death lay all about. Not until the illness had run its course would the Diné and the holy beings return to their earlier ceremonial practices that had proven effective in the past.*

As the last cold months of 1918 drew to a close, the bloody annals of World War I became a part of history and a prelude to hopes for peace. Another enemy, however, was stalking the living to spread death and sadness throughout the world. Even in countries that were technologically advanced in healthcare, such as the United States, the disease known as Spanish Influenza took its toll, killing over 21,000 Americans in the last week of October alone.[1] Transmitted primarily through the respiratory system, the sickness leaped from person to person, community to community, and region to region—inflicting the masses with an often not lethal but invariably difficult illness that infected patients for as long as a month.

One of the best general studies of this contagion and its impact is Alfred W. Crosby's *America's Forgotten Pandemic*, which takes a global view of this illness that lasted less than six months. During that time, however, Crosby points out that a highly conservative estimate of deaths in the United States is 550,000, far more than all American battlefield casualties sustained in World War I, World War II, and the Korean and Vietnam conflicts (423,000 total).[2] The oft-cited figure of 21 million deaths worldwide, he feels, is "a gross underestimation." As for Native Americans in the United States: "American Indians suffered hideously in the pandemic. According to the statistics of the Office of Indian Affairs, 24 percent of reservation Indians caught flu from October 1, 1918, to March 31, 1919, and . . . the case mortality rate was 9 percent, about four times as high as that in the nation's big cities."[3] The reason for this larger death rate, Crosby points out, was associated with the culture, its belief systems, the way it responded, and how quickly it reacted. Nothing was more true than the case of the Navajo.

This chapter compares and contrasts reactions to the 1918–1919 Influenza Epidemic in a limited geographic area—primarily southeastern

Utah and the neighboring Four Corners region—and shows how the cultural response influenced the severity of the disease. This area is ideal for analysis because of its demographic diversity, ranging from Euro-American to Native American and from scientific medicine to folk remedies to religious and ceremonial practices. What emerges is a more complete understanding of the cultural values that pervaded the societies in the Four Corners area during this time.

The origin of Spanish Influenza is still not clear. Although this strain carries the title of "Spanish," it most likely started in the United States and spread to Europe. Healthcare providers in Fort Riley, Kansas, reported the first cases of sickness when dust and smoke from burning manure infected soldiers, over 1,100 of whom became sick with 46 dying.[4] Later, some of the troops training at Fort Riley deployed to Europe for service in the final stages of the war, and with them traveled the virus-causing disease. Influenza, identified as having three major strains, spontaneously shifted into different types, making it difficult for the body to create immunity.[5] The disease spread rapidly, first to the soldiers fighting on both sides of the war and then to the civilian masses who welcomed them home.

Sickness and death followed, with the flu acting as a gateway to other forms of illness—especially pneumonia—by lowering people's resistance. Symptoms of the disease included severe headaches, chills, fevers, leg and back pains, intense sore throat, labored breathing, and total lassitude. Once infected, a person had little desire to do anything but rest and avoid exertion.

ANGLO TOWN RESPONSE

Rural as well as metropolitan areas suffered from the disease, with the Four Corners region no exception. Moab, Utah, first reported the outbreak of influenza on October 18, 1918, when three cases appeared in the John P. Miller family.[6] The town's reaction was immediate. Fearing the effects of the sickness sweeping the nation, Dr. John W. Williams, the town's health officer, ordered the closing of schools, churches, and other places of public gathering. The community fully supported his actions—especially the children, half of whom were withdrawn from school as soon as the disease's presence was reported.

The State Board of Health next went to work, outlining precautions and publishing them in Moab's *Grand Valley Times*. While most of these instructions were common knowledge, such as having plenty of bed rest, eating healthy food, and seeking a doctor's care, other practices were more innovative. For instance, the board encouraged people to keep their bedroom windows open at all times, to "take medicine to open the bowels freely," and to wear a gauze mask that covered the nose and mouth when entering a sickroom.[7] How many people complied with these initial instructions is not known, but within a week the town lifted the ban because no further cases had appeared. Monticello, however, located fifty-five miles south of Moab, reported its first two incidents.[8]

The respite from influenza was short-lived. By November 1, newspaper headlines and subtitles splashed warnings across the pages: "Influenza Spreading at Alarming Rate," with two deaths in Moab and two in Monticello. The disease attacked sixty miners in Sego, a coal camp near Moab, while the newspaper reported at least six new cases within city limits. Dr. Williams and the city council took prompt action again, posting guards on the outskirts of town to stop and direct visitors to the local hotel. There, they were quarantined for four days, inspected by the doctor, and released if they showed no signs of illness. Failure to comply with these regulations resulted in being found guilty of a misdemeanor and fined up to $100. Within the town, Dr. Williams and the city council prohibited all public gatherings and applauded the fact that many people were wearing gauze masks outside their homes.[9]

Normal activities in rural Moab ceased. The election of Grand County political candidates became more difficult, and campaigning stopped. The drafting of soldiers for the final phase of the war slowed down, and because the flu was raging in the cantonments in northern Utah, the seventeen men already qualified for service remained in Moab until the epidemic abated. When District Attorney Knox Patterson became ill, the District County Court of San Juan and Grand Counties was also postponed.[10] The town sheriff, William J. Bliss, and Marshall Abe Day enforced the new local law of wearing masks and prevented people from attempting to gather in large numbers. Even funeral services were delayed or canceled because of the quarantine.

Still, the epidemic raged. Particularly hard-hit were occupations that required people to work in large numbers at close quarters. Sego reported 100 cases, while a uranium camp on Polar Mesa stated that everyone was sick in bed. In Monticello the Mexican population was hardest hit,

Courtesy, Utah State Historical Society.

Travel in southeastern Utah during the first quarter of the twentieth century was often challenging, as this motorist can attest. Transportation during the 1918–1919 Influenza Epidemic compounded issues in providing medical assistance.

with 40 cases of sickness.[11] Livestock owner Ed Taylor accompanied his large herd of sheep to a marketplace "back East," where he contracted the disease. While returning home he stopped in Grand Junction, Colorado, sickened, and died.[12] Thus, business practices often opened the doors to affliction.

During late November, however, the citizens of Moab started to congratulate themselves on having beaten the contagion. The disease appeared to have run its course; no new cases were reported, and the satellite mining communities suggested they were about to resume production. With this sense of security, the doctor lifted the quarantine, and there the matter rested for a little over a month. The control of visitors continued in effect, but school and public gatherings resumed. Influenza seemed a thing of the past, and with the advent of the Christmas season, peace and goodwill replaced the fear of the previous month.

Yet during the Christmas gatherings a new onslaught of influenza got its start. On January 3, 1919, banner headlines again proclaimed 100 cases of influenza raging in Moab; one week later the number jumped to 250. Cold weather and seasonal moisture encouraged incubation of the disease, causing it to soar again to epidemic proportions. Dr. Williams telegrammed for assistance, receiving another doctor from the State Board of Health and two nurses from Colorado. After again suspending any type of public meetings, Williams established a fifty-bed hospital in the high school for the seriously afflicted. Two nurses operated the facility, while physicians handled the vaccinations. Although the doctors claimed the serum was "an almost infallible preventative," the various strains of influenza proved too versatile to be brought under control.[13] The type of vaccine used is not clear, since a number of varieties were available at the time. Some of these included a mixture of organisms from influenza patients, diphtheria antitoxins, and anti-tetanus and anti-meningitis serums.[14] The problem of providing immunity is described in a report: "A number of people who had the disease a month ago are again stricken, indicating that no one is immune from it."[15]

One interesting sidelight during this second period of affliction was the change in approach by Moab citizens. In the first bout of influenza, a strict external quarantine sealed off the town from the outside world. On January 3, however, the *Times* reported that "travel to and from Moab is in no way restricted, so far as local authorities are concerned. People from the outside will be free to come here and transact their business. The neighboring towns, however, have indicated that they will establish stringent quarantine against people coming from or passing through Moab."[16] This attitude was at least in part a result of the large number of sick in Moab; Williams estimated that two-thirds of the town, or about 500 people, were afflicted.[17]

Another interesting aspect of the epidemic involved some of the cures—advertised and unadvertised—used to fight the malady. Whiskey was one of the more desirable, and Williams ordered ten gallons from state sources. Because the Eighteenth Amendment requiring Prohibition was in the process of ratification, legal sources of alcohol were drying up. The assistant physician, Dr. C. Clark, was supposed to bring ten gallons with him to deliver to the sheriff, who would in turn dispense it under doctor's orders, thus circumventing the state law forbidding the shipment of alcohol. The whiskey, however, was not released to the physician's care, which prompted another flurry of letters from the concerned citizens of Moab. Statements such as "ship whiskey. Have eleven down with flu" and "have two children and wife in bed. Come through if possible" were attached to a petition signed by "every businessman, county and town officers, and the Baptist minister." Acting governor Harden Bennion relented and sent a special courier to Moab with two gallons of the illegal brew.[18]

Commercial sales of medication skyrocketed. Advertisements warned: "Druggists!! Please Note Vick's VapoRub Oversold Due to Present Epidemic . . . Last Week's Orders Called for One and Three Quarter Million Jars—Today's Orders Alone Number 932,459 Jars."[19] The ad explained that an anticipated national year's supply of this product was depleted in a matter of weeks and that the firm was stepping up production in a valiant effort to meet demand. The company called in all its sales representatives to work in the office and the factory because twenty-four of its staff members were currently in the "service of Uncle Sam." Present orders could not be filled entirely but would be in the near future. The Vick's VapoRub Company also produced a booklet outlining the history, symptoms, and cures for influenza "and particularly the use of Vicks VapoRub as an external application to supplement the physician's treatment."

Other companies also used the bandwagon approach. Dr. Kilmer's Swamp-Root "heals and strengthens the kidneys after an attack of grip . . . A trial will convince anyone who may be in need of it." Eatonic helped "millions [who] are now suffering from the after effects of the deadly flu . . . by giving attention to the stomach—that is removing acidity and toxic poisons." By using this product, "a great deal of suffering would be saved to humanity."[20] The Moab Board of Health also gave advice, warning that "two or three days lost from work or business has a distinct advantage over paying the undertaker." The announcement concluded by stating, "The Creator provided all the oxygen necessary in the fresh air; therefore, don't shut this out of your home and then in case of sickness pay good money for a tank of oxygen in an effort to save somebody's life."[21]

By January 17, the epidemic in Moab had started to abate. During that week, reports indicated that only five new cases had broken out while many of those previously afflicted were on the mend. Dr. Williams estimated that 250 people in the town had not contracted the illness, in comparison to "the great majority of the people of Moab [who] have already had the disease."[22] The townspeople heaped praise on Doctors Williams and Clark for their round-the-clock efforts, while the doctors lauded the work of the nurses in their temporary high school hospital and the serum made available for vaccinations. The hospital was the most expensive of the efforts, amounting to almost $1,700 for less than a month's operation during which it handled only ten truly critical cases.[23]

In summarizing Moab's experience, one finds an organized, orderly approach to combating the effects of influenza. Two doctors, two nurses, and an active board of health were combined with an effective program of quarantine, vaccination, hospitalization, home healthcare, and informational services. Cooperation proved to be the rule and not the exception, the end result being that fewer than a dozen people died during the combined November and January outbreaks. By January 31, the Moab Board of Health lifted the ban and allowed normal town life to resume.

RURAL MORMON COMMUNITY RESPONSE

Smaller communities to the south, such as Monticello and Blanding, had nothing close to Moab's organization and medical care. Because of their size and Mormon population, cooperation of a different nature helped many to survive. For instance, when the owner of the Grayson Co-op became sick, customers opened the store and took what they needed, with a promise to pay later.[24] Although most of the town was afflicted with illness at one time or another, a number of men and women made a daily practice of helping their neighbors. The men hauled wood, fed livestock, and performed heavier chores, while the women plied their knowledge as accomplished midwives.[25] Outside help was limited to infrequent visits from the doctor in Moab. To speed his travel to Monticello, town members met him approximately halfway with a fresh team of horses.[26] For people in Blanding, there was no doctor.

As in Moab, public meetings and classes in schools came to a halt, although in many outlying areas, some activities had to continue. One woman told of living in the community of Dove Creek, Colorado, just over the Utah border. In 1918 she ran a combination store and post office while her husband was in the Cortez hospital fighting typhoid fever. She remembers how she "saw them bringing in big, husky young men. They were bringing them in delirious and maybe in an hour or two they'd be dead . . . One fellow came and stayed overnight . . . The next day or two later, he was dead."[27]

Courtesy, San Juan County Historical Commission.

Unlike Moab, rural towns like Monticello (pictured here) and Blanding were predominantly Mormon and closely knit through family and religious ties. Although they lacked the professional help available elsewhere, the people depended on each other to handle the chores of daily life and relieve the suffering of the sick.

Folk remedies were an important part of the healing process. Beyond bed rest and warm food, a common cure was mustard plasters to provide heat for the patient's chest.[28] Quinine helped break fevers, hot packs and olive oil relieved the pain of earaches, and wild sage boiled in water and sweetened with honey loosened a congested chest. One man, caught in a lonely campsite, doctored himself back to health by eating a big gob of pine pitch.[29]

Preventive medicines were also used, with people eating wild garlic and hanging asafetida around their necks. This latter substance is an offensive-smelling resinous material extracted from the roots of several kinds of plants of the genus *Ferula*. One survivor of the ordeal of wearing asafetida around his neck swore that "it's the stinkingest stuff you ever seen . . . but it makes a good coyote bait."[30] Unfortunately, no statistics exist for these outlying areas, since there was no newspaper, no doctor, and no official organization to record the number of patients and deaths. A general impression from oral interviews indicates that most families in these communities were afflicted, some more seriously than others, and that the mortality rate was higher than that of Moab.

NAVAJO RESPONSE

Of all the people in the Four Corners area affected by the disease, Native Americans—especially the Navajo—seemed to suffer the most. Oral tradition has kept alive the trauma that accompanied the "Great Sickness," and though much of what was done to prevent it may appear ineffective to an outsider, the main issue for the Navajo was a religious one. To them, much of life and its accompanying problems carries supernatural significance that must be dealt with in both the spiritual and physical realms of this world. The result is a practical, logical approach to disease prevention and cure according to traditional beliefs.

Events do not just happen. There are omens that appear beforehand but that may not be recognized until after the fact. So it was with the epidemic. On June 8, 1918, a solar eclipse occurred, presaging misfortune. The sun, an important Navajo deity, hid his light from his people because of anger, warning that a catastrophe would soon take place.[31] During the summer and fall, dawns and sunsets had pronounced reddish hues that bathed the landscape in an ominous red.[32] The tips of cedar and juniper trees started to die, a sign indicating that sickness was in the area and would be visiting humans, and some Navajos had bad dreams portending disaster. Informants indicate that the holy people sent the disease to make room for a growing population of the younger generation; others suggest that poisonous gas or the smoke and fumes from artillery rounds fired in World War I somehow infected the Diné.[33] Whatever the reason, the Navajos were ill-prepared for the ensuing sickness.

Because their reservation is spread over a large geographic area, with many access routes and a mobile population, it is difficult to identify the initial entry of the epidemic. For instance, Louisa Wetherill (Asdzáán Ts'ósí, or Slim Woman)—the wife of John Wetherill, a trader in Kayenta, Arizona—tells of visiting many Navajo homes in southern Utah and northern Arizona to solicit sheep for the war effort. As she traveled from hogan to hogan, she became increasingly tired and suffered from severe headaches, which later proved to be symptoms of the flu. Louisa noted that the first death from this disease was in the area of Black Mesa, not far from where she was visiting. Within a week her Navajo host had died, and by the time she arrived back at her trading post, stricken Navajos filled her front yard. The Indians reacted by destroying the dwellings where a death occurred, so that "soon all over the reservation, smoke was rising from the hogans of the dead."[34] Louisa may not have been the first person to introduce the disease, but she was most likely an unwitting vector for transmitting it.

Other examples indicate how the disease spread. Some Navajos tell of a Yé'ii bicheii ceremony held in late October at Blue Canyon, approximately eighteen miles east of Tuba City. Large numbers of people congregated for the performance, contracted the disease, but showed no symptoms for a week or two. Navajos in the Monument Valley area claimed to have received the sickness from Paiutes and Utes as they moved from Navajo Mountain to Allen Canyon and the general vicinity around Blanding.[35] Gilmore Graymountain encountered some of these Paiutes in the Oljato area. The Paiute man had four women and some children with him in a wagon. He asked Graymountain to help him build a fire as he constructed a shelter: "They were just under a tree and it was very cold, with the wind just breezing through the spot."[36] By the time the Navajo returned with a wagonload of wood, two of the women were dead.

Another source of illness came from Silverton and Durango, Colorado, when infected Navajo miners returning to the reservation passed through various towns. This spread the disease to the northeastern boundary of Navajo lands, first reported by the Shiprock Boarding School during the week of October 6: "About one week prior to its advent on the agency, the towns to the east, north, and south had been recipients of their first cases in varying degrees of intensity, but these are all located at such distances and with such slow means of communication that the disease here spread as rapidly as the news."[37]

Hastiin Klah, a famous medicine man, also became sick after a visit to Durango when he appeared at the Blue Mesa Trading Post run by Arthur and Franc Newcomb. He was the first in the area to contract the disease, so he self-medicated with herbal teas and fumigants burned in his isolated hogan. He healed himself during this initial wave of influenza, which proved mild compared to what struck three months later in February, the "Hunger Moon." Food was scarce, cold was intense, and sleet and snowstorms were frequent. Entire families died, while the living barricaded the doors and blocked the smoke holes from the outside to keep wild animals from entering and eating the corpses. Later, Indian agents sent teams to burn the hogans and bury the dead, but in the meantime, those who survived fled to other people's homes for refuge. Klah traveled about helping neighbors and relatives, having remarkable success with those he treated. He brought herbal medicines to Art Newcomb when he became sick and rode sixty miles over the mountains to rescue and adopt a three-year-old boy and a five-month-old baby girl who were the children of his dead niece. Many other surviving Navajos also cared for children of the deceased.[38]

Franciscan fathers Berard Haile and Anselm Weber, with the Saint Michaels Mission, placed their facility under strict quarantine as soon as the illness appeared. They wrote lengthy reports of their travels and experiences that illustrate the assistance they rendered and how Navajo people acted during the initial onslaught of the disease. Father Weber visited the schools in Fort Defiance and Gallup between November 6 and 12. During that time what had started as 5 children with normal colds mushroomed into 250 children in Fort Defiance and 300 in Gallup bedridden with influenza.[39] Because of the quarantine at Saint Michaels, its 250 students avoided the disease, while in Gallup the demand for coffins was impossible to meet. Railroad crews were put to work burying large numbers of dead. If the sick could get to the hospital at Fort Defiance, their chances of survival increased dramatically.[40]

Father Berard Haile, meanwhile, was in the hinterland of Lukachukai and reported many men who had been working on the railroad or been employed in Cortez, Colorado, returning home and unwittingly infecting the community at ceremonies and other gatherings. Some died outside their tent or hogan exposed to the elements, while others died in shelters. He noted that the living, when in the presence of the dead, put sprigs of sagebrush in their nostrils to keep the spirit of the deceased away. Haile provided last rites for many as they took their final breaths but were still conscious enough to repeat the prayers. Burial followed, with expensive grave goods accompanying the dead in their journey to the land beyond. Haile recorded the interment of Mark Mitchell by his brother-in-law, who bathed and dressed the corpse:

> This we lifted into a large box into which we placed a good saddle, blankets, and a buckskin rope, then nailed the lid. We deposited Mark by his mother. A cloud of smoke down the valley showed that the

> family had moved and left the neighborhood. Apparently, too, it must be unsafe for the herds of the deceased to pass the "death line," that is to say, the route the corpse is to take. For when the car was about ready to move on, the driver was asked to wait until the herd could be driven to the right side ahead of the car.[41]

Haile closed his account by saying that some of the medicine men said that they as well as the priests had survived because they understood the power of prayer. They did not die like the rest of the people, which to the priest was "blissful ignorance and presumption." He felt the decision as to who survived was totally up to the Lord and that although the medicine men may view it their way and proclaim their prowess in combating the disease, "none of us can defy death, and he [who thinks he can] had better be modest in his claims!"[42]

The effects of influenza dragged on. Some of the best eyewitness accounts come from traders living on or near the reservation. Indian clients knew and trusted these men and women and came to them for assistance in their dire need. Ken and Hilda Faunce ran the Covered Water Trading Post in northern Arizona. Near their establishment, large groves of piñon trees bore a heavy crop of nuts, attracting numerous Navajos to the harvest. Exposed to cold temperatures and driving rains, the unsuspecting, infected victims attempted to collect the nuts until the disease quickly overpowered them. Entire families died next to their wagons, seeking shelter from the storms and relief from the flu.[43]

Even those who remained at home were often deprived of their warm winter hogans, abandoning them after a person had died inside. This was in keeping with the Navajo tradition that the spirit of the deceased remained in the vicinity where the death occurred to haunt the living because of loneliness. Laura Thapaha near Todalena first lost her father as he worked his way through small towns bordering the San Juan River looking for work. Next her baby sister died, her mother wrapping the infant in a blanket and depositing her in a nearby cliff crevice. Her grandmother—sensing the end was near—returned to the crevice, removed the stone barrier, took a small container of water and some cornbread, then wrapped herself in a blanket and lay down next to the dead infant while Laura's mother rebuilt the rock wall that sealed her in her final resting place. Shortly, her mother directed Laura to fix a lunch for herself and her two brothers, saddle the old gray mare down by the waterhole, and then pile poles and brush against the hogan door in which the ailing mother rested. Laura then traveled to the home of a nearby missionary who cared for the children. The next day he went to the hogan, buried the mother, and burned the dwelling, later sending the children to an Episcopalian orphanage near Fort Defiance.[44]

The results of abandoning homes during severe weather were inevitable. Influenza raged across the landscape, destroying entire groups at a time. One eyewitness reported:

> Whole families were wiped out, leaving their flocks wandering over the hills at the mercy of the wolves. Several related families living together all died but one small boy who was found herding the combined flocks of sheep . . . A Paiute woman died on their reservation north of the San Juan River. Fleeing from the place of the dead, the husband and five children crossed the river into the Navajo country with their sheep where they died one by one along the trail. Only one little boy survived and he is so small that he is unable to give his parents' name.[45]

Fear associated with the dead drove the Navajo into temporary brush shelters that proved to be ineffective protection from the cold and rain.[46]

Louisa Wetherill reported a constant flow of Navajos to her trading post, seeking help with burials. Although it took two weeks for her husband to recover from his bout with the flu, both she and John spent considerable time interring the dead and nursing the living. John estimated that by December 6, in Kayenta alone, he had buried over 100 Navajos.[47] Hilda Faunce helped a woman who requested a wooden box in which to bury her child. Although this was against traditional practices, the bereaved mother explained that her son had gone away to school in California and watched the burial of some Navajos, after which no building was destroyed or deserted: "He had not noticed [that] any ill luck had followed such burials, therefore he thought it was perhaps the box that kept the gods from being angry because the buildings were not burned."[48] In most instances, white traders dug holes for a final resting place, burned the deserted hogan with the dead inside, or simply closed the doors after shoveling dirt on the deceased. One government stockman riding the range in April buried two influenza victims who had died in their hogan the previous fall. Another man remembered parties of white volunteers from Colorado, New Mexico, and Utah going into the remote

Author photo.

Death within a home forced the living occupants to abandon it for shelter elsewhere. Severe winter weather compounded problems created by cultural practices.

canyon lands of the reservation to bury the dead.[49] Thus geographic isolation and traditional beliefs combined to make suffering and death a lonely experience for the afflicted.

The Navajo response to this catastrophe came in two forms—spiritual and physical. To them, the roots of the epidemic lay in religious beliefs, and it was on this level that the most successful prevention and treatment were to be found. There were two types of ceremonies to cure patients' illness or to prevent people from becoming ill in the first place: the Blessing Way (Hózhǫ́ǫ́jí) and the Evil Way (Hóchx'ǫ́ǫ́jí). The former is a ritual that encourages beauty, health, and harmony to surround a person and was generally used as a prayer for well-being and protection. The latter ceremony fends off evil, particularly associated with the spirits of the dead, and was used for those surrounded by death and involvement with burial. Both ceremonies share the ultimate outcome of protecting a person from harm and providing prayers acceptable to the holy people, who in turn give necessary help.[50] However, there was no specific ceremony to deal solely with influenza, a white man's disease that had never before taken its toll on the Navajo. Still, medicine men remained busy traveling about, performing ceremonies, and praying for the sick; how much of the disease was spread through these unwitting vectors and the close contact required in the rituals will never be known, but in the minds of the Navajo, these healers saved many lives and performed a valuable service comparable to the work of the doctors in Moab. Prayers, not vaccine, held the cure.

Ada Black from Monument Valley described how dependent her family was on prayers. Her maternal grandmother used them to "shield" off the sickness: "At the break of dawn she offered white cornmeal, at noon she offered mixed (multicolored) cornmeal, then at twilight before the golden glow passed she offered yellow cornmeal, and at midnight she offered blue cornmeal."[51] Ada recalled that red skies in the morning or evening portended the approach of the disease, so her parents told her to offer cornmeal and pollen with prayer to stem the tide of death. Her grandfather had the sweat lodge ready for the women to enter to cleanse themselves by perspiring in the intense heat three or four times in a row while drinking specially prepared herbs to fend off the illness. By the time the sun had risen, the women were finished and ready for the day's chores so the men could have their turn. No one in this group caught the disease.

Although the major emphasis to combat the malady was on religion, the Navajos also employed a number of physical cures. As mentioned, sweat baths provided both an external cleansing and a spiritual preparation for prayer, but the cramped space and intense heat put those infected in extremely close quarters. Because influenza was primarily a respiratory disease, the sweat bath, like the ceremonies, encouraged its spread for those who were infected. Medicine men and herbalists provided bitter plant remedies made from boiled sagebrush or juniper trees to wash the body and cleanse it internally. Sagebrush tea soothed sore throats, while juniper pitch mixed with a red ocher was plastered on the outside of the throat, forcing pus from the infected area.[52] Another medicine came from the juice of Arizona jimson (*datura*), which caused the pulse to quicken and the patient to become delirious. One person who took jimson as a cure had a recorded pulse of 240.[53]

Physical treatment also included either fasting or eating for satiety. Extremes in either case could prove fatal:

> At one place on the reservation, during the plague, meatballs the size of one's thumb were forced down the patients who were too weak and sick to eat until no more could be forced down them. The stomach of an influenza victim at another place, who had been abandoned and partly eaten by the wolves, was seen to contain about a quart of corn which had probably been boiled before it was forced down him. Such stuffed patients usually died.[54]

The same report also mentioned that massage and a series of contortions could be part of the treatment: "As the disease usually terminated in pneumonia and consequently the lungs became `tight,' the medicine man jumped on the chest to loosen up the lungs."[55] Thus in some instances the "cure" was as painful as the affliction.

Improvisation against this unknown illness took other forms as well. One Navajo man remembered:

> In those first days when the rains were cold and the Deneh [Diné] were sick and died everywhere, two of my boys had very hot bodies and could not get up. I went for a medicine man, and another, and another, many of them, but they were sick themselves or were singing the chants for others who had the sickness. All of two days I rode but could find no one to go to my hogan to save my boys. At home I found the women and all of the other children, nine altogether, were very, very sick too . . . I rode away again, seeking a medicine man. Where the cedar trees grow thick on the hill that stops suddenly, I got off my horse to pray. I prayed to several Deneh gods that know me; then I knew I must be the doctor for my family and I took berries from the cedar trees and gathered plants here and there. It was slow work in the rain, but there were those nine sick ones in my hogan.
>
> The plants and the berries I boiled with water in the coffeepots and gave each of my family [members] a drink. I sang one of the songs for healing and gave another a drink. So I timed the doses until the medicine was gone, and I rode out and got more plants and made medicine and the sick ones drank. There were days when no one came to my hogan. I did not sleep but sang the prayers and gave the medicine until all of my family was well.[56]

An old medicine man and his wife had another simple cure. They would appear at the home of people who were sick with "something that looked like a piece of tree bark" and have everyone who was ill spit into it. They went around to other homesteads; although people did not know what the medicine man was doing with his specimens, two days later everyone felt better and returned to daily life.[57] Harvey Oliver of Aneth recalled people "dying by the household" and, later, that white men came to burn the homes with the dead inside. He told of a cure where Navajos boiled herbs, and "they drank pine tree gum mixed with shortening oil or put it on their bodies. Then if that did not work, they used skunk fat on their bodies, then prayed to the disease to leave them alone."[58]

Yet the best individual account given by a Navajo person who lived through this horror is provided by Rose Mitchell (Asdzáán Nééz), who tells of a mixing of physical and spiritual procedures. Rose, who was approximately forty-four years old at the time, recalled how entire families perished overnight while diagnosticians like hand tremblers and stargazers could not determine what was wrong. Navajo families buried live babies with their dead mothers because there was no one to care for them; thus many graves had multiple occupants. Rose felt the sickness was like measles or chickenpox but that the characteristic pustules actually turned inward instead of erupting on the skin's surface. Once she became ill, her body swelled to the point that she could not open her eyes or talk, sores covered her, and she became so weak that people had to carry her outside in a blanket. She lost all awareness of time and surroundings, a state of being that lasted for a lengthy period.[59]

Her father, Man Who Shouts (Hastiin Delawoshí), a Blessing Way singer and community leader, sprang into action. He told the people to move together so they could help each other, and he prepared herbal remedies to be taken internally or applied externally as a healing paste or a compact. He also created herbal remedies to apply in the sweat house but warned that the people should not wash themselves because doing so would lower their temperature and open the door to sickness. Man Who Shouts had many of his horses killed, providing meat to make broth and fat to render into a paste mixed with herbs and red ocher. He encouraged everyone to use the Blessing Way prayers for protection, since none of the other ceremonies were effective against this disease. He and others who were not sick buried the dead. Weather and health conditions combined so that Man Who Shouts determined that his people's annual move to Black Mountain should be cancelled and they should remain where they were.[60] But above all, "He believed that the Blessing Way was our main guide, and where we could get strength to withstand all the hardships we would face every day and also, in the future . . . He really stressed those things to his grandchildren, the ones who had not passed away during the flu."[61] Rose credits his efforts with saving many lives of family members and neighbors.

Although a multitude of protective symbols were invoked through formal ceremonies, two objects served as primary means to ward off the disease. Arrowheads and fire pokers embodied defensive values repeated often in Navajo mythology and religious beliefs. Arrowheads, for instance, were first used long ago by the Anaasází to kill enemies and protect their people; similar reasoning led the Navajos to use these projectile points in ceremonies as protective devices to ward off the disease that was killing them. They served as "a shield to the patient and those who are involved in the [healing] ceremony . . . and the things that are not seen just go back where they come from."[62] The points can be left in the hogan for up to four days following the ceremony.

The fire poker (*honeeshgish*) was another important symbol of protection, delineating a line across which evil and sickness could not pass.[63] This concept harks back to physical warfare, geographic boundaries, and sanctified territory; but during the epidemic the hogan was the major spiritual realm demanding protection. Used both in ceremonies and as a general talisman, the poker represented "forked lightning, rainstreamer, and zigzag and straight lightning, symbols that prevent the enemy [evil] from crossing."[64] One woman reported,

> At night my father would lean a wood fire poker against the north side of the hogan. He would sit up and tell us, "Sleep my children, but do not go on the north side of the hogan. If you want to go outside, go out on this side [south to east] only." He would pray all through the night. What prayers he prayed I do not know. No illness came over us, not even a headache.[65]

The poker also had prayers said over it, adding to the already potent association of fire and its role in protecting and serving the home. At the conclusion of the Evil Way ceremony, the medicine man took four fire pokers from the ritual to the east and, along with plants and other materials, placed them in a tree. If they remained secure for a month or two, then the participants knew the holy people had accepted the offering of prayers and chants.[66] Some Navajos today believe that these offerings and protective devices were so vital that those who did not have them were the ones who died.[67]

Dreams, as omens, continued to play an important role during the sickness. One Navajo approached Louisa Wetherill and thanked her for visiting him in his hogan while he was ill. When she told him she had not seen him lately, he assured her that she had come in a dream and said that he must not die. The man firmly believed her spirit made the visit. A patron told another trader that he had almost died, but "when I got to the other side, I saw my brothers. They came to get me. They were all riding horses. But I had no horse, because there was no one left to kill my horse. I couldn't join them without a horse. So I came back."[68]

Louisa Wetherill tells of solving such a problem early one winter morning when a man appeared at the trading post asking for a gun to kill a horse. He explained: "Two days ago my little boy was buried . . . but they killed no horse for him to ride. Already he has nearly completed the second circle on foot, and he is only seven years old. He will be tired now. Lend me a gun that I may kill a horse."[69] He received the rifle.

UTE RESPONSE

Utes living in the Four Corners region were also affected by the disease, but apparently not to the same extent as the Navajos. The Ute agent headquartered at Towaoc outside Cortez, Colorado, reported a population of 300 Indians on his reserve. Many of them traveled off their lands and so had ample opportunity to contract the disease. On November 14, 1918, the clerk at the Southern Ute Boarding School reported that all 45 students were kept in school, not quarantined, but they were later sent home after being exposed: "Now there is or has been someone sick in nearly every home. To date there has [*sic*] been seventeen deaths from 'flu' all but one since the fourth of this month. As it is now, the sick are scattered over a radius of several townships, making it impossible to give them the attention necessary."[70] But by December 27 the dying had slowed because the Utes had "yielded readily to medical treatment [which was not nearly as available to the Navajo], and seemed to suffer much less than their Indian neighbors."[71] A possible explanation as to why the Utes did not suffer as much as their neighbors is that in addition to medical help, their curing practices did not stress congregating to perform ceremonies. In fact, "When the flu was bad, most of the Indians left the agency, some going to Mesa Verde and some to other parts, [even though] their ponies are so poor and weak they can neither ride nor drive them."[72]

The Utes still had struggles with influenza, however. Like the Navajos, they fled from their tepees when someone died inside them, thus falling prey to the elements and the disease. Many of them had trouble understanding how white men could get sick, take medicine, and get better while the Indians took the same medicine and died. Apparently, by the end of the epidemic white doctors had less easy access to the Utes, who suggested "maybeso medicine given Indian was coyote bait [poison]."[73] They turned mistrustful and ran from their camps to hide whenever a white man approached, fearing he might be a doctor. By February 21, 1919, the epidemic had subsided and the dying ended, so government officials held hearings to ensure that a fair inheritance of property was allowed to families with members who had died from the flu.[74]

As previously mentioned, the Paiutes living around Navajo Mountain appeared to have been decimated by the disease. Perhaps one reason for this is that many followed Navajo healing practices that encouraged people to congregate; also, there was far less medical attention available because of isolation. Anecdotal accounts suggest the overall impact. Fred Yazzie, a Navajo living in Monument Valley, recalls groups of Paiutes and Utes traveling from Navajo Mountain to the Allen Canyon area, dying along the way: "The sick slowly made their way here [Oljato]. Whole Paiute and Ute families died off. Some babies had no effect from the sickness. In one place a mother had died two days before and the baby was still sucking on her. That is how the baby was found."[75] Because of the visiting between the two groups, some Navajos suggest they received the illness through their interaction with the Paiute. Cold, wind, exposure, and hunger took their toll as the groups moved to the shelter of Allen Canyon, with some left behind as others moved on.[76]

CONCLUSION

The end of the epidemic on the northern part of the Navajo Reservation raised the question of how many deaths occurred. Because of the lack of records, a definitive answer cannot be given; even ballpark figures are difficult to ascertain. For instance, one trader, John L. Oliver, who lived

Courtesy, Milton Snow Collection, Navajo Nation Museum, Window Rock, AZ.

Introduction of the germ theory of disease and medical education based on that theory became more widely spread starting in the 1930s and 1940s. Navajo people added these health practices while maintaining strong faith and extensive ceremonial knowledge to combat sickness.

in Mexican Hat, suggested that reservation-wide, at least 3,000 Indians had succumbed to the disease.[77] Both the *Walketon Independent* and the *Indian School Journal* [Chilocco, OK] reported that 2,000 Navajos in the southern part of the reservation perished, a figure considered too high by some based on the total tribal population, estimated at between 31,390 and 35,000.[78] Trader Franc Johnson Newcomb wrote that "government reports state that one-fifth of the Navaho tribe perished during the winter months, but we who lived on the Reservation were sure that the percentage was much higher."[79] The Northern and Western Agencies, which extended from Shiprock to Tuba City, had population estimates that ranged between 6,500 and 8,000, with a suspected incidence of disease of 75 percent and a death rate of between 8.75 and 15.00 percent. The overall tribal population showed a 5.5 percent decrease between the 1918 and 1919 agency figures.[80] Still others, using population estimates from the *Annual Report of the Commissioner of Indian Affairs,* provide more specific figures per agency: Leupp, 114 deaths out of 1,411 people

(10 percent); Southern Navajo, 780/12,080 (6 percent); Western Navajo, 200/6,087 (3 percent); Eastern Navajo, 500/2,724 (18 percent); and Northern Navajo, unknown out of 6,500.[81]

The agency schools provide a much more accurate picture of the disease's effects on the children, but their living conditions and access to medical attention were far different from those residing in the rough canyon country of southern Utah and northern New Mexico and Arizona. For instance, the Shiprock Agency School had 225 pupils, 200 of whom were sick and 18 of whom died—a mortality rate of 9 percent. The Toadalena Boarding School had 81 students, 100 percent affliction, and 10 who died—a mortality rate of 12 percent. At the Tuba City Boarding School, 138 students were sick, but only 2 died—a mortality rate of 1.5 percent.[82] The varying death rates from one institution to another seemed to be in direct proportion to the amount and type of care rendered the sick. As an illustration, the Toadalena School had the highest mortality rate, though it had the smallest student population. The reason for this is that the principal proved to be highly neglectful in meeting the needs of sick students and was chastised accordingly through a special investigation.[83] In contrast, Max Hanley, a student at the Shiprock Agency School, reported that he and the other students had to remain in bed for two weeks before they could return to their normal work schedule.[84] In the meantime, adults shouldered the students' work responsibilities until they could be up and about, a luxury most Navajos in sheep camps could not afford. For the vast majority of those living at-large, their needs, struggles, and deaths were never investigated or recorded.

In summarizing the effects of the Influenza Epidemic on the various populations in the Four Corners region, one sees the importance of cultural beliefs, social practices, and economic patterns. For instance, the people of Moab viewed the epidemic in terms of a respiratory ailment that could be avoided by limiting contact with others, following contemporary medical practices, and leaving major decisions to medical and government professionals. Newspapers advertised cures; the board of health organized a hospital; and outside aid in the form of nurses, vaccines, and commercial products became part of the healthcare regimen. Even the legal system joined the fray by passing laws and requiring the sheriff, marshal, and volunteer citizens to enforce them. All of this was done in a rural town with a small population.

Monticello and Blanding were even smaller communities with even more limited access to professional care. Because these towns had a predominantly Mormon population, they turned inward for their succor. Cooperation and help were of greater necessity, placing the burden of healthcare and farming chores squarely on the shoulders of those men and women who felt compassion and were not afflicted. Home remedies and self-doctoring eased the suffering of many and were generally aligned (though not in every case) with an understanding of what the physical disease was and how it was spread. There is no indication that religious practices intensified; indeed, organized religious services came to a halt.

The Navajo had an entirely different response. Many of the issues fell within the realm of religion and spirituality. Forewarned by omens, the Navajo reaction was intense and culturally defined. The disease, like other illnesses, became personified and was attacked on a spiritual level, with familiar objects used in mythology that connote intense symbolic meanings of protection as part of the preventive and curative practices. From the Anglo-American point of view, many of the ceremonies were derived from the "darkest superstition," as the newspapers of the day proclaimed, but to the Navajos they were the first line of defense, comparable to the doctors in Moab and the home remedies in Blanding and Monticello. Superstition is always the other man's religion, and so it was for the outsider viewing Navajo practices.

Influenza appears to have been far more traumatic for the Navajo population than for those of the white man and the Ute. This is true for a number of reasons. First, the isolation of Navajo dwellings, because of involvement in a livestock economy, for the most part did not afford the same type of community support found in Moab, Monticello, and Blanding or even the boarding schools. Often, the sick had no choice but to perform necessary labor in the elements, which weakened their resistance to the disease.

Second, the means of transmittal was not understood, and so the disease spread rapidly and was actually encouraged by ceremonial practices. The Utes seemed not to have suffered as much as the Navajos because their general reaction was to get away from others, thereby decreasing chances for infection. Once a death occurred, however, both the Utes and Navajos compounded the problem by leaving their secure winter homes, which exposed them to the elements and created a weakened resistance to the disease.

Third, the physical remedies were, by Anglo standards, only marginally successful in alleviating the victims' suffering. Many of the practices were based on the principles of "like begets like," "opposites cure," or "the more bitter the better." All of these concepts are common elements in religious belief and shamanism prevalent in non-industrialized cultures. Known in anthropological circles as "sympathetic" or "imitative" magic, a food, plant, object, or action parallels the affliction in such a way that it can control or heal as a remedy. To the Navajo, these were effective cures and, when coupled with prayer and ceremony, completed a logical system of defense. In fact, those who did not have the prayers, chants, and herbal remedies were the ones most often believed to have died.

By March 1919 the total number of Americans killed by Spanish Influenza was recorded at 548,452.[85] It took years to recover from the sadness and trauma left in the wake of this catastrophe, while for the Navajos the event also became a historic landmark in the tribal memory. Yet it is on the individual level, the experiences of men and women, where one finds empathy beyond cold statistics. The response elicited by the epidemic in each case was tied to the culture within which it was made, at a time when much of humanity suffered.

NOTES

1. Joseph E. Persico, "The Great Swine Flu Epidemic of 1918," *American Heritage* 27 (June 1976): 28.
2. Alfred W. Crosby, *America's Forgotten Pandemic: The Influenza of 1918* (New York: Cambridge University Press, 1989), 207.
3. Ibid., 228.
4. Ibid.
5. William H. McNeil, *Plagues and People* (Garden City, NY: Doubleday, 1976), 289.
6. "Influenza Breaks out in Moab," *Grand Valley Times* [Moab, UT], October 18, 1918, 1.
7. Ibid.
8. "No Further Cases of Influenza Make Appearance in Moab," *Grand Valley Times*, October 25, 1918, 1.
9. "Influenza Spreading at Alarming Rate," *Grand Valley Times*, November 1, 1918, 1.
10. Ibid.; "Court Postponed on Account of Influenza," *Grand Valley Times*, November 1, 1918, 1.
11. "Flu Epidemic on Decline," *Grand Valley Times*, November 8, 1918, 1.
12. "Influenza Claims Prominent Stockman," *Grand Valley Times*, November 22, 1918, 1.

13. "Influenza Raging in Moab," *Grand Valley Times*, January 3, 1919, 1.
14. Persico, "Great Swine Flu Epidemic," 82.
15. "Influenza Raging in Moab," 1.
16. Ibid.
17. "250 Cases of Influenza Develop during Week," *Grand Valley Times*, January 10, 1919, 1.
18. "Influenza Raging in Moab," 1; "Troubles Had in Getting Whiskey for Influenza," *Grand Valley Times*, January 10, 1919, 3.
19. Advertisement, *Grand Valley Times*, November 15, 1918, 4.
20. Advertisement, *Grand Valley Times*, January 31, 1919, 4.
21. "Influenza—Play Safe," *Grand Valley Times*, January 10, 1919, 4.
22. "Flu Situation Much Improved," *Grand Valley Times*, January 17, 1919, 2; "Epidemic Has Been Stamped Out in Moab," *Grand Valley Times*, January 24, 1919, 1.
23. "Epidemic Has Been Stamped Out in Moab," 1; "Flu Hospital Expense Totals Nearly $1700," *Grand Valley Times*, January 31, 1919, 1.
24. Margie Lyman interview with Helen Shumway, April 11, 1986, San Juan County Historical Society, Blanding, UT.
25. Ibid.; Mae Black interview with Janet Wilcox, July 15, 1987, San Juan County Historical Society, Blanding, UT; Ray Redd interview with Jody Bailey, July 16, 1987, San Juan County Historical Society, Blanding, UT.
26. Redd interview with Bailey.
27. Pearl Butt interview with Jody Bailey, July 2, 1987, San Juan County Historical Society, Blanding, UT.
28. Ibid.
29. Lyman interview with Shumway; Mae Black interview with Wilcox; Seraphine Frost interview with Deniane Gutke, July 6, 1987, San Juan County Historical Society, Blanding, UT; Rusty Musselman interview with author, July 6, 1987, San Juan County Historical Society, Blanding, UT.
30. Musselman interview with author.
31. Gladys A. Reichard, *Navaho Religion: A Study of Symbolism* (Princeton, NJ: Princeton University Press, 1950), 19; Ada Black interview with Bertha Parrish, June 18, 1987, San Juan County Historical Society, Blanding, UT.
32. The color red signifies a number of beliefs in traditional Navajo thought. Reichard points out that when it is reversed from its normal role in sand paintings, it can represent evil associated with lightning or storms. In contrast, "White apparently differentiates the naturally sacred from the profane—black or red, for instance—which through exorcism and ritual, must be transformed to acquire favorable power"; *Navajo Religion*, 182, 187. Thus the red dawns and sunsets warned of the approach of evil, as opposed to having the white and yellow light associated with the normal beginning and end of day and the directions East and West, respectively.
33. Ada Black interview with Bertha Parrish, 1–2; Rose Begay interview with Bertha Parrish, June 17, 1987, San Juan County Historical Society, Blanding, UT; Tallis Holiday interview with author, November 3, 1987; Fred Yazzie interview with author, November 5, 1987.
34. Frances Gillmor and Louisa Wade Wetherill, *Traders to the Navahos* (Albuquerque: University of New Mexico Press, 1953), 222–224.

35. Scott C. Russell, "The Navajo and the 1918 Pandemic," in *Health and Disease in the Prehistoric Southwest*, ed. C. F. Merlos and R. J. Miller (Tempe: Arizona State University Press, 1985), 385; Fred Yazzie interview with author.
36. Gilmore Graymountain interview with author, April 7, 1992.
37. L. L. Culp to Commissioner of Indian Affairs, "Report on the Influenza Epidemic at the San Juan Indian Agency," March 1, 1919, Letters Received by Office of Indian Affairs, New Mexico Superintendency (Washington, DC: National Archives, 1919), 2.
38. Franc Johnson Newcomb, *Hosteen Klah: Navaho Medicine Man and Sand Painter* (Norman: University of Oklahoma Press, 1964), 144–148.
39. Howard M. Bahr, ed., *The Navajo as Seen by the Franciscans, 1898–1921: A Sourcebook* (Lanham, MD: Scarecrow, 2004), 440–441.
40. Ibid., 442–446.
41. Ibid., 457.
42. Ibid., 460.
43. Hilda Faunce, *Desert Wife* (Lincoln: University of Nebraska Press, 1928), 296–297; Albert B. Reagan, "The Influenza and the Navajo," *Proceedings of the Indiana Academy of Science* 29 (Fort Wayne, IN: Fort Wayne Printing Company, 1921), 246; Gillmor and Wetherill, *Traders to the Navahos,* 227.
44. Franc Johnson Newcomb, *Navaho Neighbors* (Norman: University of Oklahoma Press, 1966), 103–105.
45. Reagan, "Influenza and the Navajo," 246.
46. Ibid., 246–247; Faunce, *Desert Wife*, 297; Gillmor and Wetherill, *Traders to the Navahos*, 226–228.
47. "Navajo Indians Are Dying by Hundreds," *Grand Valley Times*, December 6, 1918, 1.
48. Faunce, *Desert Wife*, 299–300.
49. Reagan, "Influenza and the Navajo," 247; Ray Hunt interview with Janet Wilcox, July 20, 1987, San Juan County Historical Society, Blanding, UT.
50. Fred Yazzie interview with author; Tallis Holiday interview with author.
51. Ada Black interview with author, October 11, 1991.
52. Tallis Holiday interview with author; Fred Yazzie interview with author; Rose Begay interview with Parrish.
53. Reagan, "Influenza and the Navajo," 247.
54. Ibid.
55. Ibid.
56. Faunce, *Desert Wife*, 301–302.
57. David Lansing, in *Stories of Traditional Navajo Life and Culture by Twenty-Two Navajo Men and Women,* ed. Broderick H. Johnson (Tsaile, AZ: Navajo Community College Press, 1977), 108.
58. Harvey Oliver interview with author, May 14, 1991.
59. Rose Mitchell with Charlotte Frisbie, ed., *Tall Woman: The Life Story of Rose Mitchell, a Navajo Woman, ca. 1874–1977* (Albuquerque: University of New Mexico Press, 2001), 128–129, 133–134.
60. Ibid., 130–134.
61. Ibid., 134–135.
62. Fred Yazzie interview with author.

63. There are extensive teachings about the origin and use of the sacred fire poker. Don Mose, cultural specialist for the San Juan School District, explains: "[The Navajo] speak to the *honeeshgish* and say, 'Grandfather and Grandmother protect our home while we are away.' When a stranger approaches a *Diné* home and the honeeshgish is at the doorway, the poker warns the stranger and gives him the feeling that he should leave the home alone. The dark charred end protects the home at night, and the lighter end protects [it] during the day. A honeeshgish can be used by a mother who needs to leave a baby alone in the hogan for a short time while she tends to her outdoor chores. She can place the honeeshgish in the dirt near the baby for protection"; Mose, *Honeeshgish: A Navajo Legend* (Blanding, UT: San Juan School District Media Center, 2006), 8–9.
64. Reichard, *Navaho Religion*, 545–546, 581.
65. Pearl Phillips interview with Bertha Parrish, June 17, 1987, San Juan County Historical Society, Blanding, UT; also Rose Begay interview with Parrish. North is the direction of death and evil and the way a spirit travels to the land of the afterlife.
66. Fred Yazzie interview with author.
67. Ibid.; Tallis Holiday interview with author; Rose Begay interview with Parrish.
68. Gillmor and Wetherill, *Traders to the Navahos*, 226–227; Willow Roberts, *Stokes Carson: Twentieth Century Trading on the Navajo Reservation* (Albuquerque: University of New Mexico Press, 1987), 26.
69. Gillmor and Wetherill, *Traders to the Navahos*, 225–226.
70. Ray H. Car to Commissioner of Indian Affairs, November 14, 1918, Letters Received by Office of Indian Affairs, New Mexico Superintendency (Washington, DC: National Archives, 1918).
71. "The Influenza among the Utes," *Mancos Times Tribune*, December 27, 1918, 1.
72. "Superstitious Utes," *Mancos Times Tribune*, January 10, 1919, 1.
73. Ibid.; "Influenza Very Bad among Indians," *Mancos Times Tribune*, December 13, 1918, 1, 3.
74. "Hearings on Indian Estates," *Mancos Times Tribune*, February 21, 1919, 1.
75. Fred Yazzie interview with author, November 5, 1987.
76. Gilmore Graymountain interview with author, April 7, 1992.
77. "3,000 Navajos Succumb to Flu, Says Indian Trader," *Grand Valley Times*, January 3, 1919, 1.
78. Russell, "Navajo and the 1918 Pandemic," 382; Reagan, "Influenza and the Navajo," 243.
79. Newcomb, *Navaho Neighbors*, 101.
80. Russell, "Navajo and the 1918 Pandemic," 382; Culp to Commissioner, 2.
81. Garrick Bailey and Roberta Glenn Bailey, *A History of the Navajos: The Reservation Years* (Santa Fe, NM: School of American Research Press, 1986), 119.
82. Ibid.; Reagan, "Influenza and the Navajo," 245.
83. Culp to Commissioner, 7–9.
84. Max Hanley, in *Stories of Traditional Navajo Life and Culture by Twenty-Two Navajo Men and Women,* ed. Broderick H. Johnson (Tsaile, AZ: Navajo Community College Press, 1977), 35.
85. Persico, "Great Swine Flu Epidemic," 84.

3

Sacred Evil

The Dark Side of Life along the San Juan

In traditional Navajo thought, control of spiritual power leads to control of physical power. How that power is used, be it for good or evil, depends not on its source but on how a person chooses to employ it. Goodness and evil are inverse images of each other, with similar but reversed principles guiding both. One brings life, the other death; one blesses, the other curses; one is orderly and prescribed, the other chaotic. Each of these qualities in opposition to the other fosters appreciation for life and the creations of the holy people. They are all sacred, are here for the People's use, and carry results and consequences.

In this chapter the reader is introduced to the sacred and profane qualities of evil. A powerful force in Navajo beliefs, the nature of evil is an important concept to understand, even if one is not a practitioner of witchcraft. That is why medicine men who wish to help and cure still need a basic knowledge of

DOI: 10.7330/9781607322177.c03

> *the dark side. Without it, there is little understanding of how to combat it. Here the reader learns about that part of life many Navajos may be aware of but do not like to discuss. Too much knowledge may indicate that the person practices antisocial behavior shunned by the culture's positive side. Yet without recognizing it, only half of the invisible world can be understood.*

Navajo Oshley came over the hill just in time to find Old Teacher, a medicine man, beating his new wife, formerly Old Teacher's spouse. The ex-husband was angry that she had left him and was delivering a sound drubbing when Oshley arrived. The two tussled before Oshley tossed the man to the ground and warned him that he had better not cause any more trouble. The disgruntled loser eventually rode away, but this was not the end of it. As a practitioner of the Hoof and Claw Way ceremony (Akéshgaan), he held powers to heal but also to harm an individual. The ceremony lasts three days and is performed for people who have a concussion, fractured skull, or broken bones. It restores strength in recovery, healing the mind as well as the body. Elements of the ceremony can be reversed, however, to witch a person—crippling the intended target in the hips or joints, fomenting a loss of mind, or breaking bones and inflicting a concussion. There is also the possibility that part of a claw, from which the ceremony takes its name, or some other foreign object could be supernaturally "shot" into a victim, requiring that it be sucked out by a medicine man. Little wonder that Oshley feared repercussions. That evening he stepped outside his hogan, sensing impending danger. Something hit his toe, he said *páá*, then something hit hard against the door.[1] He went back inside but emerged the next morning to find his favorite spotted horse dead. His mother, a hand trembler, divined that the incident was the work of Old Teacher, who shot his power against Oshley but had it deflected from his target into the horse.[2]

Encapsulated in this incident are a number of important concerns in Navajo culture discussed in this chapter. The first and most obvious is that witchcraft is a powerful force to be reckoned with, in both a physical and a spiritual sense. Oshley immediately shifted from the physical beating of his wife and the sparring match with her ex-husband to fearing the less tangible use of witchcraft in the realms of unseen power. Old Teacher, as a medicine man, was practiced in drawing upon that power, which had the ability to both help and harm. In the same sense, the ceremony he knew could both heal and hurt, a veritable two-edged sword waiting to be employed through words that held the power to either inflict or protect. Finally, it was through supernatural power that Oshley's mother detected the perpetrator of the crime and was able to protect her son. Thus as much was taking place in the realm of the unseen as there was with that which was tangibly visible.

ORIGIN AND TYPES OF SACRED EVIL

Every culture has its means of defining what is good and acceptable or bad and undesirable. Navajos are no different. However, unlike Western, Christian thought, the Diné do not draw a sharp line between these polarities based on a God of good who opposes Satan, the embodiment of evil. Indeed, power to the Navajos is more a state of being used for either good or bad, depending on the intent of the user. Electricity warms homes, cooks food, and provides transportation, but it can also destroy or maim with apparent ease; likewise, supernatural power exists to both bless and curse those who come in contact with it. Respect, balance, and orderliness become the means by which positive forces are controlled, while the rituals of evil and witchcraft (*'iinížiin*) are based on excess, lack of reverence, and chaos. The power is there; what one does with it determines the outcome.

This duality in Navajo eyes highlights the importance of the phenomenon as it operates in the lives of people living in the San Juan Basin of the Four Corners area. Since healing ceremonies, individual prayers, and avoidance taboos center around the concept of inherent supernatural powers with beneficial or harmful qualities, it is not surprising that witchcraft utilizes these same culturally approved or credible means to achieve its opposite goals. As Harry Walters, an elder and retired instructor at Diné College, said:

> In the Navajo world everything is organized in terms of female and male, known as Hózhǫ́ǫ́jí (Blessing Way) and Naayée'eejí (Protection Way). The two forces do not oppose but complement each other in the same manner as all female and male species interact in nature. Evil is not a separate quality but is viewed as an integral part of Naayée'eejí. When used appropriately, it serves as protection but where it is abused, it becomes witchcraft (evil). Self-protection is a necessity in nature, so all things have an element of evil. Therefore, one must always go about life with great caution and respect.[3]

Thus the quality of good cannot exist or be known without evil. The two are inseparable.

Clyde Kluckhohn, in his classic study *Navaho Witchcraft*, identifies four types of black magic—witchery, sorcery, wizardry, and frenzy witchcraft. Witchery depends on "corpse poison," or decayed flesh, bones, or sexual fluids ground into powder and used to curse a person. This material serves the reverse function of corn pollen, which blesses with life and happiness. Diagnosis of the illness through hand trembling, crystal gazing, or other means determines which prayers and ceremonies will protect or heal the sick person. Sorcery creates sickness and harm by taking hair, nail clippings, clothing, or some other object that has been in close contact with the intended victim. The item is prayed over so that hardship enters a person's life. Wizardry occurs when an individual magically shoots a stone, bone, or foreign matter into a victim; the cure is achieved by sucking out the object, Oshley's experience as a case in point. Frenzy witchcraft utilizes two forms of delivery: plants, such as datura, or prayers and chants that cause a person to lose self-control and become degraded. Excessive sexual activity or gambling results. The Excess Way (also known as the Deer Way or, less acceptably, the Prostitution Way) usually provides the cure, although other ceremonies may also serve the purpose. While Kluckhohn performed the yeoman's task of identifying, classifying, and interpreting for anthropologists the elements of witchcraft, he ignored the positive side of those same forces within the culture.

To the Navajo, all of these forms of power started in the four worlds beneath this one during the times of myths. The ambivalence existing between good and evil originated there and was embodied in two beings—First Man and First Woman. In the first, or dark, world, this couple created four pillars in the cardinal directions to hold up the sky. A fifth column, made of various colors, arose from the center place. A basket nearby contained red and white stones and held all types of fatal diseases First Man could use to kill through witchcraft and wishing. The varicolored pillar "represents the diverse evils that are visited upon present day humankind, the source of all evils."[4] The Upward Moving and Emergence Way Chant, from which this explanation comes, is used for blessing and protection, is the "first of all rites," and is closely related to the War Rite Enemy Way ('Ana' Ndáá'). Both of these ceremonies are also connected to the

Blessing Way ceremony, all three of which may be used as protection from destruction or, in other circumstances, to destroy the enemy.

Although First Man helped create this negative side of life, he also made and used protective powers to defeat it. In the red underworld, various animals shot arrows at him, representing the evils of sorcery and wizardry; but he caught the missiles, shot them at his opponents, and killed many of them. He refused to bring them back to life until they paid him with songs, some of which can be used in hunting deer. The people became angry at First Man's ways and spoke harshly of him. Coyote, overhearing what they said, reported to First Man, who confronted the people but had to admit, "It is true, my Grandchildren, I am filled with evil. Yet there is a time to employ it and another to withhold it."[5] From this time forward, Coyote served as a messenger to First Man. Herein lies the dichotomy of witchcraft. Father Berard Haile, an early but highly proficient ethnographer of Navajo culture, pointed out a continuation of this ambiguity: "The children of First Man and First Woman are known as 'ant'iihjí są'ah naagháii bik'eh hózhǫ' 'witchcraft way long life, happiness.'"[6] How can witchcraft way lead to long life and happiness when it inflicts pain and death? Something seems amiss unless one understands foundational Navajo thought.

First Man spread his knowledge of protection and destruction to plants, animals, insects, and the elements. Ants, bumblebees, wasps, poisonous snakes, yucca, different types of cactus, various forms of wind, and lightning all contain evil power to cause sickness or death. Each of these ills has prayers, plants, and sacrificial materials to turn away the harm. After the plants, animals, and elements had received the evil and left the hogan where they were meeting, First Man took down the structure, patted and rolled it into a small ball, and put it aside.[7] The ability to shrink an object so one can carry it off is yet another power associated with black magic.

Hunting, sex, and conflict were other aspects of life influenced by First Man. A story tells how he supplied his corpulent wife with lard-laced deer meat, one of her favorite meals. After eating, she wiped her greasy hands on her dress and spoke to her vagina, giving thanks. She told her husband "she was only acknowledging the motive of everything that men do."[8] Later she engaged in infidelity, as did her children, who practiced incest. This gave rise to the belief that "witches always . . . marry

Courtesy, Utah State Historical Society.

First Man and First Woman established the basis for good and evil in this world. The two behaviors, while appearing opposite, are dependent on each other for contrast—a person cannot understand one without experiencing the other.

those too closely related to them . . . [and so] keep their unlawful marriages secret."[9] Navajos explain the effects of this behavior by describing a moth, which also committed this crime. The insect is said to crawl beneath the skin on the forehead of a person who has had intra-family sexual relations. The moth irritates the head and drives the person insane until he or she acts like the bug and destroys him- or herself in a fire.[10]

Events in the underworld consistently took a turn for the worse as witchcraft forced the creatures to abandon the couple. The practice of evil became increasingly dangerous. First Man and others decided that it should be done in complete secrecy, so now it is. Today, First Man and First Woman live in their home in the direction of the northeast, from whence evil originated. Their influence is still felt, however, for as First Woman warned, "When I think, something bad will happen. People will become ill. Coyote will know [and presumably carry out] all my thoughts."[11]

SACRED EVIL AND ITS PRACTITIONERS

What, then, is the nature of evil? From an intellectual standpoint, the power that drives good and bad is similar and inseparable, although the ends of this continuum result in a duality. The most important element that gives definition to either end is the quality of order or the lack of it. Thus evil is chaos; goodness is a controlled and well-kept existence. When events or natural elements arise in unexpected ways or at undesirable times, it is because of evil. Even excessive good or flamboyant emotions offer the possibility of being out of control. Ritual provides the means by which things out of bounds can be brought back to safety and order.[12]

While anyone can be accused of practicing witchcraft, definite patterns or types of people are most frequently identified. Kluckhohn provides a quantifiable basis derived from 222 cases of people blamed for practicing the dark art. Of this number, 184 were adult men—131 of whom were classified as "old," as were all (38) of the women. One hundred forty of the men and 12 of the women were ceremonial practitioners, while 21 of the men were "headmen" or "chiefs"—a number Kluckhohn felt was "an exceedingly high figure," given the proportion of leaders found throughout the general population. One hundred fifteen men and women from the total group were considered "rich." All older people wearing medicine pouches at gatherings were feared, and many of the Navajo people surveyed felt the tendency to practice witchcraft runs steadily through family lines.[13]

John Holiday, a Blessing Way singer from Monument Valley, received instruction from his grandfather as to what type of person became involved in witchcraft while John apprenticed to become a medicine man. The teacher told his grandson that he was not that kind because of his boisterous personality: "It's never revealed to the loud ones, the one who is part of the crowd and laughs out and jokes around. For those who do such things, they tend to carry out cursing rituals through other people . . . It is for the quiet one, male or female, young or old or loner;

the one who doesn't mingle with the crowd. They are the ones who perform all the witchcraft, make deadly potions, and collect one's belongings to bury as waste."[14] He warned that the dark side was not for John; the practice was worthless, would lead to a shortened life, and he should not talk about such things. His role was to help and protect people and to avoid any contact with this evil.

The context in which a person performs an action, uses a symbol, or says a prayer becomes important in establishing an outcome. For example, the color black is often associated with evil, but in the Evil Way ceremony the black ashes rubbed on the patient protect and hide him from malevolent spirits.[15] John Farella in *The Main Stalk* describes this duality as a series of "packages," many of which First Man created as "sets or entities that were necessary to Navajos, even if embodying both good and evil."[16]

Translations of Navajo interviews can often be misleading because of the frequent use of the word *sacred*. There is no single word to describe the feeling of awe, reverence, and fear—emotions often closely associated with each other. Perhaps the nearest approach to the correct meaning and feeling one can achieve in English is "forbidden," in the sense that an object or event is invested with supernatural power that must be controlled. For the uninitiated, disease, tragedy, and death await those who do not know how to handle this power. "Sacred" or "holy," then, takes on a new connotation in that it is not necessarily allied with either good or evil but is something that must be used with caution.[17]

Take, for instance, the phenomenon of death. Literature about Navajos is filled with examples of avoiding the deceased, of asking white men to bury the body, or of medicine men performing a ceremony to prevent ill effects. Yet Navajos consistently refer to the handling and burial of the dead as "very sacred." Women and children could not go near the body; the men who buried the deceased had to return by a circuitous route, jump over cactus and bushes with sharp points so the spirit would not follow, and remain in a separate hogan for four days. The relatives sat at home for a similar number of days but could not lie down until dark; they also could not talk loudly.[18] From the outset, ritual allowed "sacredness to take over. The person was placed anywhere, but there was sacredness with it."[19] As long as people handled the burial according to the prescribed formula, there was no danger. Today, however, participants sometimes come to funerals in truckloads, are inebriated, lie around leisurely with the opposite sex, and do not remain isolated for four days. The result is that death is on the rise, people suffer from physical ailments, and transgressors are plagued by ghostlike spirits.[20] Loss of control has led to chaos.

Navajo medicine men can use destructive power for good. In times of war, ceremonies are performed to confuse, frighten, and kill the enemy. During the Long Walk period (1860s), a band of Navajos fled from a group of Utes and Mexicans. The Diné climbed atop a high bluff near Red Mesa, Arizona, but soon realized their entrapment. Surrounded by the enemy, parched with thirst, and cut off from escape, they performed Enemy Way medicine, directing power against the foe. The Ute leader died, allowing the Navajos to flee.[21] Hunting provided a similar use of sanctioned power. The leader of a hunting party was responsible for directing the men in song and prayer so "the minds of game shall be drawn to this point, where its lungs, its death blood shall be. The finest and largest of game shall be drawn in here."[22] To create the proper state of mind, the men cleansed themselves before and after the hunt, but during the activity they were to "let nothing enter their minds but the desire to kill the best game." The men prayed with pollen, even tossing some into the fire, ordinarily a sign of disrespect. Because their spiritual status changed while hunting, forbidden behavior now became appropriate.[23]

W. W. Hill, an anthropologist working in the 1930s, identified a lesser-known technique called Witch Way, similar to the war incident just cited. When the track of a large deer was found, the medicine man asked his companion if he wanted the animal killed. A positive response caused the singer to dismiss the uninitiated while he picked two or three spines from a broad-leaf yucca plant, sprinkled the tips with dirt from the spoor, placed four pieces of iron ore on top, and prayed. When the chant ended, the deer was dead—killed, presumably, by the yucca tips. Once the hunters found the carcass, the uninitiated companion had to leave while butchering and an accompanying ritual took place.[24] This practice harks back to the time when the animals had to pay First Man so he would not destroy them. The wolf people gave him songs to capture or kill deer using the pith from bayonet yucca.[25] The connection between hunting this way and wizardry, the injecting of foreign objects into a victim, is obvious.

Wizardry follows a prescribed format when "shooting" a person, depending upon a supernatural power called *álílee k'ehgo*, discussed in chapter 4. The type of object may be fashioned from stone, bone, or wood; regardless of the substance it is called an arrow (*bi k'aa*). The individual shooting the object puts corpse powder (*'áńt'į́įh*) on the "arrow" and, through chants and prayers, projects the missile into the person. The songs are particularly important: "Skinwalkers chant all the time; the songs cannot stop or their power ceases. Somebody has got to be singing while they are using their supernatural power."[26] Once the object is inserted, the victim becomes sick until it is removed or the individual dies. Jim Dandy, who also apprenticed to become a medicine man, explained that this practice was developed by Navajos a long time ago to defeat their enemies from other tribes and, later, the white man; now, Navajos have turned it around to use against their own people.[27]

An example of how the practice works was given by Tall Singer from Shiprock, as recorded by trader Will Evans in the early 1900s. Tall Singer had been chanting over Good Singer's Grandson for some time with no effect. His patient was losing weight, could not eat, and was suffering intense pain on the right side of the back of his neck. Tall Singer sliced into the swollen area with the sharpest arrowhead he carried in his medicine pouch and began to suck on the large slash. At first there was only blood, but eventually the medicine man retrieved a piece of charcoal with human hair wrapped around it: "The object was about the size and length of half of the first joint of your little finger. Some witch had secured a piece of charcoal . . . from the remains of a hogan which had been burned because someone had died in it . . . Then this witch had gone to the resting place of a dead person and plucked hair from the decaying head."[28] Once Tall Singer had removed the object, the patient rapidly improved.

Claus Chee Sonny, a noted medicine man, links hunting and mating with the use of songs and prayers. To summarize a lengthy treatment of the Bringing-Home Way ceremony (Ajiłee), Snake and Bear seduced two young maidens through supernatural means. The love magic they used to create frenzy witchcraft (Kluckhohn's term) caused the girls to lose their sense of propriety and "go crazy." Just as deer can be lured into entrapment, so were these girls—who happened to be virgin Hopis, a rival of the Navajos. Hunting, sex, and war combine in this myth to obtain positive results for the Diné. From it comes the knowledge needed to obtain a bride (in a positive sense) by creating unbridled passion (negative sense). Talking God and Black God provide the curative knowledge through the plants of the deer people. These remedies are still effective for those plagued by excessive lust or wanderlust.[29] Even the ability to stare at or think about a desired outcome can cause a person to either be attracted or harmed by one controlling this power. An old medicine man is often accused of attracting a young woman to be his wife or cursing a person just through staring.

Jim Dandy told of visiting an Enemy Way ceremony held in Kaibito, Arizona. Extensive preparations were under way, with a large group of people cooking in the shade hut. The aroma of roasting sheep ribs attracted an old medicine man, hungry for traditional food. A beautiful young lady, dressed in finery and well-educated, approached the elder and told him the food was for the workers and he would have to wait. He stared at her and she passed out, then dropped to the ground. One of her grandmothers placed herbs in water and washed the woman's face until she regained consciousness, while others went in search of the old man, who had disappeared. At the conclusion of this account, Dandy explained, "I was nervous, wondering if he put something in the food. Once revived, she was alright but weak so her relatives took her home. They did not want the old medicine man coming back to bother her again. With some of these very powerful medicine men, things like that happen."[30]

PLACES OF POWER

Geographic places are often tied to powerful sites by mythology. Just as Christians hold the Holy Land with special reverence and believe specific sites draw them closer to deity, so do the Navajo live in a land filled with the power of holy people established there since the time of creation. One of the most notable sites in southeastern Utah is the Bears Ears, with stories from the Mountain Way and Upward Moving and Emergence Way associated with it. This latter ceremonial cycle contains the myth of Changing Bear Maiden, who married Coyote and learned his witchcraft. She eventually killed all but one of her brothers, lived by trickery and deceit, and used her evil knowledge to defeat others. Her youngest brother killed her and separated her body parts, tossing them in different directions. The Bears Ears are the upper portion of her head.[31]

This prominent location still plays a role in fostering good and creating evil. Plants used to cure witchcraft and incest are picked there, while a person who suffers from loneliness, sadness, or excessive weight loss might go to this site to have a medicine man sing songs of comfort. But just as good can derive from the powers at this site, so can evil. Some people mention that at the top of one of the "ears" is a hole where bones of dead people are found, the remnants of witchcraft practices. Others suggest that Comb Ridge to the south is a site where black magic is performed.[32]

This pattern of locations connected with dual powers is replicated throughout Navajo lands. A brief survey of sites found in or near southeastern Utah includes Eagle Mesa in Monument Valley, where the spirit of dead people may go. One can hear the voices of the deceased and see their bones and footprints there, while skinwalkers (witches) climb to the top for ceremonies. Until recently, a braided yucca rope hung near the rim, made by skinwalkers to assist their ascent. Other gathering places include a small gray hill northeast of Bluff; a trail that stretches along the San Juan River near Sand Island; a monolith known as Designs on the Rock that has a flat ridge where witchery practices are held; a place called Standing Black Rock, whose powers can cause starvation; and Black Mesa, where there are caves that host practitioners.[33]

In addition to prominent geographic features, less dramatic sites also hold power. For instance, a steep rock wall, a petroglyph or pictograph in an Anaasází ruin, a rock "where the sun shines the hardest," a burial site, or a juniper tree all offer potential power.[34] A hidden cave, a bend in the river, or any place associated with an element of Navajo mythology has the possibility of both healing and cursing. Claus Chee Sonny tells of witches who use carvings on rocks to work against people. To counteract this, he says, "Some people will shoot at these rocks, but I use arrowheads to scrape off such engravings . . . Then I just burn it [the rock]. You can handle it with an arrowhead only. You apply songs and prayers to undo the spells while you do this."[35]

Blessing Way singer John Holiday believed in strong connections between Anaasází sites and witchcraft. He interpreted an ancient Anaasází road leading to a stone *herradura* (horseshoe-shaped) shrine high on Comb Ridge as a location of power, saying: "Only places like that, situated high and in hidden places, were for witchcrafting activities

Courtesy, Utah State Historical Society.

Leon Bradley stands outside a male hogan in Monument Valley. Local people say a cleft on the other side of this rock formation is a place where people practicing witchcraft have been known to go. Hundreds of other locations are spread across the reservation where residents have identified similar activities.

for skinwalkers. They say that is the type of trail and rocks and rock formations they have . . . And they said that the trail leading to a skinwalker's dwelling was made of stepping stones, which they used."[36] He also linked petroglyphs and pictographs to harmful practices, commenting that a carefully defaced anthropomorphic figure was likely carved up to curse someone by killing him, destroying his health, or causing him to lose his wealth. Marks were cut across the base of the arms, legs, and neck. John responded to this disfiguring by saying, "Look at me. I could have had that done to me. I can't walk well . . . It causes a person to be crippled or a quadriplegic or [to] be totally paralyzed and shaky. That is how those types of witchcraft affect you . . . Witches probably think Anaasází artwork is more powerful and effective [than more contemporary artwork]."[37]

Perhaps one of the most interesting phenomena is the *áńt'į́į́h ba'hooghan*, interpreted literally as "home of witchcraft medicine" and glossed as "witch home." Navajos tell of an entryway that is a slim crack in a rock, opening into a spacious chamber where black magic is performed. Sometimes a normal person cannot gain access without the help of supernatural powers. Two stories illustrate how they function.

The first story sounds like a chapter from a Tony Hillerman novel, the incident occurring near Shiprock, New Mexico. A group of police officers went to a cave to investigate some reportedly strange practices. They found bones with traces of grease and other objects tied together, placed in rows, and lying on goat skins. The police heard rocks falling as they left the cave and the whirring sound of projectiles flying overhead. One officer fainted and had to be assisted before the group reached safety. As far as the men were concerned, they had been chased off by powers that were both "sacred" and "scary."[38]

Richard Van Valkenburgh, a noted anthropologist, recorded a similar incident with a clearer description of a witch home. He went with an eighty-four-year-old medicine man, Slim Singer, to visit an aged couple plagued by witchcraft and extortion payments. Van Valkenburgh and his guide camped below the mouth of a cave resting high in a canyon wall. As they sat around the fire, Slim Singer told how, as a boy, he had climbed into the cave and watched the skinwalkers perform their magic. Since his "blood was full of flint," he lay behind a fallen slab of rock and saw them press a turquoise bead onto the stomach of a doll and wish death upon a person. After the chanting and prayers had ended and the light of dawn appeared, the men left the cave. Slim Singer reported what he saw to his father, who later killed one of the men involved.

Van Valkenburgh listened to the story then dozed off, only to be awakened by the crash and thud of a large boulder careening down the scree slope. He jumped to his feet, finding refuge on the far side of the canyon, while Slim Singer headed home. As he watched the mouth of the cave, he thought he saw "two dim forms" crawl toward the opening. Not until the sun provided full light did he venture up the steep slope to the chamber. In his words, "As the light swept across the walls it finally came to rest on a row of human figures. Graduating from those almost obliterated by age to one recently executed in charcoal, they all had been drawn with their heads pointing downward. And when I stood before them, I saw in each there was a small hole where once had been stuck a turquoise bead or chip."[39] He also found wrapped in calico and buried in the dust a doll fashioned from lightning-struck pine, with an arrowhead attached by human hair. A piece of turquoise was embedded in the left breast. The anthropologist departed and returned to Slim Singer, who urged that he destroy the figurine, which he eventually did. Slim Singer also asked that this story not be told until he died, so his request was honored.

MEDICINE BUNDLES AND SKINWALKERS

Stories concerning witch activities are tied to specific locations, providing a strong connection to daily reality. Indeed, it is the everyday elements grafted into these narratives that emphasize their reality in a parallel but inverse image of the Navajo universe. So it is not surprising that those involved in witchcraft, as with medicine men who perform for the welfare of their people, also have medicine bundles (*jish*). In these containers are the materials necessary to perform evil rites. The importance of these objects in the ceremony is illustrated in a story told by John Holiday.

It seems there was a man who lived in the vicinity of Table-Shaped Mesa near Many Farms, Arizona, a site known for its witchcraft. One day as he was traveling about he found a lot of tracks leading to red sandstone on the mesa. He next encountered two men who told him that a group of witches was performing a ceremony there and that if the man went to investigate, he would find that each of the evildoers had left his or her medicine bundle at the entranceway. The oldest, shabbiest bundle held the most power, and that was the one the man should snatch and flee with.

The man followed the instructions, entered the "witch's home," observed them chanting their songs, and watched a man and woman struggling to put on their coyote skins. They complained, "Something is wrong; maybe someone is looking at us, someone who does not belong here," but they could not detect the intruder. The man grabbed the oldest medicine bundle and ran down the slope, through a nearby wash, then hid in a copse of greasewood. The witches dressed in coyote skins searched about, even going to the man's home, but they never found him. He eventually returned to his hogan with the old mountain soil bundle. John explained, "People say that the leader of this group of witches had always lived in that cave. He was born there, married there, and ate there, too. The man found out later that this 'master' had died of a heart attack the moment he stole the bundle. Many people were astonished at the brave man's act and named him Boy with the Witchcraft Bundle (Ashkii Anit'į́įhii)."[40]

The activities of skinwalkers and other witches take a variety of forms, many of which have been discussed elsewhere.[41] Still, a review of how they operate is helpful in understanding the powerful beliefs they generate. Navajos explain that witchcraft has been in this world from the beginning, and it will not go away because there "is a birth every moment." When it ceases to exist, so will this creation. The world is steadfast because, through witchcraft and skinwalking, rain comes to the earth. Practitioners put *ntł'iz*—a mixture of sacred white shell, turquoise, abalone, and jet—near water seeps so clouds will form and rain will nurture the soil.[42] There are also two powers—*yishtłizh* (brown), the ability to obtain wealth, and *łibá* (gray), a curse to inflict abject poverty.[43] Skinwalkers have control over these forces and may wax rich while causing people around them to become beggars. The knowledge is "a dangerous thing to handle, and you do not teach anyone that you do not know. In return for this knowledge, you must kill your mother or brother or sister" as part of the covenant.[44]

The power associated with this wisdom is illustrated in the story told of a man who was hunting and shot a coyote. The animal ran into a clump of bushes, so the man charged in after it. There sat a woman bleeding from the wound, coyote skin beside her. The hunter cleaned and treated the gunshot with cactus, then fed and cared for her until she recuperated. At the end of a month she prepared to leave, but she could not get back into her animal skin while the man watched. He went over the hill and looked back to see the coyote running away. The woman told him before she left that he should visit her father, who was "very knowledgeable," at a place called Burnt Corn. Later, the man visited their home, where he received forty sheep and a coral necklace for not disclosing the woman's identity. Everyone seems to have benefited from the agreement.[45]

Since the identity of witches must not be revealed, their activities take place at night when it is windy and when a family is alone or no one is home. Sightings are often made at a distance or when tracks of a wolf or a coyote turn into impressions of moccasined feet. A number of informants mentioned seeing a strange-looking dog with broad shoulders, thin back legs, and an unusual lope. Skinwalkers have the ability to communicate with coyotes, dogs, and bears and can intermingle with animals around a home. Although domestic dogs recognize a person who practices witchcraft, it is also believed that they know part of the Enemy Way ceremony. They can sing some of these songs and kill a person, so one should not beat dogs. Again, there is the potential for both good and evil.[46]

A few incidents illustrate the perception of how skinwalkers operate. A man tells that his family sent him out one morning to get a goat to butcher. As he searched for the grazing flock, he passed a hogan from which a coyote emerged: "It had an awkward trot, and everything vibrated when it ran." The man threw a rock, hit the coyote's stomach, then watched the creature dash out of sight. After he found the goats, he returned to investigate. He saw that the animal had "jumped two levels of cliffs," continuing to walk along the base until it reached two large boulders leaning against each other. A black bucket, used only for bathing, rested beneath them, and nearby, under another rock, was the animal skin. The person who lived in the hogan, because of this discovery, died before the year ended.[47]

One of the most detailed descriptions of a witchcraft incident is provided by Navajo Oshley, a longtime resident of southeastern Utah. Initially, he did not believe in witchcraft, asking some of his close relatives, "How could someone come up with such stories?" He did, however, become increasingly aware of strange events occurring around him and sought an answer in culturally prescribed ways. Oshley tells what happened.

> This was in the spring, when the wind blew hard and we sometimes lost sheep in this kind of weather. One time a ram was missing and I could not understand why, especially when it happened three or four other times. All I found were coyote tracks while the animals disappeared only when the wind blew. Soon another one was missing, so I went back to where they had been grazing and found a set of coyote prints and big dog tracks. There was only a little bit of wool on the rock but no sign of blood anywhere.
>
> I told my aunt, Lady with a House, what had happened. She was really good with hand trembling, so she did a ceremony and told me that it [the coyote] would come back in two days. I wondered how it was possible to know when this thing was going to happen in the future. As the night for its return approached, the question arose as to who would enter the sheep corral and wait to destroy it. They

selected me and did a ceremony on me and my rifle, using a sacred name for each to give protection and power. They put something on me called 'atł'izh to protect me against the 'áńt'į́įh [corpse poison] used by skinwalkers to kill people. When they [witches] are in the process of getting 'áńt'į́įh, they do it behind some sort of curtain, where they take out the dead person's saliva, pinch off pieces of skin at the joints, and make a fine powder that is very dangerous and powerful. Atł'izh was used in the old days and was made of bile from a bobcat, wolf, and mountain lion. I think now they use bird [eagle] bile. My aunt had the bile given to her, which was passed down from generation to generation. In the ceremony they told me that skinwalkers were like us; they travel upright, some are in animal form, and they have a song that allows them to pat things into a small package so that they can carry it away. This is what happened to the missing animals.

That morning we put the lambs into a cave and the sheep into the corral. My family gave me a sheepskin, water, and food [and] told me to stay in the corral the whole day and not to leave for one minute, while the children were told that I had gone somewhere. I was in a sitting position that made my body ache. I sat there until early morning when the breeze began to blow and the sheep became restless, making a snorting sound. The dogs whimpered, then quieted down. I put the bullet in the gun. Then I heard it [the skinwalker] coming. It made the sound of a horse running. By the moonlight I could see it was as big as the finest large dog. It had red fur and a white streak down its face, with a tail that did not look like it was even connected to the body. Maybe it was just sewn on. I smelled something very strong and it made a sound like a packrat. I think it was either his tail or his claws making that sound. It was in the corral trying to get the sheep into a corner. As it walked by, I shot it and it let out a howl like a human. The dogs chased it up a canyon, and later my brother followed the blood trail to a clearing where the skinwalker had sat and cleaned the blood off with some plants. It did this a second time, as it bled on a trail that went past El Capitan. My brother followed until it started to get dark.

When I returned home my aunt used hand trembling, then said that in five days we would know what had happened. In five days a man came to visit us and told us that a man had shot himself while getting at a lynx with the butt of his rifle. He was dead by the next sunset. So it was really him. I still wonder about it and how it could be. I asked another person, who said it was very holy. This is when I was told about how sacred it was. These things were only discussed behind "closed doors." From that day on, I took extra care of myself.[48]

Precedents for many of the elements of Oshley's story are explained in the previous discussion of mythology. Shrinking objects, the effects of weather, use of songs and prayers, the sacredness of this power, and the "illegal" obtaining of wealth are part of this cultural repository of understanding as to how the world functions. Even Oshley's skepticism is normal; many people have the same feelings until they encounter a situation that is interpreted in supernatural terms. Religious man views the world through religious eyes.

MEDICINE MEN: DETECTION AND PROTECTION

Yet being a believer in traditional teachings does not guarantee acceptance of witchcraft as a reality. Frank Mitchell, a Blessing Way singer, struggled with these ideas, just as Oshley did. One person told him that shooting rocks, bones, or "beans" into a person through magical means originated in the old days when medicine men wanted to coerce a family into surrendering one of their daughters for marriage. Stories about skinwalkers started when poor Navajos dressed in coyote skins with the paws attached to their moccasins to fool owners who had lost livestock into believing that the prints belonged to an animal or a supernatural being. Mitchell summarized his views by saying that the younger generation is outgrowing these beliefs because there is no need for them. As for the elders, they are like sheep bedded down with a goat that refuses to relax. He stays awake all night listening and waiting for a noise, and when it comes, he springs to his feet and startles the others: "The Navajos are like that; somebody gives the alarm and they all stampede. This witchcraft is just a false alarm, and yet the People will stampede that way."[49]

Other medicine men do not dismiss these beliefs so readily. John Holiday was trained by his grandfather, who taught that even though John would be asked to heal the effects of witchcraft induced by other practitioners, he should avoid ever using his songs and prayers to hurt the offending practitioner. To do so would cause his power for good to diminish, leading to a lonely existence filled with evil. When singing against a person who has cursed another, John warns, "You never say the accused person's name straight out, especially if you are not sure if he is practicing witchcraft. The patient might say, 'So-and-so is doing witchcraft on me. Can you counteract the situation and reverse the spell?'. . . Never name the accused person unless you absolutely witnessed his actions and know he is at fault for your patient's sickness."[50] Otherwise, there is a good possibility of harming the wrong person. John learned also that there is a limit as to how much a person can work against those performing evil. When a medicine man uses his powers to stop the cursing, "You are limited to only four [times]. If you destroy a fifth time, it will be you who will die. If you don't die, you'll likely end up paralyzed or a total beggar . . . All of your happiness, wealth, and sacred knowledge of prayers and songs will become as nothing, and you will be walking in an empty life, having lost your sacredness, your mind, your voice, and your body to evil."[51] Those trained in the Blessing Way should use their powers for good.

Jim Dandy, raised near Red Lake, Arizona, was also being trained by his grandfather to become a medicine man. Then the instruction stopped. His grandfather urged him to get a white man's education rather than pursue his present course. He reasoned that many of the traditional practices were fading out and that soon there would be no need for people with these specialized skills. Even more important, he did not want his grandson to have to dabble on the side of evil to understand what was necessary to defeat it. Jim remembers him saying, "You have to have some experience with evil before becoming a medicine man if you are really going to be able to help someone. You're going to have to do some evil things. I can't do that to you, Grandson. A real medicine man has to deal with some evil things because that is what you are going to be working against. Without this kind of knowledge you cannot work well."[52]

For those who do believe in witchcraft, ultimate safety is achieved through detection of and protection from the culprit. One fear would-be practitioners must face is that supernatural means will be used to expose them. Either hand trembling or crystal gazing can uncover a witch's activity. For instance, Ba'álílee, a medicine man who lived in the Aneth area at the turn of the twentieth century, died when his boat overturned on the San Juan River. Nearby residents believed it happened because a sick woman had had a shielding ceremony to cure her. The medicine man saw Ba'álílee during the ceremony, which caused his life to end.[53] The evil power that originated from him was deflected and returned to kill him. Stargazing and crystal gazing also unleash powers of light that identify a witch. Although explanations concerning these techniques vary, the general consensus is that a holy being or an animal, such as

Author photo.

The contents of this medicine man's bundle are used to heal and protect a patient. The power provided by a lightning-struck piece of wood, a wooden rattle with star designs, a buffalo-tail rattle with eagle plumes, and the protection of flint (chert) arrowheads speaks from teachings that extend back to creation.

Gila Monster found in mythology, help expose the culprit. Either a light from the stars will illuminate the guilty party when seen in a vision, or an image is viewed in the crystal.[54] Once the source of the sickness or problem is found, either direct or indirect action can be taken to counteract the wrong. Again, responses vary, with some informants suggesting that just knowing who is guilty is enough to destroy them; others insist that ceremonies, prayers, and charms may turn the evil; still others may kill the witch directly. Whatever the means, the first step is to identify the source of evil.

One night as he lay in bed, Navajo Oshley buckled over with excruciating pain in the upper part of his body. Not even his mother's sacred herbs retrieved from beneath a lightning-struck tree offered relief, so the family decided to have a Blessing Way ceremony. A medicine man performed the ritual, singing songs and saying prayers in sets through the night. As dawn approached, Oshley, whether awake or asleep he could not tell, saw a man enter the hogan: "He was a small, kind of fat man, with hair tied beautifully in a knot with red ochre on his face. He fell right in front of me when I recognized him. I looked up and I heard people singing, then I sat up straight."[55] Oshley told the medicine man what he had seen and was comforted to learn that he would get better; that even though this man had been friendly in the past, he was the cause of the sickness; and that the malefactor would soon die. Oshley and his family went outside, faced the dawn, then offered corn pollen and prayers to the new day. He felt better, "like a plant that was growing," while simultaneously the other man sickened and died crying.

Left Hand, son of Old Man Hat, suggests that some people intentionally announced they were witches because they were tired of living and wanted to be killed: "When a man wants to be killed he begins to claim that he is the one bewitching the people, killing the people with his witchcraft, and that is why the people believe him and want him to be killed right away."[56] The opposite effect can also be achieved, as seen in chapter 4 about Ba'álílee. This powerful medicine man used witchcraft and the threat thereof to intimidate many into following his lead in opposing the government. The more publicity he received, the greater the effect in coercing people to obey his plan of resistance. Not until he was confronted by an equal in controlling supernatural power was anybody able to ceremonially stop his practices and predict the means of his death.

After detection comes protection. One of the fundamental assumptions in defeating witchcraft is the ability to turn the bad power to good use. For example, a Blessing Way prayer, when said backward, can be used to afflict; but when said in the proper sequence, it can protect by turning the evil into good. The power associated with Ajiłee prayers to cure frenzy witchcraft is so strong that they cannot be used in the wife's or children's home if they are present. When they hear these prayers, "they may go crazy and simply run away."[57] Thus that which afflicts can cure and vice versa. The holy people developed all of these cures, just as they did the evils in the underworlds. At least thirty-two forms of sickness and death grew from this knowledge, with as many remedies. Among the various forms of relief are white shell, turquoise, abalone shell, jet, iron ore, harebell pollen, "ordinary (corn) pollen," and other types of plants and roots. The holy people inhale these offerings, accept them as gifts, and help effect a healing.[58]

Plants that hold good or bad powers include squirrel-tail (*Sitanian hystrix*), said to be dropped in a sleeping person's mouth so he will choke to death. Datura is used to drive a person insane and so is connected with sex, hunting, gambling, and trading. For example, an angry lover might take a sample of his girlfriend's saliva or dirt from her moccasin and rub it on the plant, causing her to lose self-control. Plants used to cure witchcraft include beard tongue (Penstemon), clematis (*Clematis alpina*), and twin pod (*Physaria newberryi*), which are usually given to the patient as a warm tea.[59] The sharp points of a yucca plant can also help fend off evil in two ways. The first concerns a person who spits. If witches can obtain one's saliva, it can be used to work against the individual. Evil avoids sharp-pointed objects, just as it does blacking on a person as found in the Evil Way ceremony (Hóchx'ǫ́ǫ́jí) and the pungent smell of desert plants. So when a person spits, he or she should do so into a yucca plant where evil cannot retrieve it. One can also carry small tips of yucca in a pouch for protection.[60]

In addition to good songs and prayers, as already mentioned, one of the most common protections is to carry gall medicine. The liquid is liver bile from an animal such as an eagle, bear, mountain lion, skunk, badger, deer, or sheep. Jim Dandy mentioned mixing the bile and strong-smelling herbs for a potent protection.[61] Particularly effective against witchery, the liquid can also be used for the effects of wizardry. As an antidote against corpse poison, the bile is applied to a person who has fainted, usually having an immediate effect. This medicine is often carried by Navajos who are going to be in large crowds because one never knows who in such an assembly might have a desire to witch them. Even if just a little of this gall medicine is applied externally, the evil influence will stay away. Kluckhohn was able to quantify just how prevalent this medicine, and hence concern for witchcraft, was. In a survey conducted in 1941, he determined that in the Navajo community of Ramah, thirty of thirty-two households had this gall medicine.[62]

Other forms of physical protection include not going out at night and not playing in hard-to-reach places or at the base of large rocks or cliffs. When one walks near these sites, 'áńt'į́įh can be sprinkled on a person to cause death or sickness. Skinwalkers can also come to a home, climb on top of it, and scatter corpse poison on the people sleeping below. One woman told how a witch pulled a small section of log from the wall of a hogan, apparently to scatter poison, but was frightened off by the family's father. The next day the family found the tracks of a dog or coyote whose "paws were sticking out every which way." The parents warned the children not to step in these prints, which "led to the cliff then upward."[63]

Gladwell Richardson, who ran the trading post at Inscription House, Arizona, during the 1930s, tells perhaps one of the most unique stories concerning protection from witchcraft.[64] It seems there was a hermaphrodite named Loolo, who escaped the normal fate of death when she was born. The family, however, wanted to rid themselves of this powerful yet cursed creature, and so they gave her to a medicine man named Jack Gambol to do what he liked with her. Realizing that she had supernatural gifts and high intelligence, he seized upon the waif as an opportunity to train a person in witchcraft. Once he had finished training her, he joined forces with Gani Choi, another medicine man, who along with a Hopi witch taught the girl all the knowledge of black magic they possessed.

By age seventeen (around 1935), Loolo's understanding and power became harnessed under the direction of Gambol, who went to work coercing money, livestock, and valuable goods from people on the Kaibito Plateau. Those who did not cooperate were witched with bad luck and death, to the point that few resisted. All this time, Loolo lived an isolated life in a medicine hogan, believing her songs and prayers were helping people rather than hurting them. The fine line between the power for good and for bad had never been explained to her. Finally, a member of the paralyzed community took action. L'Chee b'Asaan (Łichí' Be' Asdzáán—Red Woman) found Loolo's home, told her that she was going to cut her throat (a normal punishment for witches), and confronted her about her evil acts. Loolo was horrified to learn about the acts to which she had been an unwitting accomplice. She, with Red Woman's help, fled the control of her masters and created an anti-witch cult to do away with skinwalkers and the abuse of power.

Loolo set out to reverse these forces. The Hopi witch died under mysterious circumstances; a small boy, "suddenly commanded" by a spirit, shot and killed Gani Choi as he was witching a flock of sheep; others died under equally questionable circumstances, while Jack Gambol fled the area to avoid a similar fate. Before long, Loolo had cleaned out most of the witches on the Kaibito Plateau.

Richardson brought a man plagued by witchcraft to Loolo for help. That night, with fifty people present, Loolo performed the ceremony. She placed a bow between the legs of a man depicted in a two-foot-long sand painting. On the string of the bow she dropped a small white bead. After the drumming and singing had reached a fever pitch around midnight, they suddenly stopped. Richardson explained:

> Had I not been close and gazing directly down at the bead, I would never have believed what followed. The instant that the sound stopped, the tiny white bead jumped from the bowstring and landed on the neck of the man-figure in the sand painting. Should I live to be a thousand years old, I shall never forget it. That was the end. Maybe it was trickery, maybe not.[65]

Loolo next identified the witch by name and said he would soon "recede from this world by falling on his neck." The following week the guilty party died when he was thrown from the back of a pickup truck south of Comb Ridge and broke his neck.

Gambol later emerged from hiding and threatened to use his powers on some people who had provided negative testimony against him in a court case. When the witnesses' family members started to die, the people approached Loolo asking for help. Since Gambol knew almost as much as she did, Loolo decided to attack him supernaturally in an area he would not anticipate—his mind. She performed the necessary rite. Richardson said, "Call it mystery, magic, or mere coincidence, but Gambol was determined to be insane in the penitentiary. Transferred to a hospital for mental defects in Springfield, Missouri, he hanged himself in his cell with a belt."[66] Good triumphed over evil, just as had been promised in the underworlds.

To summarize the beliefs surrounding witchcraft, there is a wide range of understanding that stretches from nonbelievers to believers. The people who have faith in its existence are most likely those who seek answers to questions through religious expression. They believe this sacred, holy power is one of many of the dualities, or "packages," that comprise the universe. Navajos often exclaim "*yíiyá*" (scary) when a person tampers with something so sacred that it can cause injury. Use of this word does not draw a distinction between handling something very good or something very bad—either way, it holds potential for equal harm.[67] Naked supernatural power without control precipitates danger just as surely as does a bare electric wire transmitting high voltage. Those who use it inappropriately stand the chance of either losing or gaining a great deal; it becomes a matter of life and death. They are the ones who choose the dark side of life along the San Juan.

NOTES

1. The word *páá* is used in the Blackening Way ceremony ('Ant'eesh) to blow away evil and send it to the north, a place of death, evil, and harmful things. In the ceremony, a person holds an arrowhead covered with ash in his palm and blows on it, saying this word to push malfeasance away. Oshley, anticipating that this was what was happening, used the word to protect himself, something he repeated often the next day.
2. Robert S. McPherson, *The Journey of Navajo Oshley: An Autobiography and Life History* (Logan: Utah State University Press, 2000), 98–99.
3. Harry Walters, personal communication with author, January 28, 2012.
4. Berard Haile, *Upward Moving and Emergence Way: The Gishin Biye' Version* (Lincoln: University of Nebraska Press, 1981), 6–7.
5. Ibid., 12–13, 18–19.
6. Berard Haile, "Soul Concepts of the Navaho," in *Annali Lateranensi* 7 (Vatican City: Vatican Polyglot, 1943), 76.
7. Ibid., 74–77, 82.
8. Gladys A. Reichard, *Navaho Religion: A Study of Symbolism* (Princeton, NJ: Princeton University Press, 1950), 434.
9. Ibid., 433.
10. Haile, *Upward Moving,* 102.
11. Reichard, *Navaho Religion*, 105.
12. Gary Witherspoon, *Language and Art in the Navajo Universe* (Ann Arbor: University of Michigan Press, 1977), 77, 185–186.
13. Clyde Kluckhohn, *Navaho Witchcraft* (Boston: Beacon, 1944), 59.
14. John Holiday and Robert S. McPherson, *A Navajo Legacy: The Life and Teachings of John Holiday* (Norman: University of Oklahoma Press, 2005), 303.
15. Ibid., 146.
16. John R. Farella, *The Main Stalk: A Synthesis of Navajo Philosophy* (Tucson: University of Arizona Press, 1984), 41.
17. Marilyn Holiday interview with author, April 9, 1992.
18. Florence Begay interview with author, January 30, 1991.
19. John Norton interview with author, January 16, 1991.
20. John Begay interview with author, May 7, 1991; Margaret Weston interview with author, February 13, 1991; Jane Silas interview with author, February 27, 1991.
21. Sally Draper Bailey interview with Aubrey Williams, January 29, 1961, Doris Duke Collection #740, Special Collections, University of Utah Library, Salt Lake City.
22. W. W. Hill, *Navaho Agricultural and Hunting Methods* (New Haven, CT: Yale University Press, 1938), 102.
23. Ibid., 103–104.

24. Ibid., 132.
25. Haile, *Upward Moving,* 13.
26. Jim Dandy interview with author, September 26, 2007.
27. Ibid.
28. Will Evans, *Along Navajo Trails: Recollections of a Trader* (Logan: Utah State University Press, 2005), 231–232.
29. Karl Luckert, *A Navajo Bringing-Home Ceremony: The Claus Chee Sonny Version of Deerway Ajilee* (Flagstaff: Museum of Northern Arizona Press, 1978), 7–10, 185–188.
30. Dandy interview with author.
31. For various versions with textual differences, see Haile, *Upward Moving,* 207–216; Raymond F. Locke, *The Book of the Navajo* (Los Angeles: Mankind, 1976), 88–101; Washington Matthews, *Navaho Legends* (Salt Lake City: University of Utah Press, 1994 [1897]), 96–103.
32. Florence Begay interview with author; Leland C. Wyman, *The Mountainway of the Navajo* (Tucson: University of Arizona Press, 1975), 20, 42, 46; Marilyn Holiday interview with author; Tallis Holiday interview with author, November 3, 1987.
33. Marilyn Holiday interview with author; Fred Yazzie interview with author, August 6, 1991; Mary Blueyes interview with author, July 25, 1988; Slim Benally interview with author, July 8, 1988; Maimie Howard interview with author, August 2, 1988; Charlie Blueyes interview with author, August 28, 1988.
34. Charlie Blueyes interview with author; Mary Blueyes interview with author; Slim Benally interview with author.
35. Luckert, *Navajo Bringing-Home Ceremony*, 186.
36. John Holiday interview with author, April 15, 2005.
37. Ibid.
38. Charlie Blueyes interview with author.
39. Richard Van Valkenburgh, "Wolf Men of the Navajo," *Desert Magazine* 11, no. 3 (January 1948): 4–8.
40. Holiday and McPherson, *Navajo Legacy*, 306.
41. Important works in addition to Kluckhohn, *Navaho Witchcraft*, include William Morgan, *Human Wolves among the Navajo*, Yale University Publications in Anthropology 11 (New Haven, CT: Yale University Press, 1936), and Margaret K. Brady, *Some Kind of Power: Navajo Children's Skinwalker Narratives* (Salt Lake City: University of Utah Press, 1984).
42. Charlie Blueyes interview with author; Slim Benally interview with author.
43. The role these colors play is not clearly defined but appears to fit in with the same concept as colors and power in the rest of the Navajo ceremonial system. Gray is associated with evil, "despicable" and "dirty." Brown means literally "speckled, dim, gray" but lacks the same intensity of evil as gray. See Reichard, *Navaho Religion*, 202–203.
44. Charlie Blueyes interview with author.
45. Navajo Oshley interview with Winston Hurst and Wesley Oshley, January 5, 1978.
46. Sally Lee interview with author, February 13, 1991; Weston interview with author; Oliver interview with author; Charlie Blueyes interview with author.

47. Oliver interview with author.
48. Oshley interview with Hurst and Oshley.
49. Charlotte J. Frisbie and David P. McAllester, eds., *Navajo Blessingway Singer: The Autobiography of Frank Mitchell, 1881–1967* (Tucson: University of Arizona Press, 1978), 262–263.
50. Holiday and McPherson, *Navajo Legacy*, 299.
51. Ibid., 300.
52. Dandy interview with author.
53. Mary Blueyes interview with author.
54. Ibid.; Charlie Blueyes interview with author.
55. Oshley interview with Hurst and Oshley.
56. Walter Dyk and Ruth Dyk, *Left Handed: A Navajo Autobiography* (New York: Columbia University Press, 1980), 514.
57. Luckert, *Navajo Bringing-Home Ceremony*, 186.
58. Haile, *Upward Moving,* 24.
59. Gail D. Tierney, "Botany and Witchcraft," *El Palacio* 80, no. 2 (Summer 1974): 44–52; medline: 11615066.
60. Dandy interview with author.
61. Ibid.
62. Kluckhohn, *Navaho Witchcraft*, 47, 53.
63. Martha Nez interview with author, August 2, 1988.
64. Gladwell Richardson, *Navajo Trader* (Tucson: University of Arizona Press, 1986), 157–163.
65. Ibid., 161.
66. Ibid., 162.
67. Marilyn Holiday interview with author.

4

"Too Much Noise in That Bunch across the River"

Ba'álílee and the 1907 Aneth Brawl

The following historical account illustrates the power of traditional beliefs as the dominant culture implemented change at the turn of the twentieth century. More than just a rendering of cultural conflict, however, it is an interesting look at a powerful medicine man who used witchcraft as a political tool to consolidate his following of rebellious individuals chafing at the government's attempt to convert them to the white man's world. Somewhat of an anomaly, Ba'álílee's open admission to his use of this spiritual power, combined with overt threats against Navajo neighbors, was as real as the physical hostility he and his cohort employed against the agent and his forces. His name, glossed as The One with Supernatural Power, spoke not only of his rise to prominence but also of his undoing.

DOI: 10.7330/9781607322177.c04

Moonlight turned the yellow cottonwood leaves silver as they drifted in the gentle current of the San Juan River. The black turbid water, low against the drought-parched banks, was easily fordable along this stretch of river near Aneth, Utah. Known as Old Age River (Są̨ Bitooh) and One with a Long Body (Bits'íísnineezí), the San Juan was the northernmost of the four sacred rivers that protected Navajo land. Viewed as a powerful snake wriggling through the desert, a flash of lightning, a black club, the river protected those on its south side as a boundary of safety.[1] Hogans, livestock corrals, and summer shades rested in the shadows under the now naked tree branches. Sheep bleating in the cool autumn air, the smell of juniper smoke and manure, the stomp of tethered horses' hoofs, and an occasional coyote's bark was all that rose above the gurgle of the river to disturb the night's peace. Everything was calm, everything protected.

Inside the hogan slept Ba'álílee, The One with Supernatural Power.[2] Confident in his ability to remain safe, he lay next to the west wall, the place of honor. He had spent the evening working against the sickness of a patient bewitched by a man and his family for winning a horse race. Through divination, Ba'álílee uncovered the evil, identified the culprits, and worked hard to ceremonially return the curse and heal the sick man.[3] Now the weary medicine man slept, secure in the knowledge that he had done his best and that he was protected from harm.

Or so he thought. He was actually resting on a stage about to erupt in conflict derived from national as well as local events. Having lived through earlier tremors of change brought on by the Dawes Act (1887) and now subject to the beliefs of the Progressive era, this strong-willed medicine man had been dueling with a determined agent and promoter of white culture, William T. Shelton. Across the nation, Indian tribes had reached the nadir of their existence as white laws and values gnawed at traditional culture. The Navajos had avoided much of this trauma because of their isolation. The events about to play out in the next few hours heralded a shift in political control, fomenting greater change on the Utah portion of the Navajo Reservation. Ba'álílee rested, having no idea that troops were on the way.

THE EARLY YEARS

Born of the Water Edge (Tábąąhá) Clan and for the Salt (Ashįįhí) Clan around 1859 in Canyon de Chelly, his earliest recollections were of war and fear.[4] His mother died shortly after his birth, and little is known about his father, Happy Man (Báhózhóní). Caught in the clash of cultures, Ba'álílee watched the US military with its auxiliary forces of Utes, Hopis, and other tribes, as well as New Mexican citizenry, fight the Navajo during what they called the "Fearing Time" (Náhonzhoodą́ą́'). Kit Carson's foray into Canyon de Chelly with a large body of soldiers must have been part of his experience before joining 8,000 of his tribal members at Fort Sumner on the Pecos River in New Mexico. Still a child, he managed to survive the ordeal and return to the lands set aside by the government in what is today New Mexico and Arizona.

Fragmentary evidence that survives in the written record suggests that Ba'álílee spent an errant early adulthood. Hastiin Klah (Left Hand—Tł'ah), a policeman at the Northern Navajo Agency in Shiprock, New Mexico, testified that he had known Ba'álílee since he was a boy, "and he was always bad."[5] Klah recounted how Ba'álílee had employed witchcraft to kill a sick woman by shooting hair into her body. His witchery led to four days' confinement, perhaps at Rock Point, Arizona.[6] Other Navajos spared his life after he confessed his guilt and promised to leave the reservation. Ba'álílee then spent two years in "Mormon country," presumably southern Utah, before returning to his people. Perhaps this is where he gained some proficiency in English, starting the rumor that he guided the Mormons to Bluff, Utah, in 1880.[7] Shortly after returning to the reservation, he attended a dance with three friends, all of whom had revolvers and "witch knives," which scared the participants away.[8]

Ba'álílee grew increasingly powerful as a medicine man. Most chanters might know two or three ceremonies, indicating a high degree of intelligence given the learning required just to know one. He knew six—Evil Way (Hóchx'ǫ́ǫ́jí), Blessing Way (Hózhǫ́ǫ́jí), Mountain Top Way (Dziłk'ijí), Wind Way (Nítch'ijí), Shooting Way (Na'at'oyee), and Night Chant (Tł'éé'jí).[9] Navajos accepted his ability to see into the past and the future through star gazing (déest'į́į́), during which he perceived events in his mind's eye. His control of this much knowledge and power allowed him to use them against those he wished to intimidate. He also could use them to help those seeking aid. Among the Navajo, even the knowledge of witchcraft and that type of supernatural power is usually denied.[10] Not so with Ba'álílee, who spoke openly of his ability.

There are numerous stories about Ba'álílee's use of power, few of which suggest a chronological sequence. Still, they give a flavor for the man, who at least by the early 1880s was living in what was later Aneth, Utah. On one occasion, Old Man Hat (Hastiin Sání Bich'ahii) summoned Ba'álílee to diagnose and cure his ailment after another medicine man had failed. He began by star gazing and reported that he had seen his patient "sitting on a bearskin. The head of the bear was toward the east, and you were sitting on the skin, facing the east too. And this whole place was black. That means no hope. You've killed yourself with your own witchcraft. You tried to bewitch someone, but you witched yourself instead . . . No one will cure you."[11] If Old Man Hat would admit to his involvement in witchcraft, then he could be healed.[12] Otherwise, nothing could be done. The patient refused to recognize his practice of any such thing, although he intimated that some time ago a person had placed a curse on him. A medicine man presumably removed the evil, and all the objects shot into Old Man Hat's body. The witch had since died, but there seemed to be some "bean" left that was causing more trouble.[13] There was no way to reverse the process. Within a day after Ba'álílee diagnosed the ailment, Old Man Hat passed away.

Old Man Hat's son, Left Hand (Tł'ah), benefited from Ba'álílee's wisdom later, in the late 1880s.[14] He had married a young woman who was supposed to be a virgin, but after sleeping with her, he realized she was not. Left Hand raised a public outcry to which Ba'álílee, a noted headman, sat in judgment. After hearing both sides, he chastised Left Hand because he knew he had other wives living in another part of the reservation. Declaring that the young woman and the young man she had slept with had not done anything wrong by being together, he told the accuser, "You ought to have better sense than that. If you want to say something bad about it, I will see what can be done. I will take all of you to Fort Defiance [Arizona], and there I will turn you over to the headman, and he will see about it. However, I know that he won't like it. He will keep you there in jail, and he will let these two young ones get married."[15] Because the woman and the young man belonged to the same clan, it was best that they not marry, so she stayed with Left Hand. Considering later events, it is significant that Ba'álílee offered to take the three to the agent at Fort Defiance.

In 1881, another opportunity arose for him to use his ability in a positive way. A five-man posse of Mormon settlers issued forth from the newly established community of Bluff in pursuit of two horse thieves. Arriving near Hall's Crossing, the groups exchanged gunfire, with Joseph "Jody" A. Lyman receiving a wound that shattered his femur and totally incapacitated him. Retreating up the trail from the water's edge and onto the desert, the posse camped and tried to dress and care for the wound while one man rode to Bluff 100 miles away for a wagon. On October 3, Ba'álílee and some Navajo friends happened upon the scene and asked what was being done to help Jody. He learned that the men traveled a long distance for water and were having a terrible time keeping maggots out of the wound. Ba'álílee took a bucket and in a short time returned with water secured from "tanks," or depressions in solid rock nearby. He ordered the men to gather prickly pear cactus, burn off the spines, and mash the fleshy part of the cactus into a poultice, which he applied to the wound. Instantly, the infection and maggots disappeared. The pain remained, accentuated by the ride in the bouncing, jolting wagon, but Ba'álílee had saved the young man's life.[16]

Three years later he almost lost his own life. By 1884 the area of Aneth, then known as Riverview, had a small community of non-Mormon settlers who arrived from Colorado to live along the San Juan River and McElmo Creek. There were at least three trading posts in the vicinity that plied their commerce with local Navajos and Utes. Henry L. Mitchell, a cantankerous, hard-bitten man, owned one of the stores.[17] On April 15 Ba'álílee—whose home was approximately four miles east of the post—with three other men and two women, entered the store to trade. One of the Navajos took an unloaded rifle and aimed it at a calf outside, then at a boy, then at one of the white customers inside. Another white man saw the move and drew his pistol, believing a threat existed. A Navajo seized the rifle from the one pointing it, showing it was unloaded. The disarmed Navajo called to Ba'álílee outside, saying, "These Americans are going to kill me." Ba'álílee strode toward the store, gun in hand. The threatened white men drew their guns and opened fire. The Navajo who had done the pointing died instantly. The sound of gunshots brought Mitchell's son and another man from the nearby fields; seeing the problem, one of them fired, hitting Ba'álílee in the forehead and knocking him unconscious. The Navajo men rushed out of the store with the whites following, firing in all directions and hitting one Indian in the elbow as he jumped a fence. Mrs. Mitchell helped the two Navajo women trapped in the store escape out a back door. Although fired upon while running, neither was hit. Ba'álílee revived and then escaped, as did the remaining Navajo man.[18]

This incident is important for two reasons. First, the Navajo scout, Herrero Segundo, reporting his investigation of the incident, said that when Ba'álílee started toward the store he uttered "all right, that is what I want." No doubt, this was in response to Mitchell's strong-willed personality, which seemed to grate on everyone's nerves. According to Left Hand, "After this shooting, the good Indians tried to give Ba'álílee good advice, but he wouldn't listen to them and was always making trouble."[19] The issue of who followed Ba'álílee and who opposed him (the "good Indians") became increasingly magnified over the years. The second point to draw from this incident is how fast the Indians mobilized once news spread. They seized twenty-nine horses belonging to Mitchell, which were later returned through the efforts of another trader, and ransacked a vacated post upriver. In a land of isolated settlements and little rule, problems quickly escalated.

Other incidents occurred. In 1900 Ba'álílee broke into a store owned by Howard Ray Antes, an independent Methodist missionary.[20] He stole a silver belt, from which he fashioned bracelets and other merchandise. Antes, fearing repercussions, refused to press charges.[21] Shortly after this incident, James M. Holley, who owned the Aneth Trading Post from 1899 to 1905 and then remained in Aneth as a government farmer, went to a Yé'ii bicheii dance at Ba'álílee's camp. Many spectators were drinking whiskey, waving bottles over their heads, and yelling "'Where are the police? Where are the chiefs? Where is the agent? Where are the soldiers?' saying they [were] not afraid."[22] Eventually, the agent from Fort Defiance visited them to demand that they send some of their children to school. Ba'álílee, as a local spokesman, refused and told the people that if the reservation police or soldiers came after the children, his men would kill them as fast as they came. The agent balked and did nothing. It did not take long, however, for the federal government to answer the questions "Where is the agent? Where are the police?" much to Ba'álílee's chagrin.

SHELTON: OPENING SALVOS

In 1903, Superintendent William T. Shelton (Tall Leader) established the Northern Navajo Agency in Shiprock, a little over thirty miles from

Ba'álílee, a proud and powerful medicine man, confronted the forces of change in traditional Navajo practices at the turn of the twentieth century. His extensive ceremonial knowledge gave him the ability to use both physical and spiritual force against his adversaries.

Courtesy, Utah State Historical Society.

Ba'álílee's camp, and instituted an aggressive policy of change. Espousing the ideals of Progressive reform prevalent at the turn of the twentieth century, the agent enforced the mandate to improve the Navajo economy, provide education for the children, remove vices on the reservation, and create stability in a region prone to lawlessness. Shelton, a man of sobriety and strong religious conviction, surged forward on all fronts. While many people have characterized Tall Leader (Naat'áanii Nééz as he was known among the Navajos) as puritanical and heavy-handed in enforcing government programs, he faced an almost overwhelming task.

Speaking about the agency's early years, Shelton recalled taking a thirty-five-mile trip to Farmington, New Mexico. During this travel he met "eighteen drunken Indians" coming from Durango. There were also those selling liquor to the Navajos, and everyone seemed to be involved in gambling. He noted that "fifteen to twenty, and sometimes more, would congregate at each of the trading posts during the day and waste their time and money gambling. At some of the posts the traders kept a 'tin horn' gambler at their store for the purpose of getting a crowd together and beating them out of their money."[23]

By the end of 1905, Shelton claimed to have put a lid on this activity by gaining the "cooperation of the older and more influential Indians, convincing them that gambling was bad business and detrimental to the best interests of the reservation." As battle trophies from the war against gambling, he collected more than three bushels of playing cards. As for the whiskey traffic, he slowed it by assigning a first-time offender ten days of work at the agency, a second-time offender twenty days, and an additional ten days for every other infraction. Over the next ten years agency police brought in only eleven drinkers for punishment, leading Shelton to boast, "I doubt if there is a community in the United States more free from whiskey, drinking, and gambling than this reservation."[24] This claim may be naive, but his control was something that had not been possible before the government established the agency to quell the liquor traffic on the reservation's northern boundaries.

Four years of Progressive change brought substantial alteration in many aspects of traditional Navajo life. Briefly, Shelton's jurisdiction extended over approximately 3,000 square miles of territory spanning parts of New Mexico, Arizona, and Utah. He was responsible for the welfare of an estimated 8,000 Navajos, 2,500 of whom were school-age children between the ages of six and eighteen and 100 of whom attended the Shiprock Boarding School.[25] He supervised government farmers hired to improve crop production, expand irrigation systems, issue all types of farm equipment, construct and maintain roads, increase the quality and production of wool, eliminate diseases such as scabies through sheep dipping, and provide individualized agricultural counsel. The agent worked with traders to ensure fair practices and to encourage blanket weaving, quality silversmithing, and an improved lifestyle.

A quick glimpse into the daily life of Old Mexican, a Navajo resident of Aneth in 1904, shows the intensity of the government program and the effect of subsidy. Old Mexican's mother received three rams to increase the quality of sheep in her herd; his older brother was given a scraper, scythe, and pitchfork for farming. Later, the government agent wished to improve the road system, so he told community members, "If any of you want a wagon, you have to work forty-five days, and for a shovel, one day, and for an ax, one day, and a saw, one day, and a pitchfork, one day, and for a scraper, five days."[26] For those who preferred a group effort, there was a different pay scale. Also instituted at this time was the precursor of the Shiprock Fair, where competition for everything—from the best woven rug and garden produce to the cleanest baby—was rewarded with food, clothing, tools, and other prizes meant to encourage industry and white values.[27]

Changing people's values, however, is not always easy or pleasant. Social issues such as the practice of polygyny, the abolition of Indian hairstyles, consumption of alcohol, and general law enforcement proved more problematic than did incorporating material goods. This effort struck at the heart of cultural practices or aberrant behavior that had not been challenged, in some cases, for centuries.[28] The three Navajo policemen initially assigned to the agency were far too few. Shelton bemoaned the fact that "crimes such as wife beating, whiskey selling, horse thieving, and even murder have gone unpunished . . . But one of the worst things we have to contend with is that when a man dies his relatives come in and rob the widow and children of all their belongings and leave them homeless and destitute. One case has been brought to my attention where the woman resisted and was murdered."[29] Armed with this type of justification, he requested funding for two more Indian judges, a captain of police, and eight additional policemen, bringing his force to twelve. He received five more police officers.

Many Navajos approved of his practices and liked Shelton. Maimi Howard, who worked for him, felt he was a "very helpful man who understood the Navajo language and was generous."[30] Old Mexican also worked for him in a variety of endeavors—such as farming, law enforcement, road building, and freighting—and thought Shelton was fair. He also disagreed with the agent on some important issues. Old Mexican, under Shelton's direction, did not like serving as the spearhead of change while having to live in a Navajo community that was not always accepting.[31] A general impression from the Navajos at this time is that they respected and liked their agent, but he could also be a stern, no-nonsense disciplinarian when faced with recalcitrance.

The white communities generally supported him. For instance, trader June Foutz noticed the "great changes that had come since Shelton's influence had been felt among the Navajos. They were driving teams, producing more and better wool and stock, all as a result of this influence."[32] Superintendent H. F. Coggeshall commented that the first thing he noticed at the agency was that everyone was busy: "He felt that this accomplishment could only have come thru great executive ability, accompanied by the cooperation of the surrounding communities. He had found the best spirit of cooperation here [Shiprock] of any school he had ever known in the Indian service."[33] Kumen Jones, a member of the Mormon community in Bluff—a group that had often been at odds with federal agents—said of Shelton's appointment, "It was a streak of good fortune for the Mormons as well as the Navajos. He proved to be a real friend towards the latter and absolutely free of prejudice towards the former. He understood the Indians' needs."[34]

Some of those in surrounding towns and at the agency had their own agendas and did not like Shelton. A former clerk at Shiprock filed seven charges against him through the Indian Industries League based in Boston, Massachusetts. Complaints included treating Navajo people rudely, hiring questionable policemen, being influenced by his "friends," lying, and breaking promises. An investigator, Charles H. Hickman, after interviewing many people at the agency and in surrounding communities, fully exonerated Shelton on all seven counts.[35] Sworn testimony gathered during this time paints a picture of an administrator who was very involved in events and with people. He was no saint by any stretch, but he worked hard and enforced unpopular policies. It was also not the last time he would be investigated.

BA'ÁLÍLEE BITES BACK

If there was an antithesis to Shelton and what he stood for, it was Ba'álílee. Much of what follows is reconstructed from personal testimony obtained by the government in sworn statements from Navajos and whites alike. They paint a highly negative picture of this medicine man. Sufficient testimony from unofficial sources, both Navajo and white, not given under government direction, indicates that Ba'álílee was very much a power broker. While the sworn statements may not be exaggerated, they are also at times uninformed about traditional Navajo practices. Nevertheless, all accounts provide a telling story that shows Ba'álílee did all he could to resist government intervention and consolidate his power. More than just a clash of personalities between him and Shelton, his resistance forced a final answer as to who controlled the lives and future of hundreds of Navajos in the Aneth area.

A medicine man in traditional Navajo culture plays a prominent role in his community. Viewed as a person of wisdom, he is often the repository of religious learning and local history, as well as a spokesperson for those who adopt his point of view. Equally important is his control of supernatural powers, which are dependent upon the number and type of ceremonies he practices. The more he knows, the more he controls, the more powerful the man. As a leader, his position may at times become politicized, and the more power he wields, both in a spiritual and a political sense, the greater his following. Ba'álílee was exceptionally powerful and did all he could to employ that power through a political agenda. Unlike most people in his position, he was not averse to claiming control of supernatural elements to both help and curse those about him. Normally, this type of aggression is not flaunted.

Many Navajos in the Aneth area believed Ba'álílee controlled rain and lightning. He charged a fee to bring showers to the parched earth and threatened to withhold them if his terms were not met. According to Holley, Ba'álílee was "a medicine man of the worst type, [making] the Indians believe that he has power to cause rain to fall at his will and [he] has made the greater part of his living requiring the Indians to pay him for singing."[36] When it did not rain, he blamed it on the Navajos who followed Shelton's advice and patterned themselves after the white man. He also threatened to kill those who opposed him with lightning, especially any soldiers who dared to attack. As for their bullets, they could not touch him. Community members credited Ba'álílee with killing those who worked for Shelton. He threatened The One with Muscles (Dohii) and Left Hand—both Navajo judges—warning that he would kill them with "darts" shot into their bodies by witchcraft. Shortly after he issued the threat, Dohii died and Left Hand spent $700 for a protective ceremony.[37] Even after Ba'álílee's death, stories about his powers persisted. Mary Blueyes remembers, "My grandfather said he performed a prayer for a Mud Clan woman. Sometime while performing the prayer, he saw Ba'álílee in a brief flash. The supernatural spirit probably said this is the person that is doing this [witchcraft]. The prayer ended and he told of what he had seen. He said, 'I saw Ba'álílee.'"[38]

Many other, more tangible things directly opposed Shelton's plans. Not only was Ba'álílee involved in excessive drinking, gambling, and bootlegging on the reservation, but he also stole livestock from Utes at Towaoc, cowboys in Colorado, and Mormons from Bluff. Saloons and individual entrepreneurs in Cortez, Colorado, supplied his whiskey trade, which provided a handy profit when charging up to eight dollars a bottle. His polygamous marriage to two wives was a common Navajo practice, but it bothered the puritanical Shelton, who espoused the Indian Bureau's belief in monogamy.[39] On many occasions, Ba'álílee told anyone within earshot that he would have as many wives as he pleased and the agent had no say in the matter. Charges were also laid against him and his cohort of selling wives and young girls to older men. In fairness to Ba'álílee, Shelton may have confused this for certain legitimate marriage practices found in traditional Navajo culture: marrying at the young age of thirteen or fourteen, honoring the practice of bride price in recognition of losing a family member, having the same man marry both a mother and her daughter, and dissolving relatively fragile marriage bonds common in matrilineal societies. For whatever reason, Shelton wanted it all stopped.

Ba'álílee gathered a growing circle of followers who basked in his power and gave him legitimacy as leader and spokesman. Estimates vary, but most sources suggest he had between thirty and forty men to call upon for support.[40] There is no mistaking that at least a dozen of these men appropriated some of his power and reputation to create their own, becoming a law unto themselves. Short Hair (Bitsii' Agodí) was such a man.[41] In spring 1906 he came upon a young Navajo girl, Hattie, herding sheep. He tied her hands behind her back with a quirt and assaulted her. Hattie eventually untied herself and went home, where she remained sick for several months before going to the agency for help. Soon after this incident, Short Hair raped Hattie's sister too.[42] Many law-abiding Navajos were shocked at and intimidated by these criminal events.

The San Juan Agency School in Shiprock opened its doors to 106 students on February 8, 1907.[43] Traders, government farmers, Navajo police, and community leaders helped in the recruiting efforts for this new experience. Some families willingly sent their children; others were coerced into filling an established quota. Ba'álílee refused to send his children and raged against what he saw as the loss of Navajo rights. He threatened to harm or kill anyone who gave their children over to the government, explaining that when children had been sent to the school at Fort Defiance, many died from disease but the government still kept requesting more. This would not be repeated in his region.[44] Parents needed their children at home to herd livestock, help with sheep shearing, haul wood and water, and perform myriad other camp chores. Turning them into white men was undesirable at best. Navajo police and Holley, now the government's "Additional Farmer" in Aneth, received the brunt of Ba'álílee's antagonism. Fourteen children were waiting at the Government Station ready to travel to Shiprock when Ba'álílee and a heavily armed contingent arrived and "persuaded" all but four of them that they had better head home.[45]

Equally disturbing was his refusal to dip sheep in medicine that removed the debilitating livestock disease called scabies. Shelton placed fifty vats of medicine throughout the northern Navajo Reservation to eradicate the sickness. Many people in Aneth welcomed the program, but Ba'álílee refused to participate and warned others not to do so. The vat arrived in the fall of 1906 and dipping commenced, but not without threats and refusals. Shelton also provided better breeding stock to improve herd quality. He admonished the recipients not to sell these animals, warned the traders not to buy them, and encouraged the Navajos not to slaughter them for food. Ba'álílee sold his for a song and told the agent he would do whatever he wished because they were his.[46] Others in his group did likewise.

With a final burst of bravado, he and his followers armed themselves heavily against any kind of intervention. Ba'álílee had never seen soldiers in his part of the reservation and was certain that Shelton lacked the nerve and the ability to order them to his location. If he did, however, there would be a fight.[47] Shelton, Holley, and the Navajo police received death threats at different times. Local traders were also put on notice. Four Navajo friends approached Hambleton B. Noel, trader at Teec Nos Pos, and warned him that if trouble arose and soldiers appeared, Ba'álílee would rob and burn the post, kill Noel, and take everything he could on his way to the hinterlands of Navajo Mountain.[48] With his armed force in Aneth, Ba'álílee controlled a formidable position not to be taken lightly.

TIT FOR TAT

Shelton measured his response to these challenges. Realizing that Ba'álílee had clan relations with another dissident group around Black

Mountain that was also opposed to change, Shelton approached the Aneth situation carefully.[49] He sent local Navajo leaders and police on a number of occasions to invite Ba'álílee to the agency to discuss problems, but he refused. Shelton dispatched other messengers and worked through Holley to convince Ba'álílee that he and his following would benefit from what the government was providing. Ba'álílee resisted strenuously. Finally, Shelton and Special Agent R. S. Connell set off on March 30 to tour the area and see for themselves what was happening there. Connell's report, which provides a graphic depiction of their encounter with the medicine man, is an interesting example of agent hype. The two unescorted agents went to Ba'álílee's "stronghold," where they found him with thirty-six warriors. Shelton spoke tactfully and encouraged friendly relations:

> Fortunately, Mr. Shelton and the agency doctor had at one time cured the mother of one of By-lil-le's warriors, who had a boil on her neck, and who was under By-lil-le's treatment until she got maggots into her head and face and was a terrible sight even to the Indians. This Indian was the first to take our side, and Shelton, recognizing another Indian whom he had helped, got them over and called all the Indians' attention to the improvements on the roads, etc., that he had made. Working along this line, we got the band divided, and finally By-lil-le had only three left on his side and then I went after By-lil-le rough; told him he was sick in the head and proved it to the other Indians. The sweat just rolled off his face, and I thought possibly he would try a gun play, but he stood the truth as long as he could and then he went off with only two friends following him and the rest of the Indians giving him the laugh; then we had a horse race, and the Indians left with a different feeling toward the Government and the Government's officials.[50]

This eyewitness account flies in the face of every other indication of how Ba'álílee would have reacted in such a situation, but it does indicate the feelings of superiority at least one agent felt. Connell summarized his sentiments by saying Ba'álílee was on the "edge [including the Black Mountain group] of the worst district of bronco Indians in the Southwest" and that as long as the government was "slack with these Indians and it does not interfere with their raping, stealing, and depredations upon the friendly Indians there will be no open hostilities."[51]

While Shelton appreciated Connell's report, he was not fooled. The meeting did not produce the desired effect, with Ba'álílee as troublesome as ever. The agent again sent some of the most influential Indians he could muster to visit Ba'álílee's camp and quiet unrest, only to have the medicine man emerge from the brush, demand a fight, and challenge everything the leaders said or offered. While the leaders parleyed, Ba'álílee's men remained close by, shooting pistols and rifles for an intimidating effect. Holley fared little better. He sent word that a Navajo judge and policeman were coming to talk to Ba'álílee, who announced his intent to kill them both. The medicine man arrived at the Aneth Trading Post with thirty-five heavily armed supporters. The judge and policeman never appeared, so Holley staged a horse race for a purse he generously provided to the winner. Following the contest, the group disbanded. Still other peacemakers traveled to Ba'álílee's camp, but with no success.[52]

Shelton then removed his velvet gloves. Realizing that his Navajo police force was woefully outnumbered and unprepared for a confrontation, he fired off a letter to the commissioner of Indian affairs requesting two troops of cavalry to either arrest Ba'álílee or remain in the vicinity of his camp to suppress his activities. He even suggested that the soldiers come from Fort Wingate, New Mexico, 150 miles away, because the roads were excellent and hay could be delivered to Aneth at $15.00 a ton and grain for $2.25 per 100 pounds. Shelton's letter was dated September 18; by October 15 the commissioner of Indian affairs, the secretary of war, the regional commanding general, and the commander of Fort Wingate had signed off on the plan. At 8 a.m. on October 22, Captain Harry O. Williard with Troops I and K of the Fifth Cavalry began their march to southern Utah.[53]

Williard's force—composed of four officers, seventy-four enlisted men, a surgeon with two medics, and three Indian scouts—arrived at Shiprock four days later. The next morning, October 27, the soldiers moved again, fearing word would spread among the Navajos that a military force was present. Shelton and Williard devised a plan that capitalized on speed of movement, secrecy, and a night march to decrease the probability of detection. Shelton let slip a rumor that the troops were in the area to control the unruly Utes and Paiutes in Bluff, masking the real intent.[54] All excess baggage remained at the agency. The quartermaster issued each man 100 rounds of rifle ammunition and 20 rounds for his revolver. Wagons loaded with six days' rations and additional equipment rumbled toward the first stop at the Four Corners Trading Post, estimated by Williard as thirty-two miles distant.[55] The cavalry accompanied them on the first leg of the journey.

At this point, a basic understanding of places and distances is helpful. Many of these historic locations are no longer identified on maps. Using estimates given by Shelton and Williard, one gets a sense of the route taken and sites encountered. The road from Shiprock was an improved dirt road, a product of Navajo labor. The first stop along the route was the Four Corners Trading Post, a rock structure on the north bank of the San Juan River. Charles Fritz operated this post. Approximately ten miles down the road and midway between the Four Corners and Aneth posts was another store run by M. R. Butler.[56] From there the road continued roughly three-and-a-half miles downstream to the vicinity of Ba'álílee's camp, from which it was then four miles to the Aneth Trading Post run by J. A. Heffernan. The Government Station, recently built by Holley, was on the floodplain below the post. The road continued to follow the general course of the river along the north side to Montezuma Creek, ten miles away, thence through the washes and over the rolling hills to Bluff.

Ba'álílee's camp sat in a sandy floodplain that extended for approximately two-and-a-half miles on the south side of the river.[57] Two washes—the larger being Among the Rocks (Tsé Bitah—on today's map—Tsitah) and the smaller Rough Canyon (Tségi Hóchx'ǫ́ǫ́jí)—feed onto this flat, where groves of cottonwood trees grow interspersed along the banks.[58] Both canyons wend their way south, away from the river. Large surrounding hills create a cove-like space known as A Place Reserved or Set Aside (T'áásahdii Náhásdoon). To the north of this flat, the San Juan River flows against the base of a hill, channeling access. It received the title Close against the Rock (Tsé Nitah). More than a dozen hogans, corrals, agricultural fields, irrigation ditches, and heavy log fences around two of the larger camps sat against a backdrop of rough ridges and boulder-strewn hills. One of Ba'álílee's wives had a hogan on the north side of the river near a ford opposite the main settlement.[59]

Ba'álílee's camp was large, with relatives living in or near his home. He enjoyed a log and a stone house, as well as a number of hogans next to his fields that were serviced by an irrigation ditch. There was also a "medicine lodge" that was perhaps a male hogan in which he performed ceremonies.[60] Around his camp and sectioning off parts within it was a

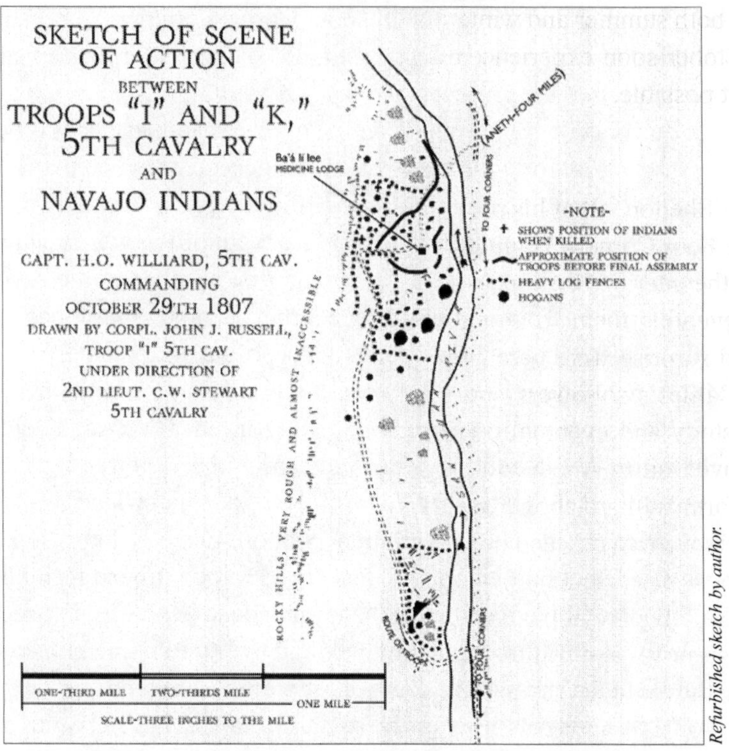

Refurbished sketch by author.

This sketch of Ba'álílee's camp four miles southeast of Aneth, Utah, was drawn the day after the battle. Today, the floodplain is bare of any dwellings, but the place name "Soldier Crossing" remains to identify the location where the last cavalry charge against "hostile" Indians took place in the United States.

heavy log fence that kept his livestock out of the gardens, confining them to the corrals where they belonged.

It was here that October night, after he had healed a man sickened by witchcraft, that Ba'álílee rested peacefully. October, however, is a time of change. Known in Navajo as *Ghąąjį'*, the term means more than "parting of the seasons" or "back to back." When the holy people created the twelve months—six of summer and six of winter—Coyote the Trickster spoke up, reserving October, the first winter month, for himself. Ghąąjį' fills the space between the ending of one way (summer planting, harvest, and ceremonies) and the beginning of something new (winter activities and a different set of ceremonies).[61] It is a time of change, when it can be both summer and winter; with it comes confusion. Ba'álílee's life that October soon experienced confusion and change on a scale he had not felt possible.

ATTACK AND CAPTURE

Shelton, all of his police, and a contingent of Navajo leaders reached the Four Corners Trading Post an hour before the military force arrived. In the interim, Shelton secured any local Navajos who came to the store, preventing them from leaving before 11:00 a.m. the next day. Security and surprise were paramount. Among those detained was Sisco, one of Ba'álílee's followers and a persistent troublemaker.[62] He remained in custody and eventually joined the group that was sent to jail. Shelton moved on to Aneth to determine Ba'álílee's exact location. He would inform Williard about the medicine man's presence; if he did not, the soldiers were to proceed on their own. The captain arrived in the afternoon, shortly after Shelton departed. Williard and Fritz discussed the situation at Ba'álílee's camp, agreed that a night march offered the greatest chance of surprise, and felt that a direct assault rather than a diversion through Aneth would net the best results.

At 1:30 a.m. on October 28, the command awakened its soldiers, who ate a hurried breakfast, quietly saddled their horses, and started down the road an hour later under the light of a half moon. Navajo police and headmen took the lead. The logistical trains remained behind, with orders to break camp in the light of day and move to Aneth. The cavalry horses trotted rapidly over the fourteen miles to a spot near Close against the Rock where the San Juan River was fordable.[63] Known as "Soldier/Police Move Across" (Siláo Ha'naa Nininá), this place was still some distance from Ba'álílee's camp, but it was inhabited by a number of Navajo families. The horses' pace quickened once across the river; the troopers pressed forward, and a half mile from the objective the formation fanned out to surround Ba'álílee's hogan.

Dawn was breaking when Williard, Navajo interpreter Robert Martin, and some of the soldiers rushed inside the hogan. Ba'álílee, Polly (also known as The Man from Spreading Water Who Is Tall—Tó Háálíinii Nééz)—a staunch supporter—and a third man stumbled to their feet. A scuffle ensued, with increasing numbers of soldiers piling into the fray. Several women, a child, and a sick man avoided involvement, but in

Williard's words, "The Indians strenuously resisted arrest and capture to such a degree that it was necessary to use considerable force before they were overcome, secured, and handcuffed."[64] Navajo accounts verify this statement but focus on different aspects. Old Mexican reported that when the soldiers took Ba'álílee outside, he refused to stop growling like a bear: "They tried to make him stop, but he wouldn't, so one of the soldiers took his six-shooter and hit him over the head with it three times and knocked him cold. They then tied him up. He was covered with blood."[65] Polly knocked three soldiers down before they subdued him.[66] Son of Red House Clansman noticed that Ba'álílee's medicine pouch had been carelessly discarded: "Rattles and feathers and many other things were lying scattered out there."[67]

By now, people in the community were gathering. Surrounded by relatives' camps, Ba'álílee was sure to draw assistance. Some came with weapons, others armed only with curiosity, but Williard took no chances; he arrested everyone, and "all resisted." Finding eight hogans in Ba'álílee's camp alone, with other Navajo homes spread over a larger area than he had planned, the captain directed Martin, the Indian police, and Troop I to secure the more distant parts of the objective. Within minutes, gunfire erupted in their direction. Little Warrior (Naabaahii Yázhí), also known as "Smarty," Ba'álílee's son-in-law, opened fire and received a shot through the torso. Although the soldiers dressed his wounds, by noon the next day he was dead. J. A. Heffernan, the trader, buried him in a shallow grave where he fell.[68] A detachment from Troop K spurred their horses toward the sound of firing, followed soon by Williard, who had remained behind to ensure all the prisoners were secured. The shooting lasted for only a few more minutes, then silence. On his way to Troop I, the captain heard a cry for help and dispatched soldiers to investigate. They found the first sergeant afoot without his rifle, which had disappeared under his wounded horse shot out from under him. The Indian assailant, Little Wet One (Ditłéé'ii Yazhí), another of Ba'álílee's sons-in-law, was out of range of the first sergeant's revolver. Another sergeant drew his rifle and shot the man in the head, killing him instantly.

Ba'álílee's camp continued to buzz with activity. In some of the hogans, women and children wailed that the soldiers were taking their men and moving them across the river. Others fled into the brush nearby, behind rocks on the hills, or up the slopes, taking what they could with them.[69] Soldiers pursued Ba'álílee's Nephew (Ba'álílee Bidá'í), also known as Fuzzy Hat (Ch'ah Ditł'oii), a medicine man. He fired two shots from his Winchester. The soldiers returned fire, wounding him in both legs before he escaped into the brush and fled through Among the Rocks Canyon. Friends provided a horse and helped him over the rough terrain.[70] News spread to other camps. Florence Norton recalled, "My father was extremely upset over the incident. He planned to encounter and kill the troops who were on their way up there [Aneth]. He had a big shotgun ready. But a woman showed up on her horse and pleaded with him and some others to please leave the place before the troops arrived . . . He said he had really wanted to shoot all the troops."[71]

Williard returned to the ten prisoners, moved his force a half mile to a ford on the river, and sounded assembly. Following roll call, the officers reported that they had met resistance from some of Ba'álílee's followers. They had opened fire on the police, not noticing the soldiers' approach. The fifteen- to twenty-minute battle resulted in the deaths of Little Warrior and Little Wet One and the cessation of all opposition. The command crossed the river with its walking prisoners and at 7:30 a.m. arrived in Aneth. The soldiers established camp near the post, secured the prisoners in a log house, purchased three sheep for lunch, and awaited the supply trains scheduled to arrive in the late afternoon. The captain took the opportunity to explain to local Navajos why he had come: "Supernatural Power spoke as though he could lick anybody. We heard that he said that whenever the soldiers came after him they were going to get struck by lightning and be killed all at once. That was the reason I came, to see if he was right. I have been looking forward to being struck by lightning. Now we are going back to see if anybody is going to take a shot at us again."[72]

Shelton and Williard then discussed the morning's events. They were pleased with the results in that no soldiers or policemen had been hurt and resistance was light, with few Navajo casualties. That afternoon the two men and part of the force returned to Ba'álílee's camp and surrounding area to search for the wounded Fuzzy Hat and to allay fears. Williard reported that the Navajos he talked to were relieved that Ba'álílee no longer posed a threat.

Rumors of a night attack faded with the dawn of a new day. At 7:30 a.m. the command rode toward the Four Corners Trading Post, prisoners in tow. The next day they arrived in Shiprock and began to refit. Word from the field filtered back to the agency. The disgruntled remainder of Ba'álílee's group insisted that the troops had fired first, there was indiscriminate killing, and property had been wantonly destroyed. Those opposed to Ba'álílee breathed a sigh of relief. Heffernan and Holley reported a calm along the San Juan that had not existed for years. Jim Joe, a Navajo who lived near Bluff, related that he was supportive of the action and encouraged others to be peaceful. John Wetherill, a trader in Kayenta, visited the Navajos in his area after collecting all the facts of the incident. He, along with Williard, Shelton, and others, were concerned that the Black Mountain Navajos might force a confrontation; it never materialized. Charles Goodman, a photographer who lived in Bluff, wanted Williard to bring the troops there and tackle some of the Ute, Paiute, and Navajo issues that community faced; Will Evans, a trader in Farmington, New Mexico, wrote a lengthy article dispelling rumors and false allegations.[73]

JUDGMENT, REVERSAL, AND AFTERMATH

On November 12, Williard received orders to return to Fort Wingate with his prisoners who, in December, continued on to Fort Huachuca, Arizona, to serve their sentences. He recommended that Ba'álílee and Polly spend ten years at hard labor and the rest of the group two years of hard labor. The ten slated for prison were Ba'álílee, Ba'álílee's Nephew (Ba'álílee Bidá'í), Silversmith (Atsidii), Many Goats Son (Tłízí Łání Biye'), Mister Coat (Hastiin Éé'tsoh, also known as He Who Smells Himself), No Teeth (Biwoo'ádinii), Polly (also known as Big Tangle People Clansman [Ta'neeszahnii Tsoh]), Son of Mexican (Naakaii Biye'), Sisco, and Mele-yon.[74] Shelton felt Mister Coat was too old to withstand the rigors of prison life, so he was released from Fort Wingate to return home. The agent was apparently right. By the time Mister Coat arrived at One with an Open Mouth (Aneth), he was exhausted. Navajos changed their local name for this settlement, from that of a trader to one that honored the returning elder—Barely Enough Pep to Make It. In January 1908 the government also released Mele-yon from Fort Huachuca because of his advanced stage of tuberculosis.[75]

Everyone seemed to be at peace with the settled issue except for Howard Ray Antes, minister of the Navajo Faith Mission in Aneth. He

Courtesy, National Archives, Washington, DC.

Opposing forces after the "brawl." Standing fifth from left, Robert Martin (Navajo interpreter); sixth from left, Agent William T. Shelton (with badge); seventh from left, Captain Harry O. Williard. Seated fourth from left, Ba'álílee, with Polly immediately to his right.

seized the opportunity to wage a crusade against Shelton. Why their relationship had deteriorated is not entirely clear. Perhaps it was because of the disagreement over building a riprap dam to protect the mission property, perhaps because Shelton had lost interest in purchasing this site, perhaps because of a growing misunderstanding over an adopted Navajo boy, or perhaps because Antes had received inaccurate information from biased sources. Whatever the reason, the missionary sent vehement letters to Henry M. Teller, a senator from Colorado, and the editor of the *Denver Post*. In his communication, Antes charged the soldiers with opening fire on "the poor, defenseless people," abusing the prisoners, shooting the Indians in the back, destroying crops, stealing corn, scaring the Navajos into the hills, and withdrawing the troops while leaving "the settlers to the mercy of bloodthirsty Indians coming from Cortez."[76]

Within six months after the incident, Colonel Hugh L. Scott, superintendent of the United States Military Academy and investigator for the government, received word to proceed to Utah and determine the truthfulness of the charges. He arrived in Aneth on April 19, 1908, where he found that Antes was staying on his farm in McElmo Canyon, Colorado, and sent for him. On April 21 the investigation started, with Captain

Williard, Agent Shelton, Navajo interpreter Robert Martin, Colonel Scott, and Reverend Antes present in the mission schoolhouse. The burden of proof rested with the minister, who first called forth Navajo witnesses. Many of them had trouble understanding what it meant to be sworn in. Antes clarified the procedure through Martin, saying, "Does he [the witness] know God heard what he said and is strong enough to punish him if he told a lie?" The reply: "He does not think so."[77] Eventually, some of the witnesses understood enough to be acceptable to all concerned; with others, the panel just agreed to let them speak.

Old Mexican told of his experience before the court. He was in the midst of lambing season when a man approached him and his older brother and asked them to attend the hearing. Although reticent, he relented and met with "an old man with white hair, dressed up in a uniform with an eagle on his shoulder." Two Indians—one an Apache, the other a Kiowa, "dressed up all in feathers"—plus five Navajo policemen and Shelton comprised the group. He commented that the agent and the missionary argued long and hard and that he was reluctant to say much about Ba'álílee because he did not know him well. As far as Old Mexican was concerned, the matter was already settled. He blurted out a stronger reason when Shelton asked him if he was still afraid of Ba'álílee, to which Old Mexican replied, "I'm afraid of him all right . . . That's all I'm going to tell you. No more."[78]

Antes eventually requested that the session adjourn to Mancos, Colorado, where a white witness named Oliver lived. Scott denied the request, saying that this man had been summoned, had not shown up, and thus was "unwilling." The investigation dragged on until almost midnight. The colonel closed by asking Antes if the missionary had the right to talk to Indians, even if forbidden to do so by a government agent. Antes said he had the right to talk to anyone he pleased when his home was off the reservation, and even though a recent boundary change had encompassed his property, it did not change this right. Scott disagreed and believed the entire problem resulted from this type of attitude.

The following day Williard and Shelton built their defense. For nine hours the two men systematically destroyed the allegations brought against them and proved that previous Indian testimony was inconsistent and inaccurate. Williard summarized his position in a detailed statement, showing the absurdity of the claims that the Navajos carried high-powered rifles but supposedly had no ammunition; that one of Antes's witnesses was too sleepy to recall certain details but could conveniently recount specific information when necessary; that Indians had been shot in the back; that the soldiers had not taken steps to bury the dead; that his men stole things; and that the crops, purportedly destroyed during the fight, had not already been harvested. Summarizing his feelings, Williard spat "that those statements made by him [Antes] were willfully and deliberately false and malicious, groundless, based on hearsay of the flimsiest character, without an iota of truth . . . [and that Williard] had been made the butt and scapegoat of a personal feeling of animosity between Mr. Shelton and Mr. Holley on the one hand and the Reverend Mr. Antes on the other."[79]

The captain next offered testimony that shed surprising light on attitudes concerning the minister. He asserted that he had made an inquiry as to Antes's character "all the way from Gallup, New Mexico, to Aneth, Utah, and failed to develop one person who spoke well of him." Dr. W. F. Fish, whose statement Antes cited as part of his defense, said he had been misrepresented. Even after the doctor made clear the misunderstanding of events, the minister retorted "'but I will make them a whole lot of trouble anyhow; I will write every paper and magazine in the country.' He said something about doing all he could to get Shelton and Holley fired."[80] Fish also caught Antes lying about a supposed police force coming to arrest the minister.

The reverend was defeated. Lack of evidence disproved his charges, his witnesses had either not testified or were shown to be unreliable, and his motives were questionable. Rather than struggle further, he tried to back out gracefully, scraping together as much dignity as possible under the circumstances. Using the guise of protecting his witnesses from the ravages of an irate Shelton, Antes chose "to suffer the humiliation of falling down on this prosecution personally rather than let any injury come to them [the witnesses]."[81]

While still in prison, Ba'álílee garnered more attention. The Indian Rights Association (IRA) sprang to his defense after Antes's efforts had died, arguing that the use of troops was illegal and that the prisoners had not been properly charged but were still arrested for questionable crimes.[82] Commissioner of Indian Affairs Francis E. Leupp sustained a direct attack for his handling of the situation and accepting Captain

Williard's recommendation in determining the jail sentences. Part of his defense is found in an article he penned titled "Law or No Law in Indian Administration." In it he argued that the incident was well handled and that there were not a lot of options in dealing with the recalcitrant medicine man.[83] The IRA fought back and managed to have the case tried before the Arizona Supreme Court. The group argued that an Indian has a right to a fair trial, the government had overstepped its legal bounds, the prisoners had been unfairly incarcerated, and they should be freed. On February 4, 1909, the government released six of the eight prisoners; on March 20, 1909, the Arizona Supreme Court voted unanimously to also return Ba'álílee and Polly to the reservation. The federal government abandoned the appeal process and in June ordered a noncommissioned officer to escort the two Navajos to Shiprock, where they were released to go home.[84]

Ba'álílee returned a changed man. He continued his medicine practice, but there was no more head-butting with Shelton. Two years later the medicine man was dead, drowned when crossing the San Juan River on his way to conduct a çeremony. Even in death, Ba'álílee attracted controversy. He had become embroiled in a fracas with a man named Cream Colored Horses (Biłįį' Yishtłizhii). Ba'álílee resorted to his previous tactics, saying, "You are going to be struck by lightning. I have mastered witchcraft and am filled with it up to here (gesturing to his throat), and according to this witchcraft you are going to be struck by lightning." Cream Colored Horses replied, "You aren't in command of lightning. You, Ba'álílee, are going to be swallowed by a big snake, and I place the San Juan River as the Big Snake."[85]

Accounts vary as to exactly what happened next. In May 1911, when the river was running exceptionally high even for flood stage, Ba'álílee crossed it with another man, He Hunted It Near Those Rocks (Tsét'ah Neiskah). The boat capsized, and the other man swam to shore, but Ba'álílee—wearing his cartridge belts and pistol—never surfaced. Some say he was chanting a witchcraft song as he crossed, but family members believe he was not involved in withcraft. Some say his body was never found; others testify that it washed ashore at Rock Nose (Tsé Achíįh) downstream: "There was a little bit of him showing and two buzzards were there. They [Navajo searchers] got him out and washed him and took him back."[86]

Jane Byalily Silas, his granddaughter who was born the night before the attack, believes her grandfather has been falsely accused of practicing witchcraft. Her family tells of stories shared by those captured by the government. For instance, the troops challenged Ba'álílee to use his powerful songs. At one point, "He prayed for rain and it rained until the camp was nearly washed out; he had to pray again to stop it. Moving on to another camp, Ba'álílee was asked to pray for a bear to come to it. He prayed, and sure enough, a bear showed up. Ba'álílee asked one of the white men to wrestle the animal, but he was afraid. The soldiers paid Ba'álílee to call it off." After performing other miracles, the troops let him go because they realized "the natives truly had a powerful God."[87] Another person described Ba'álílee's resistance against both government programs and Shelton. When the cavalry pursued the medicine man and his people, he used his powers to part the rain-swollen river so his followers could safely cross.[88] These stories, and others, say as much about the people sharing them as they do about the man.

CONCLUSION

What can we learn from events that took place 100 years ago? There is no missing the rapidity of cultural change that challenged traditional Navajo beliefs and practices. When physical powers overwhelm us, spiritual solutions become an obtainable means to address challenges. Ba'álílee was adept at playing upon the deeply religious nature of the Navajo people to resist both physically and spiritually. How much of it was self-serving and how much was justified remains for the reader to determine. But Holley, who spoke Navajo, reported that "Ba'álílee repeatedly had told his people, 'We are Navajos; we are Navajos; we want nothing to do with the agent, the Government, or the whites but want to stay away from them'; but to continue all their old Indian customs."[89] It was an uphill climb the tribe is still addressing today—how does one maintain the values of traditional culture in a sea of contemporary change?

Shelton, in contrast, was a spokesman for the Progressive era, with Shiprock his flagship. When he bemoaned Ba'álílee's presence and negative impact on the Indians' attempts to follow the agency's lead, Shelton viewed the struggle in terms of diametrically opposing forces—there was no gray. The conflict was "between the two classes, the progressive and the unprogressive," and for the latter "something more than kind talk and persuasion would have to be used."[90] Something was, and after the troops returned to Fort Wingate, the government increasingly intensified imposed change. Regulation of trading posts, further dependence on a federally sponsored Navajo government, more programs to assist with agriculture and livestock production, additional boarding schools with greater enrollments, oil and mineral exploration, the nascence of the wage economy, heightened desire for consumer goods—the list goes on. Shelton took the first step of introducing change in an isolated and heretofore ignored area of the vast Navajo Reservation. Conflict soon arose.

There is another way to look at this struggle. Historically, Aneth has seemed to attract people with strong personalities. Henry Mitchell, Ba'álílee, his followers, William Shelton, Captain Williard, James Holley, Howard Ray Antes, and others were distinct in their approach and did not hesitate to speak their minds. In an area where people had few restrictions placed on them, it had not been necessary for them to feel a bit in their mouth and the pull of restrictive reins. Once enforcement of change began, personalities took over, playing a prominent role in issue resolution. Shelton wanted peace and quiet; Ba'álílee thrived on confrontation. His power came from magnifying conflict and enlisting, either willingly or otherwise, his army to oppose the government. Shelton refused to accept intimidation and drew the line. Mexican Man (Naakaii Diné), a resident of Aneth, summarized the situation succinctly when he testified that "there was too much noise in that bunch [Ba'álílee] across the river."[91] Shelton quieted it.

NOTES

1. See Robert S. McPherson, *Sacred Land, Sacred View: Navajo Perceptions of the Four Corners Region,* Charles Redd Center for Western Studies Monograph 19 (Provo, UT: Brigham Young University Press, 1992), 49–51.
2. Spelled in various primary sources as Bai-a-lil-le, Bah-leel, Be'élilee, Bia-a-lil-le, By-a-lil-le, Bylillie, and Ba'ililii, the name has been translated as The One with Supernatural Power, He Who Knows Many Ceremonies, and The One with Magic Power. Using contemporary standardized rules, the name is spelled Ba'álílee. The basis for this name comes from the Navajo term *álílee k'ehgo*, meaning literally "According to His Supernatural/Magical Power," which refers to his ability to use unseen power for either good or evil. It is the force by which things are done supernaturally. For instance, Jesus walking on water or a Navajo skinwalker (witch) running at superhuman speeds are examples of a divine ability to control this force. The power is not discussed or flaunted, and its existence is recognized

with reverence. Marilyn Holiday discussion with author, September 23, 2007; Jim Dandy discussion with author, September 24, 2007.

3. Walter Dyk, *A Navaho Autobiography* (New York: Viking Fund Publication in Anthropology, 1947), 138. Another explanation of what happened the night of October 28, 1907, is offered by Jane Byalily Silas, Ba'álílee's paternal granddaughter. She claims he was assisting another medicine man named The One Who Sucks out the Evil (Ats'ǫǫsí). The two sang songs and prayed to remove an object shot by witchcraft into a woman's body by her jealous husband. At one point, a scuffle broke out between the medicine man and the patient's husband. They exchanged blows before the distraught husband left, allowing the ceremony to continue late into the night. Jane Byalily Silas interview with author, February 27, 1991, in possession of author. Ba'álílee is Jane's paternal grandfather; she was born the night before this incident. Her story is corroborated by Son of Red House Clansman, who said the two medicine men were "singing over a woman who was sick"; Red House Clansman, "The One with Magic Power," in Robert W. Young and William Morgan, eds., *Navajo Historical Selections*, Navajo Historical Series 3 (Lawrence, KS: Bureau of Indian Affairs, 1954), 35.
4. Silas interview with author; Florence Begay interview with author, April 29, 1988.Navajo society is matrilineal, emphasizing the mother's clan for descent (born of), with the father's clan (born for) a secondary source of kinship ties.
5. US Congress, Senate, *Testimony Regarding Trouble on Navajo Reservation*, 60th Cong., 2nd sess., March 3, 1909, Klah Testimony, p. 43 (hereafter information from this source is cited as *TRTNR*).
6. Florence Begay interview with author.
7. J. Lee Correll, *Bai-a-lil-le: Medicine Man or Witch?* Biographical Series 3 (Window Rock, AZ: Navajo Historical Publications, 1970), 4.
8. The reference to "witch knives" most likely refers to a ceremonially treated piece of sharpened flint, perhaps one that has been touched by lightning or a bear. This is "shot" into an individual through witchcraft. Cures include prayers that reverse the evil, sweating or sucking the object out, or using some kinds of witchcraft-induced vomiting. See Gladys A. Reichard, *Navaho Religion, A Study of Symbolism* (Princeton, NJ: Princeton University Press, 1974 [1950]), 610–611, 727.
9. Ibid.; Silas interview with author; Correll, *Bai-a-lil-le,* 49.
10. See Clyde Kluckhohn, *Navaho Witchcraft* (Boston: Beacon, 1944).
11. Walter Dyk, *Son of Old Man Hat* (Lincoln: University of Nebraska Press, 1938), 272–273. Bear is a powerful creature with supernatural abilities inherited during the creation to both protect and curse.
12. When a person knows he or she is being witched, the individual can obtain a medicine man, who through prayers and songs establishes a protective shield around the victim. The shield turns the evil back on the originator, who is then cursed by his or her own power. Ba'álílee is implying that this is why Old Man Hat is dying.
13. The "bean," like the witch knives, was an object, probably a round smooth stone about the size of a piñon nut, shot into the victim. See Reichard, *Navaho Religion*, 594, 610–611.
14. There are two men named Left Hand (a common Navajo name) in this story. They should not be confused. The man introduced later was a judge who worked for

Shelton, while this man was primarily a farmer and shepherd who had few dealings with the agent.

15. Walter Dyk and Ruth Dyk, *Left Handed: A Navajo Autobiography* (New York: Columbia University Press, 1980), 389.
16. Albert R. Lyman, "History of San Juan County, 1879–1917," unpublished manuscript, Special Collections, Harold B. Lee Library, Brigham Young University, Provo, UT, 26–27. See also Albert R. Lyman, "The Old Settler," *San Juan Record,* November 30, 1972, 3, 11.
17. See Robert S. McPherson, "Navajos, Mormons, and Henry L. Mitchell," *Utah Historical Quarterly* 55, no. 1 (Winter 1987): 50–65.
18. Report of Herrero Segundo submitted to Agent D. M. Riordan, April 29, 1884, Record Group 75, Letters Received by Office of Indian Affairs, New Mexico Superintendency, 1884, National Archives, Washington, DC (hereafter cited as Letters Received–NM).
19. *TRTNR*—Klah Testimony, 43.
20. See Robert S. McPherson, "Howard R. Antes and the Navajo Faith Mission: Evangelist of Southeastern Utah," *Utah Historical Quarterly* 65, no. 1 (Winter 1997): 4–24.
21. Statement by James M. Holley, Government Farmer–Aneth, n.d., J. Lee Correll Collection, Navajo Nation, Window Rock, AZ (hereafter cited as JLC Collection).
22. Ibid.
23. William T. Shelton to Commissioner of Indian Affairs, December 5, 1913, Letters Received–NM; James McLaughlin Papers, Assumption Abbey Archives, Microfilm #5, on file in the Denver Public Library, Denver, CO.
24. Ibid.
25. William T. Shelton, "Report of Superintendent of San Juan School," July 23, 1907; Shelton to Commissioner of Indian Affairs, July 23, 1907, both in JLC Collection.
26. Dyk, *Navaho Autobiography*, 97–98.
27. Ibid., 86.
28. Ibid.; George W. Hayzlett to Commissioner of Indian Affairs, July 25, 1902, JLC Collection.
29. William T. Shelton to Commissioner of Indian Affairs, October 20, 1903, JLC Collection. Shelton did not understand that a man's or woman's family could claim ownership of the property that belonged to the deceased relative as long as individual ownership had been recognized when that person was alive.
30. Maimi Howard interview with author, July 19, 1988.
31. See Dyk, *Navaho Autobiography,* for a yearly, sometimes daily, account of life in Aneth at the end of the nineteenth and beginning of the twentieth centuries.
32. "The Shelton Reception," *Farmington Times*, May 4, 1916, 1.
33. Ibid.
34. Kumen Jones, "The Writings of Kumen Jones," unpublished manuscript, Special Collections, Harold B. Lee Library, Brigham Young University, Provo, UT, 30.
35. Charles H. Hickman to Commissioner of Indian Affairs, January 9, 1905, JLC Collection.
36. Holley Statement, JLC Collection.
37. William T. Shelton to Commissioner of Indian Affairs, March 29, 1907, cited in *Report on Employment of United States Soldiers in Arresting By-a-lil-le and Other*

Navajo Indians, 60th Cong., 1st sess., May 25, 1908, 7 (hereafter information from this source is cited as *ABONI*); Harry O. Williard to Adjutant General, October 30, 1907, *ABONI*, 17; Shelton to James M. Holley, September 3, 1907, JLC Collection; Williard to Adjutant General, November 3, 1907, JLC Collection; Frank Mitchell Testimony, *TRTNR*, 49; Dyk, *Navaho Autobiography*, 134; Klah Testimony, April 25, 1908, *TRTNR*, 44. The One with Muscles was also known as Black Horse (Łį́į́ Łizhiní).

38. Mary Blueyes interview with author, March 20, 1992.
39. Sworn Testimonies from Sisco, By-a-lil-le Bida, Mele-yon, Frank Mitchell, Pit-ce-cote, and Att-city, March 19, 1909, JLC Collection.
40. R. S. Connell to Commissioner of Indian Affairs, April 6, 1907, *ABONI*, 9.
41. Short Hair was also known as Ba'álílee's Son in Law (Ba'álílee Bidá'í).
42. Hattie Testimony, April 23, 1908, *TRTNR*, 51.
43. Shelton, "Report of Superintendent," July 23, 1907.
44. James R. Garfield to Commissioner of Indian Affairs, November 22, 1907, *ABONI*, 26; Dyk, *Navaho Autobiography*, 111–112, 124.
45. Shelton to Commissioner, March 29, 1907, *ABONI*, 7.
46. Dyk, *Navaho Autobiography*, 122–126.
47. Nah-ki-Den-Na Testimony, April 23, 1908, *TRTNR*, 50; Statement of Jimmie Noland, March 19, 1909, JLC Collection.
48. Frank McNitt, *The Indian Traders* (Norman: University of Oklahoma Press, 1962), 344.
49. In 1905 Agent Reuben Perry, reacting to a rape incident, traveled from Fort Defiance to Winslow, Arizona, where two Navajos forced him to sign a pardon for the accused man, Black Water (Tółízhiní). Perry returned to the agency, requested soldiers from Fort Wingate, then marched with Captain Harry Williard and K Troop to Chinle to make the arrests. Eventually, seven Navajos went to Alcatraz then Fort Huachuca, Arizona, to serve their sentences. Williard is the officer who later arrested Ba'álílee, who was also sent to Huachuca. The seven men arrested from the Black Mountain area left others behind who resisted encroachment by the government. This region, like southeastern Utah, was isolated from the main population of Navajos. Many of those living in these locations had never known the chastening lesson of Fort Sumner. For a synopsis of the incident, see Bill Acrey, *Navajo History: The Land and the People* (Shiprock, NM: Department of Curriculum Materials Development, Central Consolidated School District no. 22, 1988), 171–175.
50. Connell to Commissioner, April 6, 1907, *ABONI*, 9.
51. Ibid.
52. William T. Shelton to Commissioner of Indian Affairs, September 18, 1907, *ABONI*, 11; Statement by Holley, n.d., JLC Collection.
53. Shelton to Commissioner, September 18, 1907, *ABONI*, 12; Adjutant General to Commanding General, Department of Colorado, October 15, 1907, *ABONI*, 13–14.
54. Correll, *Bai-a-lil-le*, 20.
55. Unless otherwise noted, the information concerning the movement and attack on Ba'álílee's camp is from Captain Harry O. Williard's report to the Adjutant General, Headquarters, Department of Colorado, October 30, 1907, *ABONI*, 14–20.

56. The post was likely located on the floodplain at the mouth of Marble Wash and along the San Juan River. On a 1903 map in the Wetherill–Grand Gulch Archives (Edge of the Cedars Museum, Blanding, UT), the old road from the Four Corners Trading Post to Aneth is shown following the river on its north side. Midpoint is a trading post called Berlin. This is likely the post operated by a man named Spencer, as well as the post where M. R. Butler traded at the time of the Ba'álílee conflict. The site is now called Burned House (Kin Díílidí) by the Navajo. Mary Jay (cited later) said, "A trader named Silver (Béésh Łigai) used to live there until he got mad at some people who threw him out. This store was located by the river below the gray hill" (interview with author, February 27, 1991). Florence Begay noted that the Utes used to trade there, too.
57. Today the floodplain is covered with tamarisk and has been scoured by the San Juan River during past floods so that nothing remains of its historic buildings. Once one moves off the floodplain, a twelve-foot-high bank buttresses the historic flats not cut by the river. Above the bank is a second plateau and then a number of large hill masses, creating the "cove" effect. The entire floodplain bench is now known as Soldier Crossing, stemming from the Ba'álílee incident.
58. Tségi Hóchx'ǫ́ǫ́jí is a difficult term to translate. The first word means a narrow canyon that is a defile through high rock walls. The second term means evil, but in this case the terrain is so rough that it is very difficult to pass over it. In English one might say, "It is a devil of a canyon to pass through." James Benally discussion with author, November 19, 2007.
59. As one travels downstream there is a collection of ruins atop a mesa and along the bank that is called Scattered Anaasází Remains (Bits'iil). Opposite Aneth is the prominent Tall Mountain (Dził Ninééz), which sits on the south side of the river. Leading to its plateau-like top, with its truncated appearance, is Reclining Rock (Tsé Biyaají), a long ridge that inclines from the floodplain. Baxter Benally discussion with author, September 24, 2007; Florence Norton interview with author, March 6, 1991; Mary Jay interview with author, February 27, 1991; Isabel Lee interview with author, February 13, 1991. North of this mountain lies Aneth, called at this time The One with an Open Mouth, named after a trader. Howard Ray Antes was the first to apply the name Aneth, a Hebrew word meaning "the Answer," in 1895. Other Navajo names were given to Aneth and Montezuma Creek, many of which are tied to traders operating there at the time. It is not clear if One with an Open Mouth refers to Holley, Heffernan, or another person.
60. The difference between a male (hooghan ałch'į́ adeez'ą́) and a female (hooghan nímazí) hogan is determined by the shape of the structure, not who uses it. The male hogan has a passageway that leads into the area where people live. The main space is constructed by using three forked poles that interlock at the top where the smoke hole is located. There is less space in the male hogan because of the conical shape of this tepee-like structure. The female hogan is more prevalent today. It is round, more spacious in height and width, constructed with a cribbed roof, and has a greater seating and storage capacity. Both hogans have doorways that face east. The male hogan, the first to be created by the holy people, is said to have more efficacy for ceremonial purposes, although both male or female hogans are acceptable for ceremonies. Ba'álílee's "medicine lodge" could possibly have been a large male hogan.

61. Jim Dandy discussion with author, October 29, 2007.
62. This phonetically spelled name is untranslatable and does not sound like a Navajo word.
63. Isabel Lee interview with author.
64. Williard to the Adjutant General, October 30, 1907, *ABONI,* 16.
65. Dyk, *Navaho Autobiography*, 131.
66. Ibid., 132.
67. Son of Red House Clansman, "The One with Magic Power," 35.
68. Ba'álílee's Wife's Testimony, April 22, 1908, *TRTNR*, 19–20; J. A. Heffernan Testimony, April 22, 1908, *TRTNR*, 32.
69. Isabel Lee interview with author; Son of Red House Clansman, "The One with Magic Power," 36.
70. Florence Norton interview with author, March 6, 1991; Dyk, *Navaho Autobiography*, 132; Mikinly Chinee Nez Testimony, April 25, 1908, *TRTNR*, 45.
71. Florence Norton interview (source of the quotation); John Norton interview with author, January 16, 1991.
72. Dyk, *Navaho Autobiography*, 131.
73. James A. Holley to William T. Shelton, November 5, 1907; Shelton to Jim Joe, November 7, 1907; Joe to Shelton, November 20, 1907; Charles Goodman to Holley, November 1, 1907, all in JLC Collection; Frances Gillmor and Louisa Wade Wetherill, *Traders to the Navajos* (Albuquerque: University of New Mexico Press, 1953), 136–138; William Evans, "The Actual Situation," *Farmington Enterprise*, November 29, 1907, 1.
74. As noted previously, some Navajo names were written phonetically and are either untranslatable or may have more than one meaning, depending upon inflection and how attuned the writer's ear was to the language. Navajos often had more than one name, which explains how the list of the ten men who went to jail differs among eyewitness native speakers. Most of the names presented here are confirmed, but two or three are best guesses or left as found in the historical record.
75. Son of Red House Clansman, "The One with Magic Power," 37; Commander Thomas telegram to Adjutant General of the Army, January 29, 1908, JLC Collection.
76. Court Proceedings, April 21–22, 1908, *TRTNR*, 29.
77. Ibid., 11.
78. Dyk, *Navajo Autobiography*, 133–134.
79. Court Proceedings, *TRTNR*, 31.
80. Ibid., 40–41.
81. Ibid., 24–25.
82. For an excellent review of the political fracas surrounding the Ba'álílee incident, the Indian Office, and the Indian Rights Association, see Donald L. Parman, "The 'Big Stick' in Indian Affairs: The Bai-a-lil-le Incident in 1909," *Arizona and the West* 20 (Fall 1978): 343–360.
83. Francis E. Leupp, "'Law or No Law' in Indian Administration," *Outlook* (January 30, 1909), 261–263.
84. Interior Department to Secretary of War, June 25, 1909, JLC Collection.
85. Cited in Correll, *Bai-a-lil-le,* 47. The San Juan River has many teachings and specific sites connected to Big Snake, a powerful Navajo deity who participated

with other holy people during the creation of this world. He is not a benevolent god but rather one connected with protection and conflict.

86. Silas interview with author; Mary Blueyes interview with author, March 20, 1992; Florence Begay interview with author; Martha Nez interview with author, August 10, 1988; John Joe Begay interview with author, September 18, 1990.
87. Silas interview with author.
88. Jerrold E. Levy, *In the Beginning: The Navajo Genesis* (Los Angeles: University of California Press, 1998), 229–230.
89. Holley Testimony, April 23, 1908, *TRTNR*, 7.
90. Shelton to Commissioner, September 18, 1907, *ABONI*, 8.
91. Nah-ki-Den-na (Naakaii Diné) Testimony, April 23, 1908 *TRTNR*, 50.

5

Traditional Teaching and Thought

Navajo Metaphors of the Elders

Navajo metaphors provide a condensed, intensified view of thought within the culture. Perception, framed through language, is embedded in a word, a phrase, or a sentence in which lies entire systems of classification and understanding. Extended metaphors expand that connective meaning even more. The comparison of two seemingly dissimilar or unconnected objects or thoughts becomes a unified expression that teaches important values for the continuation of society. Language is the means of transmission, giving rise to the necessity of its preservation. Without it, the unique worldview specific to a culture is lost, something the Navajo Nation now struggles to reverse.

The next four chapters illustrate various aspects of Navajo language and thought, starting with traditional guidance

DOI: 10.7330/9781607322177.c05

through metaphor. This chapter suggests that even with the younger generation's immersion in American society, many of the teachings from the past—associated with objects and activities common to traditional culture—still hold powerful, valuable lessons highly relevant to today's youth. Next come lessons learned from the efforts of Father H. Baxter Liebler, an Episcopalian missionary who adopted many of those teachings, objects, and religious practices to instruct Navajo parishioners in his faith. Explained from their perspective as to what they saw taking place, these Navajo converts discuss their appreciation for his efforts and yet the difficulty inherent in combining the two religions. Chapter 7 is a history of the Pectol shields and their eventual repatriation to the tribe because of the oral tradition that explained their origin and use. Navajo history and culture proved vital in their return. The last of the four chapters revisits the discussion of how metaphoric language works, a comparison between old and new metaphors developing on the reservation today, and suggestions as to why this shift is occurring. Thus language tied to thought is the recurring theme throughout all four of these chapters.

"Cartoons. Did my grandpa tell you any of those cartoons he has running around in his head?"

I winced. The young teenage boy gazed into my eyes without a ripple of a smile. He was serious. I looked over in the corner where, sitting beside a small wood-burning stove, rested an older Navajo man—silver hair cropped close, his eyes gazing into the fire. I was glad that he probably did not understand what his grandson had just said, since what was a cartoon to one person was the essence of life for the other.

As I made my way across miles of sandy desert road and slick rock, then eventually to the serenity of asphalt, I had time to reflect upon what had been said. The interview with Charlie Blueyes had been informative, but the brief dialogue with his grandson had also been enlightening, though of a far different nature. In that two-room, gray stuccoed house planted in a sea of red sand and gray-green sagebrush, three people had assumed roles that typify a problem inherent across the Navajo reservation today.

Charlie Blueyes, a man in his mid-eighties, spoke only broken English. Although he understood more than he let on, he was so fluent in Navajo that our interview was conducted entirely in his language. The interpreter who worked with him understood the importance of what he said. The grandson, in contrast, spoke English well, but his Navajo was a struggle at best. School and the dominant society had captured his native tongue and replaced it. As for me, I was desperately interested in reconstructing elements of the history of the Utah Navajo as seen through the eyes of someone who had lived part of it. Oral history gave a slant to the historical record that could be obtained and preserved in no other way.

So there we sat: Charlie in the twilight of his life (he died two years later), a white man with the help of an interpreter being taught everything from religious beliefs to historical events, and a young boy who saw little value in any of it. My impression is that although many youth do not fall into the category of the latter, it seems that today far too many do. What should be held as sacred or at least important gets pushed aside for the less valuable "trinkets and baubles" of contemporary American culture. In a sense, the grandson had sold a cultural Manhattan Island for twenty-four dollars worth of trade beads.

Before going further, it is important to point out that many Navajo youth are vitally interested in their cultural heritage. Also, the age-old theme of a white man preserving Navajo culture before it disappears is trite and one I do not presume to take on. Yet in a very real sense, as today's elders die, a certain essence of traditional Navajo culture is lost. This is true of every generation, no matter what the culture, but in spite of the valiant efforts of institutions like Diné College, the Navajo Academy, and curriculum demonstration projects on or near the reservation, Navajo elders still complain about the growing gap in young people's understanding of traditional values.

For people like Charlie Blueyes and other elders raised in the traditional lifestyle of the livestock economy, change has been ever-present on the horizon. For the elders, there is comfort in sharing their teachings with today's youth. Charlie's grandson, however, represents the present generation, which finds difficulty in bridging a widening gulf between the deeply religious values rooted in the elders and their existence in a mechanized, fast-paced world where traditional teachings become confusing, unrealistic, or inapplicable. While the complex religious oral tradition of the past serves as the foundation of Navajo perception, there are many things still familiar—from gophers to fire pokers to baskets—that teach important values. One of the most enjoyable parts of discussing these symbols with older Navajo people is being introduced to and learning of the metaphorical meaning attached. This often results in walking away with a feeling of surprised agreement based on something unfamiliar compared to the known. Here are two short, light examples followed by more serious ones.

I was driving down the road one day with a Navajo friend when we passed a hitchhiker. My friend, Baxter Benally, remarked that a hitchhiker is occasionally referred to in Navajo as a prairie dog. When I asked why, he said that just like a prairie dog, they stand by the side of the road, hold their hands by their waist, and watch the traffic go by. Sometimes, when a driver is not careful, they also get hit. Now I can't see a hitchhiker without making the connection. The metaphor has become a mnemonic device or memory jogger that revisits my mind every time.

Another metaphor revolves around the bluebird, which according to Navajo association is drowsy and nods off to sleep. When a person who is tired fitfully fights against the opening stages of sleep, he or she is referred to by the bird's name. The sudden jerks back to consciousness parallel the quick movements of the bird's head followed by a slow-paced downward slump.

TEACHINGS OF THE FIRE POKER (HONEESHGISH)

The same act of association occurs with more serious things, too. Take, for instance, the fire poker. While there are a number of ceremonial teachings about this object, it is a common tool used by a member of a family to stir the embers of a cooking fire and to bank the coals at night. From a nonreligious vantage point, what could be more practical than to use this device to teach a teenage girl as she prepares for marriage. An older woman put it this way: "Her life is compared to the fire poker, or honeeshgish, made from wet juniper branches and used to stir the red hot ashes. It can withstand this hard use and so is known as a `home sitter.' A person cannot do without one, they say. When a woman returns home, she says, `Where is my fire poker because it is indispensable.' This is the way a wife should be."[1]

Now, taking this teaching and broadening it with thoughts from other elders, one soon has an interesting description of a model wife and

Courtesy, Milton Snow Collection, Navajo Nation Museum, Window Rock, AZ.

The fire and fire poker are two of a woman's tools to fight hunger. Their teachings are part of what is collectively called *habeedí*, the essential tools of the home. Other objects in this category that provide education for life are the grinding stones, hairbrush, stirring sticks, door covering and frame, and bedding.

mother. For instance, one man noted that "we would not put our hands into the fire without getting burned; that is the purpose of having a fire poker. It can walk into a fiery furnace and retrieve an object without getting harmed because it will not easily catch fire."[2] So, too, should a wife and mother be that way when temptation and difficulties arise.

Now more than ever before, Navajo elders are concerned about the young people who display a lack of commitment and place self-fulfillment above family responsibility. Betty Canyon described her view of youth—married and single—when she said, "Today, the people in our society live as if they were small children, tending a household while the parents are away."[3] Unlike a seasoned honeeshgish, all too often, according to the Navajo elder, youth catch fire and burn, unable to withstand the heat from temptations of status, material possessions, and peer pressure.

Another person recalled how Grandmother Red Woman added emphasis with her fire poker as she taught: "She gathered us children and lectured us about character and attitudes. She'd say, `When you herd sheep don't look at each other but go on either side of the flock and take care of them.' All the while she would be tapping the fire poker in front of us . . . `Then some day, when you find a husband, you will be protected. But if you are incapable, you will run off on him. You will then get another husband, but he will be worse off than the first one. Pretty soon you will be homeless, with no place to go. It will be a disgrace."[4] Home, as symbolized by the fire and a honeeshgish, would lack warmth and help.

The fire poker also serves as a shield and protection. It is an object that holds power through prayers. Jenny Francis said, "You pray and pray with the fire poker. Everything goes according to the way you pray. If you pray in the good way, without harsh words, it is good for your children. You pray for them from the bottom of their feet to the top of their head[s]. You even pray for the alien teacher who is instructing your child. My children will walk in beauty."[5] Thus the fire poker becomes a physical reminder of good thoughts and prayers offered for loved ones.

Even when a parent must leave for a short while, a honeeshgish can be used to watch over a sleeping child. It is placed next to the infant to protect it through the love and prayers left behind. In the old days, when a hogan was abandoned for a season, the occupants placed a honeeshgish in a crevice between the logs to protect the home until they returned, addressing it saying, "Grandfather or grandmother, protect our home while we are away."[6] The hogan remained safe from harm because of the prayers. Protection for the home through the fire poker can also be achieved by stirring dog food with the end of the stick. By doing this the charcoal ash from the fire-hardened end mixes into the food and helps the dog "remember the home and his duty to protect it, [making the pet more able to] see and sense negative energy so he can chase it away."[7]

Conversely, the fire poker, as a symbol of love and blessing, should never be turned against a child. To strike a youngster with it is to turn the power of the home against him or her. Not surprisingly, the child's mind will go "empty," and he or she will have a hard time "thinking straight" and processing information.[8] One elder pointed out that the honeeshgish and the fire together represent the "hope and faith of the Navajo that they will continue to live on this earth forever."[9] To beat a child with this object very literally is to beat the future "hope and faith" of the Navajo Nation.

Ada Black summarized the importance of this symbol, with its link to home and unborn generations: "Even though you might not have much, you say your prayer this way. When you are pushing back the used hot coals, you pray that harmony will come. Do this after you eat, too. With this there is growth for future generations. In this way there is a home. I have a fire poker with me under my wood stove. It is right here where the prayer is said."[10] Thus the essence of what it means to be a Navajo, to maintain one's identity, and to hold a share in the future can all be summarized in the lessons surrounding this simple piece of wood, this object of power.

HOGAN AS UNIVERSE

What follows is a broader survey of teachings that hint at the depth and strength of Navajo metaphorical thought. Starting with the origin of life and continuing through to death, there are mental images that accompany every phase. In the beginning, when the gods fashioned this world, sacred powers came together to form both the physical and spiritual aspects of life. To the Navajo, these two elements—spiritual and physical—are inseparable and intertwined as a part of the creative process. This incident of creation is referred to as "the palm of time," a sacred period that should be held in the "palm" of our memory and handled with respect. One person characterized this feeling as similar to when "one holds a tiny rabbit—it is something holy and to be cherished."[11] It was also a time when important things happened: the gods formed patterns and "stretched" the world so it was habitable for man.

Navajo teachings also employ extended Navajo metaphors in which a multiplicity of meanings is attached to the same object. No better example exists than that of the hogan, a structure the People have used to instill important values of life. Jim Dandy, raised by his medicine man grandfather and grandmother near Red Lake, Arizona, explained his experience with metaphorical thought concerning this type of home:

> As a child my grandparents taught me at an early age about this structure [hogan]. Grandmother especially had extensive knowledge about it that reached into many aspects of my life. These teachings helped me understand the world of my grandparents. The holy people designed the first male hogan in the beginning of the world for ceremonial purposes, while the female hogan is mainly for family and

daily life. This sense of greater power is comparable to the teachings about the difference between the male and female hogans. The sweat lodge has the same shape as the male hogan with its posts coming to a point. The female hogan is built by overlapping logs and has a calmer power because it is not pointed. When building a female hogan there are six main posts, while in a male there are five, but in each instance the four cardinal directions are represented. These logs are partially buried in the ground with prayers for protection and assistance before anything else is added to the structure. This is called "addressing the mountains," where each post represents and is blessed to hold the powers of one of the four sacred mountains. Each of the four directions has a mountain associated with it: to the east is Sisnaajiní [Blanca], the south is Tsoodził [Taylor], the west is Dook'o'oosłííd [Humphrey in the San Francisco Peaks], and the north is Dibé Nitsaa [Hesperus]. There are two poles for the door that faces east. These posts represent wealth on each side of the door and bring all kinds of good things to the people living there. The foundation, or the legs and other logs at the bottom of the structure, are aligned with the four directions and represent the whole hogan. There are an additional twelve posts in the female hogan, symbolizing the twelve people who comprise the main part of the foundation, forming the circumference of the home. They are holy people, the same ones involved in the Yé'ii' bicheii [ceremony and dance], who serve as primary deity, participated in the creation of the world, and represent different things such as water, colors, and teachings.

My grandfather was a pretty quiet man and did not get after us unless we really did something wrong. He did not say a lot, but he was very knowledgeable about sacred things to do with ceremonies and healing. My grandmother, on the other hand, was more outgoing in her discipline and taught [us] about things around the home. Whenever we entered the hogan we had to behave ourselves. She taught us a lot and I miss that. One of her teachings was about how the hogan is compared to the body, with the fire being the heart of the home, the floor like one's back, and the opening of the smoke hole symbolizing a person's navel. She also taught about the four directions and how to do things in a respectful way, especially during a ceremony and the blessing of a hogan. Each one of us had our turn to learn.

The hogan represents life. A person comes in from the east with birth; goes to the south, which is life; enters old age to the west; and ends with death and spirit-travel to the north. While life starts in the east, west is where the heart sits. When a person follows a circular direction in a hogan, he follows the path of growth through life.

When one enters he moves clockwise, especially when there is a ceremony being performed. If there is a stove, one always puts the food either on it or in the center of the hogan in front of the medicine man to show that you are going to be feeding the people.

Fire, like a grandparent, is a provider and must be respected.[12] My grandfather started his teaching about the home by saying, "I'm afraid I'm not going to live forever. Your grandmother has taught you that as she cooks she prays for you as part of your life. By doing this the fire becomes your grandfather also. When she sings about you there is a light involved in that process, and the fire, as the great-grandfather, keeps everything alive in the universe inside the hogan. As with the sun the fire sits there, where there is moisture and air, and everything that makes you alive is found within the hogan. The fire represents the sun because everything that is cooked for you becomes a part of you. When your own fire dies out, you will be just like your grandparents and pass on. It is our job to share these teachings with you to carry on. Keep the light going all the time; that is your responsibility, and as a father you should teach your children."

Every time my great-grandmother cooked, she would stir the coals with her fire poker, pray, then place in the fire any food that was left over so that the fire, too, could eat. She thanked it for being a holy person, a great-great-grandfather who provides. When my grandparents prayed, the fire was always addressed as a male in the prayer, thanking it for its help. The fire poker, like the fire, is a help and guide. There should be one in the hogan at all times; a person should not live without one. There are two different kinds—one is used for cooking, the other for ceremonies. The fire poker used for cooking is female, the one for ceremonies male. They are shields that protect the home and must be cared for as living beings.

Grandmother started with the ground inside the hogan and likened it to the Navajo wedding basket. When the hogan is compared to an upside-down basket, the point of communication and connection is the smoke hole. The logs in the cribbed roof become smaller as one moves closer to the top; they become smaller each time, step by step. The rainbow is like the inside of the roof as it surrounds above and arches over the people below. One cannot go beyond its sides, but on every sacred mountain the rainbow reaches over it, just as the roof inside the hogan does.[13] So the rainbow for the hogan goes from the floor up to the smoke hole and down to the floor on the other side.

The stove or fire, with its opening, is in the center. There are the mountains, which are the upright logs; the roof like the rainbow, with the sky and clouds above. The roof beams are similar to a ladder that leads step by step to heaven. When the sunlight comes in the

> top through the smoke hole, it is a part of the heavens entering. The outer rim of the wedding basket is like the dawn that goes around it, with the two stitches on the rim that gets bigger the same as when one moves closer to the floor of a hogan. Beyond that point a person does not really know what is there. When building a hogan, an opening (smoke hole) is always left, just as in a basket.[14] It represents the knowledge one receives from the heavens, and so this hole for learning should never be blocked. The same is true when making a rug; there should be an opening somewhere in it. One does not just put a rug together without a string or a pathway to keep the rug open so that one can learn a lot about what is on the other side, beyond the object.
>
> A person should never write his name on a hogan or make other marks because it is disrespectful. To do that is similar to writing on one's hand, which is like putting a curse on oneself. A hogan is also like a person; when the mud comes off, it is like one's skin peeling. If there is no fire, it is as if the heart has stopped and the hogan cannot stay alive and functioning. It should be cared for just like a human.[15]

Dandy's teachings are instructive regarding the extent and power of traditional thought. The hogan's connection to the holy people since the creation of this world, its inherent powers, and its various interpretations—whether associated with the sacred mountains, a basket, rainbow, human body, or life path—add to this structure's meaning. Metaphorical thought reaches deep into its tradition.

THE BODY AS METAPHOR

Once while I was attending a ceremony, a Navajo acquaintance decided to inform me about an aspect of Navajo culture concerning the creation. He had started talking about problems and eventually made reference to an incident involving witchcraft. I asked him why this form of evil did not seem to bother white men but was of great concern to Navajos. His reply took us back to the "palm of time." He pointed to his hand, then to mine, and asked what the difference was. Size and texture were not the concern but rather the color. Next he pointed to the reddish-brown sand at our feet and let me know that the Navajo people had come from the soil and the worlds beneath it, their skin color being proof of their origin. Next he asked where my people had come from. Across the ocean, a different soil, was the reply. His answer to my question (and answers in Navajo are rarely short or simple) eventually led us to the belief that the problems particular to his race were engendered in

Courtesy, Kay Shumway.

The female Navajo hogan offers powerful metaphorical teachings that range from its representing everything from a womb to the universe. For an elder who uses its characteristic shape to instruct, he or she may include anything from the placement of its logs and the protection of the four sacred mountains to its smoke hole and east-facing door.

the origin, the soil, the very essence of Navajo being and that the problems my race faced were derived from its own creation, which had not involved emerging from the ground. Along this same line of thinking, Mother Earth is made of the same things humans are. She hurts as we hurt. The things that are within her are within us. Water is like her milk, and so people are suckled by her.

The hand itself is also filled with teachings. Navajos refer to all humans as either earth surface people or the five-fingered ones. The five main posts of the Navajo sweat lodge, a "male" structure designed by the gods, are referred to as "fingers." When people are in the sweat lodge, it is said they are in the hands of the gods. Sacred thoughts and prayers remain in the structure, creating a holy place where people can return to be renewed. Nothing can bring greater peace than to be removed from the "world" and placed in the hands of the gods.

Four fingers used in traditional thought can serve as a mnemonic device that represents earth, sky, water, and fire; birth, puberty, marriage, and old age; the physical, emotional, mental, spiritual; or corn, squash, beans, and tobacco, the four main sacred plants. Fingers, when combined with the sacred number four, can teach some of the most profound concepts concerning life from birth to death. Yet sometimes, when death occurs, fingers can be used to comfort and explain why it happened. One medicine man taught: "Counting only one joint from the thumb and three joints from the finger, our joints represent the thirteen moons of the year. With these fingers we make a living. Look, your fingers aren't the same size. They grow at a particular rate to be a certain size. There is nothing that we can do about it. In the same way, we cannot control when people die. Not everyone reaches death at the same time. Life extends into infinity even though people pass away."[16]

Death, old age, poverty, and hunger have other explanations for their existence. Joe Manygoats tells of Monster Slayer, a mythological warrior, going about killing monsters that inhabited the earth. Four were allowed to live to bring appreciation for the things of life.[17] The first ones, called the Hunger People, pleaded, "Let us live. Who can eat and live on one meal forever? Let us be the hunger that exists in humans so that one will crave the taste of all the different varieties of food. It is good for everyone's well-being." So they were allowed to live. Next the Death People begged, saying, "Let us live. We will fill the void, the boring hours, even if one is at home." They, too, were not killed. Next the Poverty People pleaded to remain alive: "It is not good to wear one type of clothing forever. It is better to keep changing and renewing one's clothes because of the wear and tear. Besides, then one will have a choice." Finally, Old Age reminded Monster Slayer: "It is not good to be born then remain as a newborn forever. Therefore, it is better to renew generation after generation through the aging and dying process."[18] All of these beings are still with us today, but each generation continues to ask why it faces these problems. The question remains eternal, the answer inscrutable.

Some Navajo people have an interesting way of connecting money and poverty in today's society. Ben Whitehorse stated:

> In early history, [George] Washington [said] that all nickels were to have an Indianhead with feathers on one side and on the other a buffalo. A dime would have a white man's head on one side with arrows on the other. The same was true for a fifty cent piece, a quarter, and a silver dollar, with the white man's head on one side and an eagle

> on the other. These Indian symbols indicate our ownership in the money. If these symbols ever change, Indians will lose their rights and authority. This is what I was taught.[19]

Many of today's elders still wear their hair in the traditional hair bun (*tsiiyéél*), which also has numerous teachings. One's blessings are tied up and sealed in the "knot," which is the means by which the holy people recognize a person. The hair is bound to keep thoughts whole and unified, with the coils of the scalp facing toward the heavens: "It is believed that the longer your hair is, the wiser and more knowledgeable you are. It is said that the holy people have already established a path for each of us . . . It is up to each individual to bring out these things [life's teachings] and learn how to use them. Our hair bun is held in place with a sunbeam, the string or hair tie that holds our knowledge and understanding together. The sunbeam gives us a sense of direction and helps us plan. It helps us move forward in life."[20]

The black stripes left by the rain on the mesas and the rain-laden clouds that blow across the desert are similar to hair that has been left to hang down. This hairstyle was only allowed in the old days during a ceremony or at the time of an individual's death and burial.[21] Ben Whitehorse recalled the sacred nature of these connections between the land and sky, husband and wife, life and death:

> The man's wife shall care for his hair, likewise the man for hers. They will sit one behind the other as they brush one another's hair . . . The hair is strands of rain by which the holy people recognize us. It is sacred and through this symbolism the rain gods—one male and one female—and also the lightning know of us as we live on this earth. They will bring no harm or threat to us . . . Likewise our earth is the female and the things made in the heavens are male. The male brings forth the water to replenish the earth with living vegetation, and thus we humans and animals are continually reproducing. This is how they interact with each other.[22]

George Tom from Monument Valley agreed: "If we were to cut our protective shield of hair, the heavens will not hesitate to hurt us. Both men and women have a right to wear a knot; it is our 'sacred law' since creation."[23] Florence Begay warned that "if you ever start cutting your hair, we will have little rain. I think this is true because we do not have much rain. Back then men and women always wore their hair in a knot. It is considered male rain and so one should not cut it short."[24] Ben Whitehorse fears that as more and more people give up their traditions and unity within the culture is lost, "death" will become a reality: "If things should turn out like this, when women start wearing pants and wearing their hair down or [shaving] their heads, our important plans for the future will be led astray."[25]

THE WEDDING BASKET AS LIFE'S JOURNEY

Another example of metaphorical thought is associated with the Navajo wedding basket. There are many different interpretations as to the meaning of its pattern, but all of them reflect the deep sensitivity that imbues Navajo philosophy. Each interpretation speaks to an individual depending upon his or her stage of life and personal circumstance. The first baskets made available for the People came from Sun Bearer (Jóhonaa'éí), who gave it to the holy people for their ceremonies. Sun Bearer agreed that this was good as long as the baskets were used for worship, so "no ceremony should be performed without the basket. Prayers and songs are set in the basket when it is first used in a ceremony. The basket is used in teaching and in all major ceremonies today."[26]

Beyond the strictly religious implications of the basket's designs of the earth, place of emergence, mountains, sun's rays, clouds, and similar elements found in the creation story, other forms of guidance are woven into these familiar patterns. In one instance, the entire design is said to represent a person's life. The center of the basket is the point of emergence, where a life in this world began. As the small coils spiral outward and enlarge, so, too, does a person's world expand, moving from family to playmates to associates in an ever-widening arc. The design in the center is small, representing the small things done as a child. As the coils widen and broaden, they show a parallel growth in the individual's accomplishments. Once the rectangular points of black are reached on the outer edge, a person's life of achievement starts to dwindle. Things done in the frailty of old age do not have the same consistency or breadth as those done during the prime of life. The red center band, or rainbow, is the harmony and foundation upon which adult life should be built, while the white line that passes through the entire design from center to edge shows that no matter what happens in life, one can get through it. There is always a way out of problems. The basket thus represents growth and

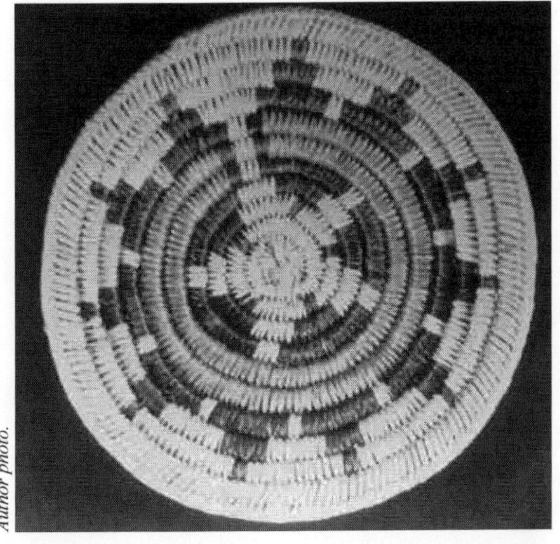

Author photo.

The Navajo wedding basket, like the hogan, has dozens of stories that speak of life's journey. Just as the holy people during the time of creation used this basket to hold sacred materials and part of their teachings, so, too, is a basket used in almost every ceremony today.

progress, a snapshot of one's life. The care with which it is woven and the tightness of its weave are left to the individual creator, just as each person makes his or her own life and determines the value and beauty within.[27] Once the basket or life is made, it must also be treated with respect. It is said that a person who spins around while holding a wedding basket will lose his or her mind. This provides a physical, visual meaning to the Anglo thought of how one's life is in a "whirl," or out of control.

The next three teachings about the basket are closely allied but share insightful variations in their interpretations. Betty Yazzie tells how the center of the basket represents the whorl on top of a baby's head, with the central white part representing initial growth. The first ring of black is one's brothers and sisters, the red is marriage, and the second ring of black is one's children. If there is red above that ring, it depicts grandchildren. As the design returns to white, "it represents how you are growing old and how you are reaching full circle in your life."[28]

Another understanding gleaned from this design begins in the center, which is said to be a newborn's umbilical cord. The start of the black design represents the time when the young child starts to speak, the next white line indicates when parents step in to teach, and the red section is a protective rainbow that shields the important knowledge the growing youth wishes to keep. The second black design depicts the time when that person shares with and teaches others the things he or she has learned thus far. As white space becomes interspersed with the black, one becomes more forgetful; by the time the totally white outer rim is reached (old age—white hair), the individual is returning to the baby stage: "The braid rim is like another seal. If you notice on a ceremonial basket, the ending rim is aligned with the beginning of the basket as if to say, 'Life ends back where it began.' All of your knowledge goes back to the beginning."[29]

A third interpretation explains the four stages of a day and how a person should follow a daily pattern of thought. The eastern side of the basket represents early dawn, illumination, and leadership. The mind is fresh and can see a long distance in planning for the future. The southern side is one of love, compassion, and humility that should be practiced around the home as family members labor at their tasks. Evening is the western side before the sun goes down. It is a time to return and gather with the family to share the day's activities, plan for the next, and listen to the elders. North is a time of introspection and rest during the night. A person should review what was good that day and what needs to be improved: "Our ancestors believed that negative behavior traits were found around your ankles. Since this is where bad behavior originates, this explains why they threw a whip at a misbehaving child's ankles. This area was always chapped, too, as people then didn't wear shoes and socks."[30] Each of these interpretations of the wedding basket design shows the creative power in Navajo thinking, helpful in teaching values important to youth as well as adults.

TEACHINGS OF HOME, MARRIAGE, AND FAMILY

The stones upon which corn is ground also teach lessons. One story tells of an old grandmother who raised her grandson from infancy. As the boy grew older, people visited their hogan and were disgusted by what they saw. The grandson was always lying about the fire, covered with ashes and lazily sleeping long after the sun was high in the sky. The visitors shook their heads in disbelief that a grandmother could be so neglectful in raising a child. They did not know that the old woman would awaken him early in the morning, massage his muscles, teach him songs and prayers, then have him run long distances, returning before sunrise. She then cared for him, rolled him in ashes, and encouraged him to sleep. The boy grew into a handsome young man mentally, spiritually, and physically—everything his grandmother desired.

He eventually became eligible for marriage and was introduced to many beautiful young women at a *kinaaldá* (puberty) ceremony. Many of the women did not recognize him and were smitten by his presence. When asked if he was available for marriage, the grandmother replied yes but added that acceptance was based on which woman could grind a handful of corn the finest, make it into a ball, toss it in the air, and have it land on the ground in one piece. Many tried but no one succeeded until one maiden stepped forward and miraculously accomplished the task. Only after she had won his hand did people learn that it was actually Spider Woman in disguise, who had surrounded her cornmeal with a web. She married the man, became jealous and mean, then placed him on a towering rock and almost starved him to death. With the help of some animals, he escaped and learned important lessons about how to select a wife, that looks can be deceiving, and how destructive jealousy can become in a relationship. The physical skill of grinding corn was just one of the necessary tasks to sustain life and not the ultimate test of who one should marry.[31]

Accompanying grinding stones in many Navajo homes are the stirring sticks used to mix ground cornmeal mush. Made from a number of peeled greasewood sticks two feet long and tied approximately six inches from the end, this utensil serves not only the practical side of moving thick cornmeal mush but also as a "weapon to fight hunger" by women, just as a bow and arrow serve a corresponding function for a man. Women hold their tool in the right hand to stir and men grasp the bow in the left hand, signifying—as throughout all of Navajo culture—the male and female duality. Nellie Grandson spoke of women praying for rain after mixing the mush and that when the sticks were not washed "it is said that there is hunger on them. The Hunger says 'Eek" when she is washing her weapon. This is what was said."[32] This lesson may help children today, who rarely want for food, to realize the problem of scarcity many elders have faced.

Sam Black noted that after a woman has used the stirring stick, she raises the implement to the east and prays for a "warm winter day so that her family will not be cold. After her prayer has been said she will squeeze the cornmeal off of each stick and eat it with delight. If a man should use the cornmeal sticks, he will be afraid and shake all over. These sticks are not to be used by a man."[33] Other things that may be prayed for include rain, long life, good fortune, acquisition of property, health, and friendly relations.[34] For Susie Yazzie, all of the teachings behind household equipment are classified as either discipline or respect.[35]

As a part of life, marriage plays an important role. The teachings of the braided rawhide rope serve as a reminder of how marital responsibility should be handled. Sam Black held such a rope in his hands and explained that each length of rawhide was braided to the other, giving the lasso its strength. When one part failed, the entire rope snapped and separated. Together, however, the braids could pull in the riches of life—sheep and goats—and hold on to them for future use. Comparing this to a man and wife's life together, Sam pointed out that when the fabric of the relationship tore apart, cooperation ended, the shared wealth departed, and soon the wife and husband separated.[36]

George Tom felt hard work was the cure for marital problems. He counseled, "Hold fast to your hoe and ax; they are the tools for the cornfield and firewood. Keep your eyes on the sheep—keep a close watch from all sides—for that is the best way. People will argue with each other, but do not take sides. Leave it alone."[37] Another piece of advice on holding marriages together has to do with knowledge and job skills. Navajo people place a high value on knowing how to do things so that economic independence and cooperation become entwined. Isabel Lee cautioned, "If your in-laws own some livestock and ask you to butcher a sheep and you don't know how, you'll get guts all over yourself. This will happen, or you will stand there and say you don't know how . . . [Then one day] you'll hang on to your husband's dirty loincloth crying and begging him to stay. This will happen if you do not learn how to do anything."[38]

Few things can keep a couple or an individual more securely on the straight and narrow path of correct thinking than prayer. In traditional Navajo culture, a day starts by facing the first sliver of white light on the horizon, praying to the rising sun, and sprinkling white cornmeal to the holy people. At the end of the day, the petitioner scatters a pinch of yellow cornmeal to the west. Throughout the day there are songs and prayers to accompany activities, which may be accompanied with pinches of corn pollen. It is therefore not surprising that the Navajo people have found an object to remind them of this duty to the holy people.

It may be surprising, however, that the object that does this is a macadam road. Fred Yazzie noted that as a person drives down the highway, there is the white, or "breakdown," lane on the right. To the far left are yellow markings and in between the blue-gray hue of asphalt. To Fred, the white represented white cornmeal; the yellow, yellow cornmeal; and the macadam, blue cornmeal—one of the food staffs of life in a traditional economy. Just as a person starts and ends a day with prayer and cornmeal represented by these colors, so should a driver stay between these lines. No harm comes to an individual who does so.[39]

When I was working with a Navajo family on an autobiography of an elderly patriarch, Navajo Oshley, I learned some important lessons.[40] The legacy he left for his family provides a fascinating glimpse into the metaphors used to discipline children for their own welfare. His daughter recalled that whenever he went out for a walk he would take a child, whom he taught using whatever he encountered. Finding a whiskey bottle on the road, he would kick it and warn that "glass" (whiskey) would "block your way" and that because it was outside of Navajo tradition, its effects were very hard to cure.

Sometimes at home, when the children were into mischief, his wife would grab a broom and start after them. Oshley would caution her that brooms were only made for sweeping, not for hurting children, who needed to be disciplined through love. He would tell the children, "Tears are dropping from your mother; is this how you want to behave?" or "This is not the Navajo way; you are not from this family if you are doing this. I don't want somebody to look at you and think it is me." He would drive the point home by saying, "The sheep are in chaos; when the mother is lost the lamb is lost. If you are misbehaving, you are like a lost sheep trying to find its mother and father." Another time he explained that children were sacred, just like corn. They should behave, but sometimes, just as corn gets worms, so do children. Worms are removed, and so is misbehavior.[41]

Isabel Lee blamed some of the problems of misbehavior on a mother's decision at a child's birth to wean the infant at an early age. She said, "Today, our children drink cow's milk from bottles, whereas mothers of earlier times breast-fed their children. It was said that breast-fed babies grew into intelligent children. But now, children are going crazy; they are still 'drinking from bottles' [alcoholic beverages]. They don't listen or obey but just act like stubborn cows [from drinking cow's milk]. There is no one who can put us back on track."[42]

Physical exercise is a means for teaching discipline and self-discipline. The well-known practice of "running to catch the sun" at dawn was institutionalized as a daily practice as well as a part of a number of ceremonies. Metaphors teach how this regimen should be performed. Isabel Lee recounted some typical advice: "Get up! It is dawn. Get up, run, get rid of your frustrations. Yell, yell while you run so you won't sound like an old billy goat being dragged along. Run more swiftly; run like a rabbit that is being roasted; that's how you should be. Curl your back while you run, and if you are clumsy you will show it."[43]

The time of day and the seasons are also used to teach youth. For instance, darkness reminds a person to go to sleep and get rest. Dawn tells one to arise, "to build a fire" and prepare for the day. The sun lends encouragement to tend to goals before sunset, suggesting that people should get busy because the sun will not wait for them. Hunger, cold, and heat are other reminders. The first warns people to look after their subsistence; freezing temperatures make them mindful to gather wood and prepare for winter; heat tells them to seek shade and rest, "just like a lizard."[44]

Parents use weather as a part of their teachings about how hard life could be at times. Buck Navajo, from Navajo Mountain, tells how his father trained him for the rigors of the future. Although it may seem harsh, what he was taught prepared him for what he encountered later in life, inculcating the patience required to be a successful father and medicine man. In Buck's words:

> My father was very assertive. He would chase me out of the hogan even though there was snow outside and make me walk. He would say, "Let your eyes get cold. Let your body get cold. Let the cold freeze your total body. Your brother is not mercy. Your sister is not mercy. You are going to be among people who have no mercy. This world has no mercy and you are going into it. The Anglos are not merciful. Everywhere you go you will encounter people who have no mercy. It is all up to you to survive." This was how I was raised and what I was told.[45]

This type of teaching proper behavior is central to Navajo thought. One person described effective parenting as she reminisced, "I guess my parents really rubbed that teaching into my ear, so I obeyed them." Etiquette in greeting relatives as they come to visit one's home is also circumscribed by dos and don'ts. Food is very much a part of the social event, and when the visit is over, those departing use a metaphor to jokingly say thanks. As the visitors get ready to leave they say, "Let's go. What else are we going to sit here for? Our roots have been cut," meaning now that they had eaten, there is no use hanging around. This is an old way of showing respect for relatives and the role they play in supporting extended family and friends.[46]

FACING CULTURAL LOSS

When these teachings of respect are forgotten, one becomes impoverished. Failure to recognize family ties and the interdependence within a community leads to hatred and strife. Abuse of healing power provided by the holy people can also lead to trouble. As one person described it, "While everyone else travels by horseback, your one-sided footprints will be seen alongside the road. So never misuse what you have learned. Use it only to help and heal your people."[47] Otherwise a person will be alone, depressed, and without assistance from others.

Some Navajo elders are concerned that the youth are failing to learn even the most basic traditional teachings. Fred Yazzie explained that this did not happen all at once but occurred gradually. He described the process: "At first their [the young people's] way is the way of doing what they are supposed to do, but pretty soon they are not practicing the religion right, and they have different goals. They no longer know the songs. It is like they have stepped out of it [traditional culture] into a new set of ideas. They only know the edges of songs and mix up the prayers."[48] Difficulty follows. A person, however, can pass tranquilly through life by paying attention to the lessons of the elders. One grandmother, Betty Canyon, spoke of how her grandchildren realized her value and importance to the family: "They tell me that I am their only root that is of strength." And so she stays, herding sheep and teaching her traditional values.[49]

Still, it is hard for the younger generation to become as totally involved as their grandparents would like in the culture of former days. One elder said, "With all of this, who will be here to take the role of the older people? No one wants to herd sheep; even this animal's smell is offensive to young people. When they go to the corral, they act like a cat trying to cross the water. It seems like they do not listen, and after they are told, they just feel like doing it more . . . They want to live their own way, do not think of their parents until [they are] in trouble, and their younger brothers and sisters follow them. I do not know if they will come back to the reality of life."[50]

One day, most of us will reach old age and become elders ourselves. One person compared life to a tree that is strong in the trunk (the beginning of life) but eventually starts to branch out in many directions that are sometimes crooked and other times straight. But in the end the tips grow together, all heading in the same direction. This symbolizes that toward the end of life the final pattern is established and becomes straightened out.[51] S. P. Jones, having arrived at that point, said, "We are worn out; that is the kind of people we are. Take, for instance, a living tree. As it gets older, some of its branches get hard and die and can no longer sway in the wind. Its covering and beauty are gone, with only a few limbs still working. That is the way old age is."[52] Eventually, the tree topples to its resting place, making room for a new generation of growth.

As the elders die, many of their stories and much of their wisdom will be lost. From their lives come teachings that entertain and instruct today's younger generation. For instance, around many Navajo camps, one may find a burro, whose form suggests a lesson in correct living. Elders tell how the holy people shaped many different kinds of animals out of precious jewels, such as white shell, turquoise, abalone, and jet. When they completed the work there was a large pile of refuse, which some children discovered and decided to play with. They created from these scraps an animal with hooves made of jet, a nose of ash, a body of valuable stones, legs striped with coal, ears of a jackrabbit, cattail fuzz for hair, and a tail of worm material. The children then sprinkled the being with stardust. They laughed at the funny sight and mocked the animal, but their parents cautioned them not to look at the creature's outside but instead at what was within. That was where the value was. So it is with people. A person should look at the heart and not the outward appearance, lest the critic pass through life without ever seeing the beauty in others.[53]

Another story entertains with a message while teaching about dogs. Anyone who has been around dogs for very long has noticed that they

Courtesy, Milton Snow Collection, Navajo Nation Museum, Window Rock, AZ.

To young people, this picture expresses a mother's love for her child. To those who understand traditional teachings, it also speaks of important Navajo cultural values, including the hair bun (thoughts), turquoise (holy people recognition), the loom (to fight hunger), dress (modesty), and the cradleboard (in the tradition of Changing Woman).

often sniff each other's tails. During the palm of time, the dogs decided to hold a meeting in a circular brush enclosure (*ił'názt'i'*). Before entering, each animal hung its tail on the cedar branches outside. Coyote (the trickster) came along, saw an opportunity for fun, and switched the tails, then howled to the dogs to quickly come out. In their haste, each animal grabbed the wrong tail. Today, dogs go around sniffing to see if they can locate their real tail.[54] Paralleling the English adage "haste makes waste," this story teaches that a person should not always arise to the "howling" of an outsider who may just be waiting to see what confusion can be wrought through hasty decisions.

Although there are many more sayings, I hope the point has been made that the teachings of the elders are filled with an infinite number of metaphors that instruct about important elements of life. For youth who take a moment to pause and listen, they will find a world of beauty and relevance. In the restless society of today—both on and off the reservation—one finds peace and reassurance in what the older people have to offer. For many of them, their days are almost over, their lives spent. But I have been impressed by their determination to pass on to subsequent generations the principles that carried them through two world wars, livestock reduction, the end of many traditional practices, and into the space age of the twenty-first century.

As Charlie Blueyes sat on his bunk in the corner of the room and stirred the embers of the fire, he doubtless felt satisfaction at sharing his understanding with the hope of having it passed to his grandson at a later time. Age has a way of causing people to look back to their roots as much as forward to the unknown. Navajo biography and autobiography is one part of this process where people within the culture can find a foundation, while people on the edge can catch a fleeting glimpse of another way, another time. Nothing, however, captures more succinctly the feelings and attitudes of the past than metaphors used to create a mental image of an inner view. Through these metaphors comes a world of learning for today's youth.

NOTES

1. Stella Cly interview with author, August 7, 1991.
2. Joe Manygoats interview with author, December 18, 1991.
3. Betty Canyon interview with author, September 10, 1991.
4. George Tom interview with author, August 7, 1991.
5. Jenny Francis interview with author, March 23, 1993.
6. Gilmore Graymountain interview with author, April 7, 1992; Ada Black interview with author, October 11, 1991; Don Mose, *Honeeshgish: A Navajo Legend* (Blanding, UT: San Juan School District Media Center, 2006), 8.
7. Dave Wilson, "Family Fire Poker Teachings," *Leading the Way* 9, no. 7 (July 2011): 10.
8. Britt Tallis interview with author, December 6, 1993.
9. Sam Black interview with author, December 18, 1993.
10. Ada Black interview with author.
11. Marilyn Holiday discussion with author, June 20, 1993.
12. Fire is a fundamental element of life, as are water, air, and Mother Earth: "All living species have fire within them. Even a flea, lice, a dog, birds, chickens have a fire within them. A puppy's fire is at the tip of its tail. This is his spirit. If you cut off your dog's tail, you shorten its life . . . The horse's fire is behind its ears . . . In humans the fire is inside, close to the heart." The hogan is viewed as a living entity and so must also have a fire to keep it well as a home of warmth.

Francis T. Nez Sr., "Fire: The Heart of Life," *Leading the Way* 2, no. 10 (October 2004): 1, 16.

13. The roof of the first hogan built by the holy people was made, in its spiritual form, with a rainbow.
14. "Weavers leave an opening in their weaving as a means of escape. In any situation, there is the potential to trap one's self. With an opening, you will never be cornered by sweet talk or appearances. All of Navajo art is this way. It is intentionally left imperfect. This represents a way out of life's difficult situations." Maggie Yellowhair, "Why Weavers Leave an Opening," *Leading the Way* 6, no. 5 (May 2008): 21.
15. Jim Dandy interview with author, October 8, 2007.
16. Kathleen Manolescu, "Navajo Morality and the Concept of Bee haz'áanii," *Navajo Times*, March 5, 1998, A-7.
17. In some versions of this story, Lice was one of the four monsters allowed to remain because they teach compassion and caring for one another as they are removed with other people's assistance.
18. Joe Manygoats interview with author.
19. Ben Whitehorse interview with author, January 30, 1991.
20. Mary Ann Clark, "The Hair Tie and the Kinaaldá," *Leading the Way* 7, no. 4 (April 2009): 18.
21. Ada Black interview with author.
22. Whitehorse interview with author.
23. Tom interview with author.
24. Florence Begay interview with author, January 30, 1991.
25. Whitehorse interview with author.
26. Buck Navajo, "Navajo Basket Teachings," *Leading the Way* 4, no. 9 (September 2006): 4.
27. Wanda Ketchum interview with author, September 11, 1993.
28. Betty Yazzie cited in Georgiana Kennedy Simpson, *Navajo Ceremonial Baskets: Sacred Symbols, Sacred Space* (Summertown, TN: Native Voices, 2003), 51.
29. Geno Bahe cited in ibid., 52–54.
30. John E. Salaybe Jr. and Kathleen Manolescu, "The Beginning of Marriage and Family: Corn Story Teachings," *Leading the Way* 6, no. 11 (November 2008): 4–5.
31. Mary Blueyes interview with author, February 9, 1994.
32. Nellie Grandson interview with author, December 16, 1993.
33. Sam Black interview with author, December 18, 1993.
34. Clyde Kluckhohn, W. W. Hill, and Lucy Wales Kluckhohn, *Navaho Material Culture* (Cambridge, MA: Harvard University Press, 1971), 125.
35. Susie Yazzie interview with author, November 10, 2000.
36. Sam Black interview with author.
37. Tom interview with author.
38. Isabel Lee interview with author, February 13, 1991.
39. Fred Yazzie interview with author, August 6, 1991.
40. See Robert S. McPherson, ed., *The Journey of Navajo Oshley: An Autobiography and Life History* (Logan: Utah State University Press, 2000).
41. Joanne Oshley Holiday interview with author, May 8, 1996.

42. Isabel Lee interview with author.
43. Ibid.
44. Manolescu, "Navajo Morality," A-7.
45. Buck Navajo interview with author, December 16, 1991.
46. Mary Jay interview with author, February 27, 1991.
47. John Holiday interview with author, September 9, 1991.
48. Fred Yazzie interview with author.
49. Canyon interview with author.
50. Susie Yazzie interview with author, August 6, 1991.
51. Karenita Atkinson discussion with author, August 24, 1998.
52. S. P. Jones interview with author, December 20, 1985.
53. Charlie Blueyes interview with author, June 7, 1988.
54. Story told to author by an acquaintance at a Mountain Way ceremony, held November 11, 1995, in Tuba City, AZ.

6

"He Stood for Us Strongly"

Father H. Baxter Liebler's Mission to the Navajo

Father H. Baxter Liebler understood the power of Navajo metaphor and cultural symbols long before he made his way into southeastern Utah. As an Episcopalian priest, he had already approached learning the language and studying the culture enough to know that if he were going to make a difference, unlike many other Christian ministers, he was going to have to approach his mission in a different way. Appreciation for, understanding of, and commitment to the people and their beliefs became paramount. Hindsight proves that the success he enjoyed came from these principles, as he meshed the teachings of the elders with his "foreign" religion. The product was a combined theology that brought two cultures together in a harmonious relationship of acceptance.

DOI: 10.7330/9781607322177.c06

> *Of equal import is the question raised of directly adapting values and practices from one culture into another in an effort to have them blend. For those Anglos—sometimes referred to as "wanna-bes"—who lacked the sophistication, determination, and wisdom Liebler attained from years of study, observation, and application, the results are ludicrous. This Episcopalian priest, however, was able to do it successfully, gathering a devoted congregation of Navajo followers who appreciated his efforts and considered him a friend. Perhaps it was his sincerity or ability to pick and choose what he could use and what should be left alone, or perhaps it was the very dedicated service—religious and nonreligious—he offered unflaggingly. Whatever it was, he was accepted and loved by the Navajo people he taught.*

The San Juan River was still running deep that July 1943. The cottonwood leaves trembled slightly in the midday heat, with an occasional breeze snaking its way along the dirt road that ran beside the red rock bluffs north of the river. Ada Benally remembers shading her eyes and looking across the brown, roiling water at the approaching dust cloud that billowed above the far bank. The hum of vehicle engines stopped, the opening and closing of truck doors sounded in the distance, and the dust began to settle. Ada wondered what was happening. The sights and sounds came from a section along the river where Navajos and Utes had traditionally picked sumac berries, wild spinach, and herbs. Perhaps these people had come for that purpose. She decided to wait and see, since the river was too high and too fast to cross on foot, and there was no boat to take her across.[1] Had Ada been able to ford the river, she would have witnessed the establishment of Saint Christopher's Mission, two miles outside of Bluff, Utah. Ada would later be counted as one among several hundred of the mission's future baptized members.

But that was in the future. At this point, the cassocked Father H. (Harold) Baxter Liebler, the director of this Episcopalian mission, stepped out of his vehicle to begin his lifelong work among the Navajo. He had come from Old Greenwich, Connecticut, leaving behind a well-established parish to pursue a boyhood vision he considered his destiny. At age fifty-three, Father Liebler set out to fulfill his dream of a mission to the Navajo. He selected an isolated part of their reservation known as the Utah Strip with the hope of finding a group of people least touched by earlier inroads of Christianity. Saint Christopher's was the ideal spot for this undertaking. The site was geographically central to the Utah Navajo population that lived on the northern boundary of the reservation. The vast majority of the people lived in hogans south of the river and occasionally came across on horseback or in wagons to trade; a general store and a twenty-home Mormon community comprised the city of Bluff.

Father Liebler wrote extensively of his experiences over the next twenty years in a book entitled *Boil My Heart for Me,* which is still in print.[2] Beneath the fascinating story of his and other people's efforts to bring Christianity to the Navajo lies submerged the even more important tale of how this message was received. Often, discussions concerning Christian missionary efforts toward the Indians tend to be one-sided—whether about Roman Catholic priests in the wake of the Spanish conquest of Mexico, Jesuits accompanying traders into the pine forests of Canada, or Protestants establishing farms and missions in the American West. Only a handful of these missionaries paid much attention to understanding the cultures they proselytized, and even fewer cared about preserving what they encountered. At the same time, little has been recorded about the Native Americans' philosophical reaction to what was taught. Even books written recently that try to integrate an American Indian perspective speak of a historical time, when those who received the lessons of Christianity have long since died.

This chapter is somewhat different in that much of it is based on oral interviews of Navajo people who encountered this missionary experience from their own traditional perspective. Thus it is an examination of the meshing of Episcopalian doctrine with Navajo traditional beliefs as they met for the first time on the San Juan River that July day. It is the story of a dedicated priest who was willing to go more than halfway into the Navajo world to bring them partway into his. It is a story of trust and respect that bridged both worlds. And it is a story told from two views that speaks of a common humanity.

ESTABLISHING THE MISSION IN THE MAN

Long before those first vehicles clanked into sight or a tent was pitched, Father Liebler had carefully laid out the mission's philosophical

Father H. Baxter Liebler, Episcopalian priest and founder of Saint Christopher's Mission in southeastern Utah. Dedicated to a life of service, his admiration for the Navajo people allowed him to move beyond the restrictive bounds of ethnocentrism to embrace cultural diversity and respect for others' beliefs.

Courtesy, Baxter Benally, family photo.

foundation in his mind. As a young boy, he read the romantic writings of James Fenimore Cooper's Leatherstocking tales, the story of Hiawatha by Henry Wadsworth Longfellow, and the more realistic works of Henry Schoolcraft and George Catlin. Yet no one had more of an impact on his interest in Indians than Ernest Thompson Seton, a naturalist who wrote and lectured extensively on woodcraft skills as well as Native American philosophy. When Seton learned that the young Liebler had formed his own "tribe" of "woodcraft Indians," he invited the boy to join him and others in annual camping events that promoted understanding of Native American ways. This simpatico relationship with the "chief" and others interested in Indian beliefs lasted for years.[3] Perhaps it was a lapse into this romantic past that encouraged Father Liebler—long after the founding of Saint Christopher's—to again don breechcloth, leggings, moccasins, and war bonnet, then whoop his way from Navajo campfire to campfire asking if the people at a local Enemy Way ceremony needed anything. Everyone appreciated the gesture, but perhaps no one more than the bedecked priest.[4]

Liebler referred to the early part of his life as a "pagan boyhood," since by age four he had rejected Christianity. Indian lore replaced Episcopalian doctrine in guiding the young man's beliefs until he was reconverted during his freshman year at Columbia University. His thoughts now centered on traditional Christian values, though he maintained his interest in Indian practices.

For twenty-five years, Father Liebler labored at Saint Saviours' Church in Old Greenwich, Connecticut. His philosophical background developed from two converging streams of intellectual tradition—Native American and Episcopalian beliefs. There should, however, be no misunderstanding of his intent. He was first and foremost an Episcopalian priest who taught the doctrines of his church as explained in the American Missal. This "high" form of the church used the vestments, ritual, and service that were closely akin to the teachings of the Roman Catholic Church. Why Liebler chose this approach will be discussed later, but the fact that he was devoted to his beliefs cannot be questioned.

At the same time, however, Father Liebler maintained his interest in Native American philosophy. Before he arrived in Utah to face the full-blown, intact religious system of the Navajos, he had already decided not only on which side of the fence he belonged but also the color and construction of that fence. He wrote, while still in Connecticut, that the religion of the American Indian had many "harmless pagan practices which were not inconsistent with belief in the True God, and where such has been the practice, the Indians have been happy to adopt and make part of their spiritual lives the revelation of God in his Divine Son."[5]

Father Liebler recognized the wisdom of building upon what was already in place rather than tearing down a culture's entire social and religious fabric. He knew that for the Indians, religion was "life itself . . . [and] a very real thing."[6] He believed that symbols, such as the Sioux sweat bath and the sacred pipe, held intrinsic values similar to baptism and the

Eucharist of Christianity, an understanding missionaries to those people had mistakenly tried to erase. Thus the challenge lay in retaining and blending these concepts, since "God is a respecter of human personality, and . . . no good is accomplished by forcing an immortal soul's decision on so important a subject as religion . . . A far more wholesome attitude would be the recognition that the Indians are different from ourselves. Why not let a Higher Being decide which is better?"[7]

Yet the reality of missionary efforts still necessitated change. Liebler looked at what had been done elsewhere and found it doctrinally inflexible, unsympathetic, and consequently unproductive. He drew upon his experiences with Seton and a talk Canon Douglas had given in theological school and concluded that the current methods of the Episcopal Church missed the spirit of true missionary work. The "clean slate" approach that advocated wiping out "pagan religion" before "teaching the true religion, true faith, and adding to it all of the cultural fringe benefits of Christianity" was wrong.[8]

He held to this judgment until 1953, when he attended a National Council of the Episcopal Church. With ten years' experience under his cassock, Father Liebler braced himself for an unpleasantly ethnocentric meeting but found instead a far more sympathetic audience composed of many religious leaders traveling their own "Saint Christopher road."[9] By this time, there was no arguing with the success he had encountered through his efforts. While he had not started out as a "maverick" priest doing everything his own way, he did believe the rules established by the Domestic Mission Board of his church were too rigid. Armed with permission from his bishop in Salt Lake City, Liebler skillfully laced Episcopalian and Navajo practices into his services. The fact that various bishops visited Saint Christopher's often to confirm newly baptized members and that in 1972 he was seated as an honorary canon in the Episcopal Church testifies that his efforts met with both official and unofficial approval.[10]

His different perspective included not falling into the same trap into which other missionaries had plummeted. For example, he did not believe in the "fringe benefits of Christianity," such as giving rides, handing out clothing, and fostering dependence; in this there appeared no firm philosophical ground upon which to stand. These problems were part of the inevitable challenge that came with living in the midst of a materially impoverished population. The worst possible scenario occurred when Christian missions of various denominations vied for "customers" who wanted material benefits from any and all. The religious confusion that arose from Navajos accepting various faiths for material rewards, or "making the rounds" as Liebler called it, resulted in a muddled understanding of the basis of life. In later years, Liebler recorded this befuddlement when he wrote of an apparent conversation with a Navajo who had experienced this problem. The Navajo stated:

> I do not believe the old stuff any more. I do not believe the things my father and my mother believe. I do not believe those gods any more—I still think there are ghosts; I still think there are things we should be afraid of, but I do not believe in the things that they [the parents] have to do all the time. I do not know what to believe because one missionary says one thing, one says the other thing. All say, "do not go any other place, just come to my church," and I do not know what to do.[11]

To summarize Father Liebler's philosophical background on the eve of his departure from Connecticut, one finds a priest whose idealism bordered on the romantic yet who was ready to experiment in new ways to bring the gospel to the Navajo. The underlying tenet of his approach was to include rather than exclude new religious possibilities—a basic tendency already existing in Navajo religion, much to the frustration of missionaries with more rigid views.[12]

To prepare for this experience, he began a course of study that continued until his death. The winter before he arrived in Utah, he ventured for the first time into the Navajo language under the tutelage of Gladys Reichard, a leading anthropologist in the field of Navajo studies. Both teacher and student realized the impossibility of Leibler's gaining any kind of fluency in such a short time, so Reichard decided to work on pronunciation, hoping that ease of speaking would come later. Liebler believed she did too good a job because when he first started to converse with a native speaker, he or she assumed from the priest's pronunciation that he understood everything in the conversation.[13] That was far from the truth.

Perhaps of even greater long-range significance was the fact that Reichard understood Navajo traditional beliefs. At least part of the contents of her book, *Navaho Religion—A Study of Symbolism*, must have been available to Liebler during these sessions, and he would have had access to all of it after it was published in 1950.[14] Reichard published a number of other substantial works concerning Navajo religion and culture based on her extensive fieldwork. No doubt her thoughts helped mold part of Liebler's understanding of ceremonial lore.[15]

There is also no doubt as to the impact of the Catholic Franciscan missionary Father Berard Haile and his associates stationed at Saint Michaels, Arizona. Haile had studied and written about Navajo beliefs and Christian doctrine as the two faiths encountered each other in the early 1900s. Haile worked among the Navajo for sixty-one years, continuing an exhaustive study of their language, customs, and religious philosophy. In addition to assisting in the production of *An Ethnologic Dictionary of the Navajo Language* (1910), he labored for thirty-five years to develop a Navajo orthography and published numerous monographs on religious aspects of their culture.[16]

Although Father Liebler never met Haile, he described his heavy dependence on these works. Especially in the beginning of his ministry, while his language was impoverished, he put together basic sermons derived from the Franciscan catechism. Six weeks in the creation, six minutes in the delivery, Father Liebler's first text was an amalgam of Christian Bible stories and doctrine he read to his small congregation.[17] He did not give a second sermon until Easter, over three months later. But from the writings of the Franciscan Fathers, Liebler eventually derived twenty-five doctrinal discourses that fit the appropriate religious season of the year. As his fluency increased, his dependence decreased, but rarely did he slacken his attempt to fortify his Navajo vocabulary and usage.

ESTABLISHING SAINT CHRISTOPHER'S MISSION

In the summer of 1942, Father Liebler began his search for a place to establish a mission. A train brought him to New Mexico, where he started from Stokes Carson's trading post south of Bloomfield, New Mexico, then wended his way on horseback through the Four Corners region. Assisted by a compass and a general knowledge of the land, he traveled through Farmington to Teec Nos Pos, then through Monument Valley, Utah, to Mexican Hat, Utah. Near that small community he told of lying on his back, head propped against his saddle, and watching the shifting shapes of clouds in the azure sky. Eventually, in "stark clarity" he saw in "pure white against the blue, arms spread in blessing over Navajoland, the unmistakable form of the Saviour, vested in alb [a ceremonial robe worn by priests] . . . From that instant there was never a doubt in my mind that all that had ever happened to me was a preparation for that which lay ahead."[18] He rode on to Bluff, convinced that he had been guided by Saint Christopher, the patron saint of travelers. The mission, founded the next year with the help of five other people, bore witness of this belief through its name.

This mystical, supernatural intervention was one of a number of such incidents Father Liebler experienced during his ministry. Interestingly, the Navajo speak of having similar manifestations forewarning his arrival. Randolph Benally, who lived next to the mission, told that one night, after the children were asleep, he and his wife were in their hogan getting ready to retire when a "strange little woman" appeared by the doorway. She announced: "There is a white man coming who will stay here for a few days and then will go away. A year later he will come back with others to do you good. Listen to what he says." She then disappeared. Randolph picked up a flashlight to track her outside, but there was no trace to follow. Similar reports came from Navajos living across the river and from people to the west.[19]

Another man, Dan Benally, explained how he understood Father Liebler's arrival. He said the priest told them that he came from "under where the sun rises" to "tell the people about the Holy One and maybe they will understand it." Father Liebler then "talked to people as he walked about . . . but at that time older men and women asked many questions" such as 'Why are you walking here among us? Maybe you are a spy' [referring to witchcraft] . . . He told them that this [Christianity] was his work, that he was a priest. So at length the older men and women as well as the younger people started to think of him in a different way. He was telling the truth. `This thing is good for us, the telling of the Holy One.'"[20]

One of the first steps in Liebler's establishing an identity was handled through keen Navajo observation. For better or worse, a person often becomes known by a physical attribute, a habit, an incident, or membership in an organization and is labeled accordingly. In Father Liebler's case, he received a number of names from different people. His most common title, translated as "The-One-Who-Drags-His-Robe-Around," was a general name given to priests who wore a long cassock as part of their vestments. To distinguish him from other clergy, he was also known as "The-One-with-Long-Hair-Who-Drags-His-Robe-Around," which at times was shortened to "Long Hair" in reference to his Navajo hair bun tied at the back of his head. Because so few white men adopted this hairstyle, he was also called "The-One-Who-Wears-His-Hair-Tight."[21]

He also picked up a name or two he would have liked to have forgotten. Not that he was in any way being abused. Indeed, in all of the interviews and research conducted for this chapter, there were never any negative feelings expressed toward Father Liebler by Anglos or Navajos.[22] This is a great testimony in and of itself. But Navajos were observant and recalled that during his reconnaissance in 1942, he drank some alkali water by mistake. For a number of days he suffered from this dietary indiscretion, giving rise to the names "Priest-with-Sore-Guts" and "The-One-Who-Soils-His-Robes."[23]

Father Liebler was not the only one to be named. He brought with him or had join him over the years a staff of faithful helpers who assisted in making the mission a success. Without going into detail about these individuals, their Navajo names help paint a picture of some of their prominent characteristics. Brother Juniper, for instance, was an easy one, since his name translated directly as "Juniper Tree." He was also called "Baggy Pants." Catherine Pickett, a nurse whose eyesight was exceptionally poor, was called "Eyeless" because of the thick glasses she wore, while Helen Sturges, a teacher at the mission, was called "The-Woman-Who-Teaches-School" or "The Counter." Joan Liebler, helper and later Father Liebler's wife, assumed the epithet "The-Woman-Who-Cries-a-Lot."[24] Yet most often, traditional Navajo kinship terms denoting "my older brother," "my older sister," and "my father" or "my grandfather" were used. Accompanying the use of these terms were implied familial responsibilities and relationships customary in Navajo society.

An important part of Father Liebler's plan to integrate Navajo and Episcopalian doctrine hinged on being taught by the local community's repository of traditional beliefs, the chanters, more commonly known as medicine men. He believed a helpful approach in bringing the gospel to the Navajo involved the "cooperating medicine man, the simplicity of surroundings, together with a scrupulous observance of traditional details of ceremony."[25] He spent countless hours visiting with medicine men or

Courtesy, Baxter Benally, family photo.

Hastiin Tsé'kizi and John Antes, two medicine men from the Bluff, Utah, area, share thoughts on traditional teachings. One of Father Liebler's many practices that won the respect of the Navajo people was his interest in sitting in ceremonies for hours to learn about these beliefs.

traditionalists like Shoodii, Hastiin Yazhi, John Antes, Hastiin Tsé'kizi, Hash'kaan, and Randolph Benally to observe their ceremonies, discuss beliefs, and take notes in his ever-present binder. He questioned the men, clarifying details, and became immersed in the teachings, songs, and prayers of the Blessing Way ceremony. One man said, "They told him the way Navajos pray, and from this he understood how to do it."[26] Fernandez Begay recalled, "This person Shorty, with his Blessing Way ritual tools, used to perform for him [Liebler]. He performed by singing his Blessing Way songs . . . [and] spoke in our Navajo language, our way of praying. That is where he learned from. It was `beauty behind me, beauty above me, below me and around me, in beauty I will walk.' That is how he prayed."[27] And that was how Father Liebler often closed his services.

CREATING AND USING THE LITURGY

Prayers are the core of Navajo ceremonial belief. They are perceived as alive, strong, and powerful when performed properly. They serve as a literal shield of protection from evil powers that could otherwise harm a person. Thus an individual is admired for his ability to converse with the holy people through prayer and may be invited to participate in blessing, healing, and protecting a person if he has the appropriate knowledge. Father Liebler gained that status. Dan Benally, speaking of Liebler's ability, said:

> For me, I walk behind this priest's teachings. He starts his ceremony by praying. He pleads with the Holy One, who is all around us. He says the Holy One is in heaven, and he holds his hand up to heaven. This is how he prays. He teaches in this manner and pleads in this way with the bread [sacrament]. This is how Father Liebler prayed and conducted his ceremony.[28]

Many Navajos told Liebler he had "good, strong medicine" and that when they went to his church they felt like "the real Holy One is here in some way, that he isn't any other place. This is what we call good strong medicine. This is what we want."[29] He went on to note that "when someone has done wrongfully, he [Liebler] would pray for that person . . . Because of him helping with this, his prayers were holy, were good, were nourishing . . . He stood for us strongly."[30] Another remembered that he prayed for the soldiers in World War II, and "because of these services I returned unharmed, the bullets missed me."[31] Jessie Shorty added her evaluation, saying "he performed good services . . . It was done in the right manner . . . and he prayed for us very well."[32]

Not only did he pray well, using Navajo patterns of thought, but he also encouraged Navajo ceremonies to be performed on or near the mission grounds. In one woman's eyes, "He liked their traditional ceremonies, so that is why they followed him."[33] He would sit in on parts of a five-day rite, attend a puberty ceremony for a young woman, participate in a Blessing Way, encourage participants of an Enemy Way ceremony to hold part of their activities nearby, and, when asked, contribute material means such as firewood, water, and herbs. From a purely practical standpoint, the priest considered all this "good publicity."[34]

The people felt Father Liebler believed in these ceremonies. From the Navajos' perspective, his actions represented acceptance, especially when "he took part in the taking of corn pollen. He did what the Navajos did while he was sitting in there. He said, 'I will not talk against this. I am already a believer . . . This is why the Navajo ceremony and the ceremony that I hold are one.' This is what he said . . . `With this we will be one.'[35] John Shorty remembers that he "prayed along with the ceremonies," "respected them," and "believed in the ritual tools."[36]

Yet Liebler's goal was to teach Episcopalian doctrines that ranged from the creation and the fall of man to Christ's life, passion, death, resurrection, and ascension.[37] He realized that the Navajos viewed healing, death, and spiritual harmony in very different terms, and so he gave much time and thought to placing Christian symbols and values in a context that was understandable. Individual Navajo explanations of what they learned may differ from what was taught, but a glimpse into their perception of Father Liebler's efforts is instructive.

Take, for instance, the sacraments of the church. Navajo traditional view shows great concern that the holy people are able to recognize a person, no matter where he or she might be. Protection from harm is another important concept derived from various ceremonies. These two ideas joined in the service of the Mass, where bread and wine become the body and blood of Christ. Navajos were impressed that "while he [Liebler] is singing, he places something in your mouth," that "it [sacrament] is holy," and that "the holiness remains in you."[38] The singing and accompanying ritual appeared similar to the actions associated with the use of corn pollen in traditional ceremonies. One man explained that the sacrament was called "*jish*," or the medicine bundle used by chanters: "The Holy One set this for us, and this is the ceremony that is to be done. The one who has become a priest will perform this ceremony."[39] John Shorty explained his understanding of the Mass, saying:

> This bread is Jesus's bread. With this he will acknowledge you and your body will be healthy. You can go anywhere with this bread . . . It is said that this bread was broken into pieces and it has revived many, and that is why we pray with it and place it in our mouth[s]. After that, this is medicine; this is something that grows . . . The grape juice is the blood of Jesus. All of this will come together and become your blood, and that is what is prayed about. He sees you by that.[40]

Father Liebler, with all of his apparent outward acceptance of Navajo beliefs, also struggled within to maintain the purity of his church's teachings. In an article titled "Christian Concepts and Navaho Words," he bemoaned the fact that the Navajo word for sacrament translated roughly as "our mouths into, a thing is put." The emphasis on the physical act detracted from the spiritual belief inherent in the gesture. The symbolic meaning of other translated terms likewise could be lost: baptism ("head-top water"), confirmation ("our interior-standing [i.e., soul] being made strong"), penance ("our sins taking-away"), and extreme unction ("holy salve").[41] Christ was called the "Holy One" or the "One-Who-Cannot-Die" and held certain qualities shared by other "holy people" in the Navajo pantheon, although Father Liebler made no direct comparison between them.

THE POWER OF SYMBOLS

The possibility of misunderstanding symbols in many respects becomes the crux of the issue in conversion. If a symbol is "an outward and physical sign of an inward and spiritual grace," then one must ask how closely the parallels in belief can be drawn around the physical object. For Father Liebler, "The lines of the life of the Church and the life of the American Indians were parallel lines, but they met in infinity which is God."[42] He believed that in this earthly existence, certain symbols were more a cultural expression than an eternal verity, but when placed in an appropriate context, they could serve as a bridge between two different philosophies.

Father Liebler used both Christian and Navajo symbols with an eye to narrowing what appeared to many outsiders to be a huge chasm between the two faiths. When he arrived in Utah, he introduced the Anglican Missal, an English translation of the Roman Catholic Mass. Liebler wanted this "high" church approach because of the colorful vestments, pageantry, and ceremonies that gave worship a very tangible, recognizable form. The Anglican Missal also contained provisions for celebrating more saints' days and the highly visual ceremonies associated with Holy Week and Easter. Joan Liebler recalls Father Liebler saying that "whether the Navajos understand the language or not is not important; what they do recognize is what they see. And if they see a service being conducted in a really reverent, worshipful way, they will respect it. But if you start changing it all over the place, they won't react. The medicine men know their job, and they don't make mistakes and change things around."[43] For at least some Navajos, the clothing itself "made" a person a priest.[44]

The Christian year, with its many holy days, services, and colorful vestments, followed a recognizable pattern, paralleling Navajo

Courtesy, Baxter Benally, family photo.

Father Liebler believed that because Navajo ceremonies were as much a visual and physical experience as they were spiritual and intellectual, he should use the vestments and ritual found in "high" Episcopalian ceremony. Here, two altar boys help serve the sacrament in the church building that incorporated many Navajo values.

ceremonies that were performed according to season. No direct correlation was drawn between the two, but the notion that "to every thing there is a season, and a time to every purpose under heaven" certainly agreed with both beliefs.[45]

The place of worship also needed to be harmonious with both beliefs. Father Liebler realized before establishing Saint Christopher's that the door of the church, to agree with Navajo practices, had to face east so the holy people could observe what took place. Anglican and Roman customs also required that the priest face east. Liebler built a freestanding altar so he could stand behind it and face both east and the congregation at the same time. This was perhaps the first church in the United States to change the location of the altar from its traditional position against the wall of the sanctuary. An additional benefit of this freestanding altar was that the congregation could observe the priest's activities. In Navajo ceremonies, everyone in the hogan is an observer-participant with the medicine man. At Saint Christopher's, the Navajo people could now watch the preparation of the sacrament.[46] The chapel itself was built in a traditional cruciform shape, but Father Liebler used concepts of Navajo etiquette such as never touching both sides of a house or hogan doorway, thus avoiding the entrapment of evil within the building.[47]

Once the chapel was completed and consecrated in an impressive ceremony by an Episcopal bishop, Liebler invited the medicine man Shoodii to perform a blessing on the structure using Navajo prayers and corn pollen—a symbol of peace, fertility, and protection: "In this manner everything will be in harmony and things will come about more easily . . . A person should not just move into a house because there will be something to harm him."[48] A medicine man "dressed traditionally and carrying his ritual tools" performed a similar blessing on the clinic as others looked on.[49]

Other appeals to the senses came in the form of incense and bells. Although incense is a normal part of a "high" Episcopalian service, to the Navajo it equated with the use of cedar smoke for purification in their own observances. The smoke also carried prayers to the holy beings and helped "the people feel good throughout their being . . . These [incense and smoke] are the same."[50] The bell summoned the faithful to worship and marked different times of morning, noon, and night. The people were told that whenever they heard it, no matter where they were, they were to cross themselves. By doing so, they would receive a blessing.[51]

Another auditory part of worship included the music sung in services. For the Navajo, the tune and the words are inseparable. Father Liebler started by using other Indian tribes' melodies with hymns and prayers for the service. The Kyrie Eleison fit into parts of some Hopi snake dance music, the Sanctus into Omaha, and the Agnus Dei into a Zuni melody. Eventually, he took part of the tune from one of the Navajo Night Chants and put the Gloria in Excelsis to it. He expressed misgivings about this action because he knew Navajo thought would automatically revert to the music's previous association. This problem was illustrated during a vesper service held at the mission. The small congregation was singing a hymn when Randolph Benally, who was passing by outside with his flock of sheep, joined in. His words were far different, but the tune was the same—that of the Night Chant.[52]

A final example of a Christian symbol adapted for Navajo use is the Virgin Mary. To make Christmas more memorable, Father Liebler obtained from a priest-friend a set of carved figures for a nativity scene. Mary, Joseph, and Jesus were dressed in Navajo clothing and hairstyles, but the wise men wore full war bonnets as Comanches, since everyone knew Comanches "came from the east." Father Liebler believed it was one of his most successful efforts to bring home the real meaning of Christmas.

Another friend made a three-foot plaster statue of Saint Mary dressed as a Navajo woman and carrying Jesus in a cradleboard. This was placed in the church and was known as "Our Lady of the Navajo" or "Madonna of the Navajo." Navajo mythology has a comparable deity, Changing Woman, who gave birth through supernatural means to twin boys. They, in turn, received powerful, sacred weapons used to destroy evil monsters inhabiting the world. Whether traditional Navajos made this connection between Christ's birth and ministry and that of the Twins is unknown, but certainly the idea was not foreign to their beliefs. As a pedagogical device, the statue served to teach of God's involvement with the Navajos, a theme that found its way into the art done by children attending the mission school.[53] The figure's significance increased in 1964; it was one of the few objects that remained unscathed when the original log church burned. For Liebler, "The God of Truth was not going to let the Father of Lies have his way without some witness . . . She seemed to declare to all who would listen, `Here I stand. Were I not the Mother of God, you would have no Redeemer.'"[54]

The physical tie between the people of the Holy Land and the Navajo was reinforced by teaching part of Genesis. Father Liebler pointed out that when God created man from the dust of the earth, He used the reddish soil in the Middle East, which was comparable to that of southeastern Utah, and that the people living in both places had similar-colored skin.[55]

Hair was of equal importance to skin. There are many teachings in Navajo society concerning the traditional hair bun first instituted by the holy people. Briefly, this hairstyle is the means by which the gods recognize their people so no harm will befall them. It serves as a prayer and protective shield from misfortune and as a means of encouraging rain with its fertility when the hair is unbound in ceremonies. Hair hanging down can also symbolize death, since that is how Navajos are buried. Cutting the hair causes drought.[56]

There are different versions of why Father Liebler adopted this hairstyle. The most prevalent one tells that there was no barbershop nearby, and so he let his hair grow for some time. But the real reason was that long hair was a sign of virility, and he had started growing it before he came to the West. Just before returning to the East for a short visit, he was approached by some Navajo men who asked if he intended to open a school. In Navajo thought, haircuts and school, based upon the older boarding school experience, were synonymous. When Father Liebler replied that there would be a school and then pointed to his long hair and told the men they need not fear that their children would be cropped, he convinced them of his sincerity and convinced himself that this hairstyle was important to keep.[57]

Whether he just stumbled upon this idea or it was more carefully planned is left to conjecture. But there is no doubt as to its effect on his parishioners. In their minds, he was told that he was no longer an Anglo and that he should wear his hair like the People, for "they will be looking at you . . . that was the way to be represented as a conductor of ceremonies."[58] With his hair tied back, he "could say his prayers easily . . . [and he probably thought] that way the Lord will know me. With that the spirit of Navajo traditional ceremonies will know me."[59] He was also taught to mix the scrapings of black lichen in yucca root shampoo to make his hair grow fast and prevent it from graying: "He said, `I remember this and am aware of this.'"[60]

Sometimes the association of Navajo symbols could overpower those of Christianity. In his early struggles with language at Saint Christopher's, Liebler hit upon the idea of using sand paintings to illustrate gospel themes. One Good Friday he took colored sands he had collected and created before the altar in the chapel a picture of the crucified Christ, Saint Mary, and Saint John in elongated form. While he drew this on the ground, he gave fragments of a sermon based on the Franciscan catechism and had Brother Michael and Helen Sturges sing appropriate hymns—all in good keeping with traditional Navajo ceremonialism. At one point in the service he covered the sun with black sand to represent the darkness that spread across the land at Christ's death. Many Navajo people were impressed that a white man would think to create such images.

But they were even more impressed with what they considered the results. Over the next twenty-four hours clouds started to build, and

Courtesy, Baxter Benally, family photo.

Father Liebler's mixing of symbols initially raised eyebrows among some of his priestly peers. The yé'iis on the altar and at his feet, the "Navajo Madonna" and adaptation of the Christmas story, his use of sand paintings, and mixing prayers with Navajo ceremonial music were effective but not without consequences.

within two days heavy, soaking rains pelted southeastern Utah, breaking a lengthy dry spell. Word spread that Father Liebler had strong prayers, could bring moisture to the land through his sand paintings, and had similar powers to heal the sick. The People talked about this event for years to come.[61]

His reputation as a rainmaker preceded him when he opened a satellite mission in Monument Valley. Little Gambler, an elderly medicine man, approached him after Mass and explained that the region was suffering from a major drought, that Father Liebler had the ability to bring rain, and that he should relieve the People's suffering. The priest heard a "voice" that instructed "you will have rain [the] day after tomorrow," which he repeated to the medicine man. Although he had trouble believing he had said that, Father Liebler stood behind his words and was overjoyed when the expected rains appeared on schedule. Later, Little Gambler offered to go into partnership with Liebler, suggesting that the priest "make the prayers for rain" and the medicine man collect the money.[62]

The sky, however, held more than rain. Father Liebler taught the concept of life after death, using as his springboard the translation of Heaven "at the other side of the sky." Traditional Navajos often held a variety of beliefs concerning what to expect in the afterlife. They generally understood that when a person died, his or her spirit lingered to haunt the living because of loneliness, then traveled on a four-day journey to a dark, drab underworld to the north. Relatives and those involved in the burial needed to take ceremonial precautions to avoid unpleasant experiences with those who had passed on.[63] Thus fear and avoidance characterized the general attitude toward death.

Christian doctrine encouraged graveside services, a hope in an afterlife, a judgment based on earthly behavior, and a future resurrection—all of which was antithetical to Navajo teachings. The Christian concept of sin was also difficult for Navajos to follow, since the gods were more concerned with violations of taboos than with personal moral infractions. Father Liebler taught Christian beliefs in relation to a personal harmony and peace between man and God. Penance through confession drove home the necessity of avoiding sin.[64]

MINISTERING TO THE PEOPLE

Father Liebler, as minister of his faith, saw the world as caught in a struggle between right and wrong. This Paulinian duality of light versus darkness, good versus evil, and God versus Satan portrayed a real, tangible battle that took a different form in Navajo beliefs. Liebler referred to himself as a "superstitious son-of-a-gun . . . but the reality of it is that the devil has had a hold on this country for a long time."[65] Father Liebler did all he could to combat these forces.

One of the greatest examples of this power was witchcraft, a common form of which involved "skinwalkers."[66] Briefly, a person who wishes to become a skinwalker learns different ceremonies that turn good power into evil. This is done by reversing what is acceptable, such as prayers for harmony, and saying them in such a way that the person has the power to perform antisocial activities. Killing a family member, making "corpse poison" from the flesh of the dead, causing sickness and loss of livestock, inflicting misfortune, and inviting sterility and death are all actions attributed to witchcraft practitioners.

Father Liebler at times faced problems because of these Navajo beliefs. He had men come to the mission and ask for baptism, but other members accused them of being witches and would not attend services if the accused were present. Since no one ever admits to this activity and a culprit is discovered only through supernatural means of divination, there was no concrete proof on which entrance to the church could be denied. Father Liebler regretted that the prayers for exorcising evil spirits had been removed from the Episcopalian Book of Common Prayer in the past. "There used to be real powerful stuff in it," where the spirit was actually commanded to leave the body.[67] He did believe, however, that baptism removed any unclean spirit from a baby and that at the spirit's departure, the infant cried and one could sometimes smell sulfur.

The priest also used holy water on at least one occasion to chase away a skinwalker. A woman in Monument Valley came to him and complained that she was plagued by a skinwalker who climbed up on her hogan and looked through the smoke hole at the family inside. The priest prayed with her and gave her a small jar of blessed water with the instructions that when she saw the creature peering in again, she should pray silently, then throw the water in his face with the words "Go! Go! In the name of Jesus Christ, go, and never return."[68] She did as she was told and was not bothered again.

Death was often a time of high anxiety for Navajo people. Burial, when possible, was left to a white man to perform—whether a trader, priest, or government employee. Father Liebler tried to explain that once a person was baptized, his or her spirit went to Heaven and was not malevolent. In one instance a man died in a hogan, so according to tradition a hole was to be broken in the north wall, the body carried through it, and the structure abandoned. The widow, one of Liebler's disciples, explained to family and friends that because the man had been baptized, this act was not necessary. The people agreed and followed Christian burial practices.[69]

As a service to the People, Father Liebler established a fenced cemetery near the mission. This was a welcome addition that removed the problem of handling the dead, hiding the body, and worrying that it might be exhumed by witches for the burial goods or body parts used in witchcraft. Sometimes, he would just receive word of where a corpse was located and would have to find it, bring it in, clean and dress the cadaver, and bury it, wrapped completely in a new blanket. The people believed in his prayers, and when he spoke of the remains returning to the land and then sprinkled dirt into the grave, the Navajo approved and quickly adopted the white man's method of burial.

Still, old beliefs persisted. According to some Navajos, Father Liebler had told them to stay away from the cemetery, that evil would overtake them and they would have bad dreams. This seems to be a misunderstanding on their part or an insertion of an earlier understanding quite different from the view Liebler expressed about death and the afterlife. At any rate, 134 graves comprise the cemetery at Saint Christopher's Mission today, a real service to the Navajo people.[70]

There were many other services, what Father Liebler referred to as "fringe benefits" of Christianity, the recounting of which lies far beyond the scope of this discussion. Saint Christopher's sprang from one man's dream; was operated by a host of hardworking, faithful disciples; and reached into many facets of the Navajos' life in southeastern Utah. Through Navajo eyes, the reason was simple—"This Father Liebler could not do any harm"; "He really loved us"; and "They call [him] the missionary that does 'em good—don't just talk."[71]

For approximately twenty years, the mission blossomed into a sort of headquarters for the region's Navajo people. Living quarters, a hospital, school, enlarged chapel, well facilities for mission and community use, and several outbuildings for storage and maintenance helped meet the needs of this growing church community. There were also satellite missions in Montezuma Creek and Monument Valley, along with visits to Navajo Mountain. Saint Christopher's continued to provide services until tribal, state, and federal agencies were able to assume responsibility for the Navajos' health, education, and welfare. Many Navajo children received their first formal education as well as their Anglo names at the mission school. The twelve-bed clinic, with 5,000 registered patients on its files, served as a birthing center and headquarters in the battle to

Courtesy, Baxter Benally, family photo.

At its height, Saint Christopher's Mission supported a hospital and an elementary school, serviced a small airstrip, and held religious services in satellite communities in Montezuma Creek, Oljato/Monument Valley, and Navajo Mountain. Here Liebler interacts with children outside the elementary school.

fight trachoma and tuberculosis.[72] An emergency airstrip south of Bluff allowed for evacuation of seriously ill patients. Father Liebler and his staff improved the water system, from a series of springs at the top of the cliff to drilled wells still used today by local families; through political sources the missionaries obtained a bridge that spanned the San Juan River and allowed children to cross to get to the school; mission staff provided rides for patients to Blanding, Monticello, Cortez, or Shiprock when no other health option existed; and workers constructed visitors' hogans supplied with firewood and a meal for long-distance travelers.

Annual Christmas celebrations drew hundreds of families from near and far to the mission, where they celebrated the season and ate deer and elk meat provided by the Fish and Game Department. Families built campfires on the mission grounds and, when the festivities ended, departed with toys for the children and clothing for everyone, donated by people throughout the United States. Father Liebler also "helped get important papers [legal documents] for us,"[73] provided marriage and family counseling, and became an impromptu judge in local disputes. Even after he left Saint Christopher's in 1966 to "retire" in Monument Valley, he continued his work in a different area for another sixteen years. Old age may have slowed the body, but the vision was still clear.

THE END OF AN ERA

In November 1982, Father Liebler passed from this life. For some, his death and burial were as symbolic as his ministry. His wife, Joan, believes he chose to release his spirit from its failing body only after he had seen his three sons and received the sacrament for the last time.[74] The funeral services, held in Oljato, and the graveside service at Saint Christopher's were conducted in both Navajo and English. An estimated 250 to 300 mourners jammed into the chapel, spilled into the courtyard, and joined in the funeral procession to the grave. His burial was at the site of the original Saint Christopher's chapel that had burned down eighteen years before. Overlooking the grave stood the "Madonna of the Navajo." John Shorty remembered that Father Liebler, when still in his prime, had said, "'I am Catholic and now I am Navajo. I have joined them and I live among them, and when I die of old age, I will be buried among them.' That is how he talked."[75] His wish had come true.

H. Jackson Clark, Father Liebler's friend and business associate, recalled what he considered an appropriate symbol. One lone cottonwood tree still clothed in the green leaves of summer stood above the grave as a "sentry," while all the surrounding trees had lost their foliage. Only a slight breeze stirred the leaves, but once the casket was lowered and the first shovel-full of dirt had been tossed into the grave, a strong wind blew in, the temperature dropped fifteen degrees, and the green leaves swirled away from their branches, stripping the tree. "The feeling of God's love was almost overpowering. The wind died down in a matter of minutes and all was calm. Father Liebler was at peace with his Maker."[76]

Yet it was not his dying but rather his living for which he had become famous. His acceptance of Navajo beliefs as a compatible expression of Christian values presaged a later view of Episcopalian theology. He dared to challenge traditional convention by using symbol and practice from a foreign Navajo worldview while emphasizing tangential points of agreement. He consistently preached the doctrines of his church without isolating himself or his mission from the appreciation and acceptance of the People. As trite as it sounds, to the Navajo he represented a love and kindness that blended faith and works. Few Native Americans or Anglos did not respect the man for his vision.

Today, the San Juan River still courses between its banks, not too distant from the mission. A dozen buildings stand beneath large cottonwood trees, planted at an earlier time for protection from the hot sun. An occasional dust devil swirls around the yard as a pickup truck stops by the well to fill a water barrel. But many of the services that had been part of the mission's daily life have been discontinued. Most of the buildings stand in disrepair, begging a fresh coat of paint and some willing hands to ply hammer and nails.

For many older Navajos, Saint Christopher's represents a place of the past instead of a refuge for the present. They recall the sense of community, the Christmas pageantry, and the clinic and school extending arms to bring health and education to the People. The old ones wish for a return to simpler times. But most of all they miss Father Liebler, his figure draped in priestly robes, hair in a bun, face lit with a smile, speaking fluent Navajo. Perhaps John Shorty's recollection portrays best the mental image older Navajos have of this priest:

> He [Liebler] would go to a Blessing Way ceremony and would bring apricots or peaches in a jar. He would sit there cross-legged with the men. And when they prayed, he would take some corn pollen. The prayer to protect would be performed at night, and he would be given an arrowhead just like they give out to the people. He would hold the arrowhead. "Massage yourself with it, that is what is supposed to be done," was said, and he would do it. He would take corn pollen and according to [tradition he would say,] "Let there be beauty toward me from the east, from the south, from the west where Changing Woman is housed, and from the north . . . Let there be beauty for me from every direction. From where the water flows, let there be beauty toward me; under the plants, let there be beauty toward me; where the gods are, let there be beauty toward me. I am your little one, your child, your grandchild, that is why I ask you. Let me walk in beauty.[77]

Father Liebler's life was a thing of beauty, and in beauty it was finished. For the Navajo, "he stood for them strongly."

NOTES

1. Ada Benally interview with author, February 2, 1994.
2. H. Baxter Liebler, *Boil My Heart for Me* (Salt Lake City: University of Utah Press, 1994).
3. Ibid., 19–20; H. Baxter Liebler interview with Daniel B. Kelly, June 27, 1972, Southeastern Utah Project, Utah State Historical Society, and Fullerton Oral History Program, California State University, 4–5.
4. Marian Huxall Talmadge and Iris Pavey Gilmore, "Padre of the San Juan," *Desert Magazine* 11, no. 10 (August 1948): 8.
5. H. Baxter Liebler, *Moccasin Tracks* (New York: Blackshaw, 1939), 59–60.
6. Ibid., 50.
7. Ibid., 54–59, 85, 94–96.
8. Liebler, *Boil*, 23; Liebler interview with Kelly, 6, 15 (source of the quotation).
9. Liebler, *Boil*, 171–172.
10. Otis Charles, Bishop of Utah, commemorative letter, November 24, 1982, St. Mark's Cathedral, Salt Lake City, UT, in possession of author.
11. H. Baxter Liebler, "The Social and Cultural Patterns of the Navajo Indian," *Utah Historical Quarterly* 30, no. 4 (Fall 1962): 320–322.
12. Other priests have had similar thoughts and experiences—for example, Fathers Pierre Jean De Smet (Flatheads and Pend Oreilles) and Peter Paul Prando (Blackfeet and Crow). What makes this study interesting, though, is not only Liebler's originality in working with the Navajo but also the response and interpretation of the people he converted.
13. Liebler, *Boil*, 30–31.
14. Gladys A. Reichard, *Navaho Religion: A Study of Symbolism* (Princeton, NJ: Princeton University Press, 1950).
15. Joan Liebler interview with author, March 4, 1994.
16. Franciscan Fathers, *An Ethnologic Dictionary of the Navajo Language* (Saint Michaels, AZ: Saint Michaels Press, 1910); Berard Haile, "Soul Concepts of the Navaho," in *Annali Lateranensi* 7: 59–94 (Vatican City: Vatican Polyglot Press, 1943).
17. Liebler interview with Kelly, 63–64; Joan Liebler interview with author; Catherine Pickett interview with author, May 14, 1994.
18. Liebler interview with Kelly, 7; Liebler, *Boil*, 23.
19. Liebler interview with Kelly, 21–22.
20. Dan Benally interview with author, February 2, 1994.
21. Ibid.; Liebler, *Boil,* 44; Ruth White discussion with author, March 14, 1994.
22. Obviously, many Navajos met Father Liebler and chose not to accept his religion. No doubt, some may have resented his "invasion" of their traditional beliefs. As one reads this chapter, a generally positive view of his work is presented. Yet in all of the interviews I did concerning Saint Christopher's, I never heard about any real dissent concerning the man or his mission. Perhaps part of the reason is that he did not force anyone to accept things not to their liking; another reason is that he often served as the Navajos' advocate in the white communities; another is that he often held large celebrations (especially around Christmastime) during which food, clothing, and children's gifts were dispensed to Episcopalian members and non-members alike; and finally, he provided medical care, education, limited

legal and social counseling, and assistance with burials to people who had very few other places to turn for such help. Thus his brand of missionary work was not invasive, as he consciously worked on social relations as much as he did on the more philosophical religious aspects.

23. Liebler, *Boil*, 16, 19; White discussion with author.
24. Dan Benally interview with author; Mary Rose Sampson and John Sampson interview with author, February 9, 1994; Talmadge and Gilmore, "Padre of the San Juan," 6; White discussion with author.
25. Liebler, *Boil*, 56.
26. Dan Benally interview with author.
27. Fernandez Begay interview with author, February 2, 1994.
28. Dan Benally interview with author.
29. Liebler, *Boil*, 114.
30. Fernandez Begay interview with author.
31. Ibid.
32. Jessie Shorty interview with author, February 9, 1994.
33. Ibid.
34. Ibid.; Ada Benally interview with author; John Shorty interview with author, February 2, 1994; Liebler, *Boil*, 82.
35. Dan Benally interview with author.
36. John Shorty interview with author.
37. Liebler, *Boil*, 91.
38. Fernandez Begay interview with author.
39. Dan Benally interview with author.
40. John Shorty interview with author.
41. H. Baxter Liebler, "Christian Concepts and Navaho Words," *Utah Humanities Review* 2, no. 2 (April 1948): 174.
42. Liebler interview with Kelly, 6.
43. Joan Liebler interview with author.
44. Ibid.; Pickett interview with author; Dan Benally interview with author.
45. King James version of *The Holy Bible* (Salt Lake City: Deseret Book, n.d.).
46. Pickett interview with author.
47. Liebler, *Boil*, 197.
48. Liebler, *Moccasin*, 71; Sampson and Sampson interview with author; Dan Benally interview with author.
49. John Shorty interview with author.
50. Sampson and Sampson interview with author (source of the quotation); Dan Benally interview with author.
51. Fernandez Begay interview with author.
52. Liebler, *Boil*, 101–102; Talmadge and Gilmore, "Padre of the San Juan," 9.
53. Joan Liebler interview with author; Talmadge and Gilmore, "Padre of the San Juan," 6.
54. Liebler, *Boil*, 62, 122.
55. Pickett interview with author.
56. George Tom interview with author, August 7, 1991; Ada Black interview with author, October 11, 1991; Stella Cly interview with author, August 7, 1991; Ben Whitehorse interview with author, January 30, 1991.

57. Pickett interview with author; Talmadge and Gilmore, "Padre of the San Juan," 6.
58. Dan Benally interview with author.
59. Fernandez Begay interview with author.
60. Dan Benally interview with author.
61. Liebler, *Boil*, 67–70; Pickett interview with author; Liebler interview with Kelly, 40.
62. Liebler, *Boil*, 97–98; Liebler interview with Kelly, 27.
63. Liebler, "Christian Concepts," 174–175; see also Haile, "Soul Concepts."
64. Joan Liebler interview with author; Liebler, *Boil*, 60–61.
65. Liebler interview with Kelly, 43.
66. For easily accessible reading about Navajo witchcraft, see Clyde Kluckhohn, *Navajo Witchcraft* (Boston: Beacon, 1944); Margaret K. Brady, *Some Kind of Power: Navajo Children's Skinwalker Narratives* (Salt Lake City: University of Utah Press, 1984).
67. Liebler interview with Kelly, 44–45.
68. H. Jackson Clark, *The Owl in Monument Canyon* (Salt Lake City: University of Utah Press, 1993), 79; Joan Liebler interview with author.
69. Liebler, *Boil*, 189; Joan Liebler interview with author; Clark, *Owl in Monument Canyon* (source of the quotation).
70. Baxter Benally discussion with author, February 9, 1994; Fernandez Begay interview with author; John Shorty interview with author; Joan Liebler interview with author; Pickett interview with author; Toni Turk, *Rooted in San Juan: A Genealogical Study of Burials in San Juan County, Utah, 1879–1995* (Salt Lake City: Publishers Press, 1995), 585–601.
71. Dan Benally interview with author; Jessie Shorty interview with author; Liebler interview with Kelly, 26.
72. Pickett interview with author.
73. Dan Benally interview with author.
74. Liebler, *Boil*, 205; Joan Liebler interview with author.
75. John Shorty interview with author.
76. Clark, *Owl in Monument Canyon,* 82.
77. John Shorty interview with author.

7

Seeing Is Believing

The Odyssey of the Pectol Shields

The issue of repatriation of Indian artifacts has become an ever-increasingly heated topic in today's culturally sensitive society. Although NAGPRA (Native American Graves Protection and Repatriation Act), initiated in 1990, established a process by which this can be accomplished, the road to do so is rarely smooth. Individual, tribal, and governmental agency interpretation of where an object belongs is not always clearly spelled out in the archaeological and historical record or in Native Americans' oral traditions. Even the tribes themselves cannot always agree. Many objects such as medicine bundles, religious masks, and other ceremonial paraphernalia have been willingly returned to the Navajo Nation for safekeeping, restoration, or use. Other items located in public repositories have been subject to long disputes.

This chapter looks at the history of the Pectol shields, a well-known story that began in 1926 and did not end until

DOI: 10.7330/9781607322177.c07

> *2003. The shields, since their unearthing, have been subject to various interpretations on origins based on different religious beliefs and social science findings. It was not until Navajo medicine man John Holiday provided testimony that the government reached a final NAGPRA ruling as to their deposition. The importance of Navajo oral tradition and culture in reaching this conclusion cannot be overemphasized. The history of the shields makes plain that it was not enough to have only a religious or scientific view of their origin; it required a cohesive cultural pattern long practiced to make the difference. Future decisions of this nature may very well call again upon the power of Navajo tradition and culture.*

Sparks from the piñon and juniper fire rose into the black night sky. Shadows danced on the low alcove's walls, flames flickering with wind currents. Nine figures crowded beneath or stood outside a low overhanging ledge, as some bent forward digging and peering into a hole in the sandy-bottomed cave. There was nothing to distinguish this particular site, a mere four feet by six feet, from any other of the countless crevices and rock niches surrounding the little town of Torrey and what would later become Capitol Reef National Park, Utah. Supervising the excavation was Ephraim Portman Pectol, a Latter-day Saint (LDS) bishop, entrepreneur, and promoter of Wayne County. His wife, Dorothy; three daughters; their son-in-law, Claude Holt; and three other men assisted with what everyone anticipated to be a Native American burial of some type. Earlier that day Ephraim and Dorothy had discovered a cedar bark covering eighteen inches beneath the sandy floor of the cave. They decided to let family members share the thrill of discovery, returning with them and others in the evening for an enjoyable outing. Growing anticipation accompanied the unveiling, with Ephraim hoping to add something significant to his burgeoning collection of Indian artifacts on display at home.

It was August 16, 1926, twenty years after the US Congress passed the Antiquities Act to protect archaeological sites from collectors and vandals. In southern Utah, however, professional archaeologists as well as avocational pot hunters burrowed into ruins, burials, and any other site that might hold objects left behind by prehistoric Indians. Today, many of the efforts of even the "trained, professional" archaeologists of the time would be classified more as looting than scientific excavation. Collecting was everyone's intent. While large Ancestral Puebloan (Anaasází) ruins like Mesa Verde (Colorado) and Chaco Canyon (New Mexico) had been under the spade and trowel of the Wetherill family at the turn of the twentieth century, what seemed to be endless smaller sites drew less attention and were easily accessible to local people. In south-central Utah where Pectol lived, the highly developed Anaasází material culture gave way to the less dramatic Fremont remains. Still, there were objects to be had and no telling what might be unearthed during a dig of discovery.

Scraping away more dirt and removing a four-inch cedar bark covering, Ephraim exposed a circular piece of hide approximately thirty-six inches in diameter. Expecting to find a body with a few primitive tools, his eyes must have bulged when he beheld three buffalo-hide shields painted in dazzling multicolored geometric patterns. Lifting the objects out of the ground and into the flickering firelight, he "unearthed three of the most wonderful shields ever seen by man. As we raised the front shield the design on two shields came to view. For the space of what seemed two or three minutes, no one seemed to breathe; we were so astonished. We felt we were in the presence of the one who had buried the shields. And these words came to me while in this condition: 'Nephites and Gadianton Robbers.'"[1] Beneath the last object was a cone of earth that maintained the convex shape of the tanned leather shields with their arm and neck carrying straps; next was a bottom layer of cedar bark to guard against moisture.

PECTOL'S AND OTHER LDS INTERPRETATIONS

What Pectol really discovered that evening was the beginning of a controversy that remains to this day. Ephraim Pectol, very much a man of his time, filtered what he saw through what he believed. His initial response to what he saw as Nephites and Gadianton Robbers was totally in keeping with his experience as an LDS bishop for sixteen years, steeped in the teachings of the *Book of Mormon*.[2] Three transoceanic crossings of Israelites before the time of Christ, the rise and fall of the Nephite and Lamanite civilizations, the belief that their descendants were directly connected with today's Native Americans, and all of the religious teachings recorded before the fall of their society furnished dramatic fare for interpreting archaeological remains. Mormons living in southern Utah did not hesitate to connect ancient Indian artifacts and sites with these events. Even the discovery of the shields took on religious tones. Dorothy, guided by the Spirit, had directed her husband, who had not received as strong an impression of where to dig: "You must dig into this and you will find something."[3] And he did.

Others soon added their interpretations of what was discovered that August night. A local newspaper, the *Richfield Reaper*, declared the shields "an archeological discovery of great value to science and hardly measurable in monetary valuation." The biggest question for the writers at the *Reaper* was how to interpret the "quite elaborate designs . . . visible on the shields, undoubtedly pictographs which have not yet been deciphered but quite evidently they tell some kind of a history or legend." Archaeologist Andrew Kerr from the University of Utah agreed that it was "one of the most valuable finds recently made," but he stood clear of any interpretation.[4]

Ephraim Pectol, however, was quite certain what the designs meant. He quickly declared that the shields were Nephite and interpreted the designs through LDS doctrine: "Shield No. 1 [now referred to in the literature as CARE (Capitol Reef) 11] . . . is interpreted as representing creation. This universe is represented in orange color; light has penetrated this universe. And in the distance we see an earth has come into existence. The light has then encircled the universe."[5] Teachings from the Bible's Book of Genesis and LDS theology emphasize the importance of light while God was creating the earth and during spiritual encounters. Pectol viewed the shields as a chronological recounting of the sacred story of the creation and other early scriptural events.

The second shield (CARE 191) "represents to me the peopling of this earth after it had been created, or the second stage of human religion."[6] According to the *Book of Mormon*, a group of people, the Jaredites, came to the Americas around the time of the Tower of Babel. They traveled across the ocean in eight barges, represented by as many lines on the shield, to inhabit the new world: "This is a very important event in the history of the Nephites. The Lamanites received knowledge of this event . . . The thought would naturally come to [them that] the earth had been created and was peopled by the Great Spirit who sent eight barges across the water and peopled the earth."[7]

The third shield (CARE 12) went further into LDS beliefs: "Shield No. 3 represents the return stage of human religion and that is what shall become of the people who have peopled this earth that had been created." Pectol saw the span of human life reflected in CARE 12. The center black stripe "represents the beginning of man's existence upon the earth as being born in sin, represented by the black."[8] Above this stripe is a succession of lines and stripes: "From our birth we have the privilege of entering the kingdom of Satan, which is represented by the lower part of the shield, or we may go into the kingdom of God, represented by the upper half of the shield. The first row of stripes represents the Terrestrial Glory; the second row the Telestial, and the third row the Celestial."[9] Latter-day Saints believe that instead of a dualistic heaven-hell in the afterlife, there are three degrees or kingdoms of glory and a fourth realm of outer darkness to which the dead are assigned as part of a final judgment. Choice during this earth life is a determinant as to where each person goes. There is no predestination, and his reference to being "born in sin" is not part of LDS theology. (A child is viewed as incapable of sinning before the age of accountability, which is age eight.) Still, family members joined with their patriarch in asserting that, as did daughter Leona, the objects "are associated and a part of our *Book of Mormon*."[10]

The shields were not the only artifacts the Pectols viewed through religious eyes. In the general vicinity of his first find, Ephraim later discovered what he called the burial robes. Made from animal skins, this clothing was allegedly discovered close to the grave of an infant. Some people believe Earl Behunin, another local collector from Torrey, actually unearthed the robes. Neither account gives an indication of when they were found.[11] Regardless of who found the robes and when, Pectol perceived similarities between them and LDS temple robes. On the "skin we call the robe we find marks similar to the marks of the priesthood." There were also "four belts, or strips of buckskin . . . an antelope skin tanned with the hair on, we are pleased to call the apron, and a piece of mountain sheep skin, also tanned with hair on, we represent as the cap."[12] Because of the LDS garment's sacred nature to practitioners, he did not delve any deeper in comparing them to the robes he found.

As Pectol's collection of artifacts grew, eventually reaching over 200 Indian objects in his museum, he became increasingly fascinated by

Courtesy, Neal Busk.

Ephraim Pectol and his two daughters, Golda (*left*) and Devona (*right*), display the three shields they unearthed in a small alcove on August 16, 1926. A devout Mormon, Pectol interpreted the painting on the shields according to teachings of his faith found in stories from the *Book of Mormon.*

the archaeological remains around Torrey. He did not hesitate to place his interpretation on those remains, either. Two ruins sprang to life as

> the remains of fortresses behind which the ancient inhabitants fought their intruding foes. These forts are about one mile apart and are built on prominent points of vantage. The myriad of broken arrow points in and around these forts and the valley strewn with hundreds of graves tells its own gruesome story of how two mighty opposing forces once fought for possession of this land. How perhaps for weeks the battle raged. We picture women and children under cover of darkness carrying food and water to the entrenched braves, and another force of skilled workmen at the ammunition factory discovered by Dr. A. A. Kerr and myself . . . about three miles west of the battleground, with another force of runners hurrying the manufactured arrows to the battle front. At last the entrenched army seeing defeat at hand demolished everything of value to the foe, and under

> cover of darkness retreated to the southwest carrying with them whatever belongings remained, and bidding "goodbye" as they passed to their homes nestled among the cliffs. Dawn finds the enemy in hot pursuit.[13]

Pectol expressed a deeply poetic sentiment that connected him as much to his own religion as it did to the early inhabitants of southern Utah.

A year after the discovery of the shields, the *Improvement Era*, a magazine published by the LDS church, printed an article titled "The High Priest's Vestments."[14] Author Frank Beckwith interviewed the Pectols and adopted their stance that the shields proved the spirituality and dignity of early Native Americans and implied a connection with Hebrew tradition. Relating how the shields were first discovered, Beckwith described the "three great circular pieces, symbolic [as] vestments of the High Priest of that land in a time of long ago."[15] One can assume that by this point the clothing and shields were linked in an interpretation that connected the two as visual metaphors of objects associated with temple ceremonies. The author's flowery monologue pictures a "High Priest, having performed the sacred duties" and a "solemn and sacred march before God," removing his "sacred vestments" and in the "dead of night when all the air seemed to breathe a secret purpose" hiding the objects from the "profane gaze of the unworthy."[16] Secret and sacred, the objects assumed contemporary religious values.

Beckwith, like Pectol, imaginatively described how these objects were used. He declared that, though the "popular mind" would see the shields as weapons,

> the thoughtful, the prudent, the student of the lore of an ancient and deeply religious people, will see in them the symbolic insignia of [the] office of the High Priest, and will in fancy, picture him in deerskin cap, fur headdress, and kilts or robes about his loins, buckskin garments clothing his person underneath, and with one of these wonderful objects on his arm. The eldest High Priest, of topmost authority, will carry the four-colored, highly emblematic one; his attendants a lesser one, in accordance with their lesser rank. And each, in ensemble, will personify symbolically the natural forces he represents in his person in the forthcoming religious rites.[17]

In addition to picturing the shields used by ancient high priests, Beckwith was eager to add his own interpretation of each shield. He regarded CARE 191 as the most important: "It has four symbolic colors, dear to the ancient Indian heart—red, black, green and yellow." These colors represented the sun, rain clouds, corn leaves, and mature corn ears, respectively. Where Pectol focused on its eight black lines for interpretation, Beckwith found deep significance in the "seven rays of green . . . The sacred number seven so outcrops among our ancient inhabitants as to cause one to pause with wonder." This number supported his theory that "the ancient Indian was descended from Judah." He also saw the shields reflected in various ceremonial dances, such as the Dance of the Ayash Tyocotz, an unspecified Pueblo Indian ceremony.[18] Beckwith's interpretation did not coincide with Pectol's, but both men were imaginatively graphic in depicting what they believed.

Beckwith's article brought the shields to the attention of the LDS community, and the news continued to spread. They became the subject of a variety of firesides and talks Pectol gave in southern Utah.[19] Lecturing in church meetings, town halls, and other public sites, he shared his knowledge and interpretation of the artifacts across Utah, with word spreading to California.[20] The Hollywood Stake Mutual Improvement Association (MIA) printed an article in the *Improvement Era* explaining that the Nephites had used shields to defend against their enemies. The Pectol shields, representative of *Book of Mormon* shields, "have been reproduced in Hollywood Stake and used in presenting the M.I.A. slogan . . . the suggestion being given that a shield in the form of our M.I.A. slogan would be probably just as efficacious and desirable today as in the time of the Nephites in protecting the more vital parts of the body."[21]

THE SHIELDS: FAME, DEFAME, AND REINTERPRETATION

A continual proponent of Wayne County, Pectol spread information about the Capitol Reef area's prehistoric treasures. He showed the Noel Morss archaeological expedition a few Fremont sites around Torrey in 1928 and 1929. Morss was the first archaeologist to designate the Fremont Indians as a distinct culture. Pectol and Morss revisited the rock shelter where the shields had been discovered in hopes of finding more objects to provide contextual clues to the shields, but they found nothing. Morss recognized that the shields were anomalous in the archaeological record, and in his report on the Fremont River drainage he expressed "the opinion that these remarkable shields date from comparatively recent if not historic times. This conclusion is based on their uniqueness among objects of ancient origin, on their resemblance to modern Athabascan shields . . . The shields, while modern from the point of view of the Fremont culture, may still be old from a historical standpoint."[22]

In addition to archaeologists, other people visited Torrey to see the shields, which Pectol shellacked for protection, as he did many of his other artifacts.[23] In August 1929, Edward Southwick visited the museum and recorded Pectol's account of finding the shields and vestments. He took pictures of the objects but did not show them until Elder George F. Richards of the Quorum of the Twelve Apostles gave him permission to do so.[24] The holdings in the museum drew others to Wayne Wonderland, a new name for the area now known as Capitol Reef and environs. Charles Kelly—writer, researcher, and adventurer—initially came to Torrey to visit Pectol's museum. In 1943 he became the first custodian of Capitol Reef National Park.[25] The artifacts were also highly revered among Pectol's family members. His grandson, Neal Busk, remembers playing a Fremont flute in the room above his general merchandise store, something that would surely make an archaeologist shudder.[26]

When asked where he found the shields, Pectol had Joe Covington, his grandson, lead the inquirers to the rock shelter by a circuitous route coming and going, making it difficult to relocate. Covington, with clear conscience, took the people to the spot designated by Pectol, who had intentionally misinformed him. The discoverer regarded the real site sensitive and sacred enough to keep it hidden from all except his closest kin. Covington was surprised years later when a family member led him to the real spot.[27]

Ephraim Pectol continued his life of accomplishment. He became noted as an avid booster of Wayne County and worked to bring federal protection to parts of it, as well as services such as telephones, roads, and an airport. Along with Joseph Hickman, he was one of the founding fathers of Capitol Reef National Monument, established by presidential proclamation in 1937.[28] This major step in preservation reached fruition following his election to the Utah State Legislature in 1933, where he used his position as a bully pulpit for the establishment of a national park during President Franklin Delano Roosevelt's administration.[29] Yet his most enduring fame is tied to the shields he uncovered that August night.[30]

As the federal government became increasingly interested in the region that soon became a national tourist attraction, it also became concerned about allegations of stolen Indian artifacts held by citizens of Wayne County. The federal government sent G. G. Frazier to Torrey in September 1932 to investigate these reports. He found little evidence of illegal collection, except for Pectol and Charles W. Lee. Both men ran informal private museums displaying their holdings. As the locals "knew nothing of the location of the lands from which they [Pectol's and Lee's artifacts] were gathered," Frazier relied on testimony from the two men to determine if the objects had been taken from public lands.[31] Pectol had found the shields a few miles east of Torrey on lands now managed by the Bureau of Land Management (BLM)—not, as is commonly thought, within what is now Capitol Reef.[32]

Frazier reported that Pectol was a "well educated man" who believed "he has connected the American Indians with the South Sea Islanders [and] also that he can prove the history of the Indian as interpreted from the shields is the same as described in the 'Book of Mormon.'" In advanced old age, Lee was "apparently very childish . . . His sole income is derived from a ten cent admission charge to view the collection." Frazier confiscated the artifacts the men had found on public lands but decided, "It is my belief that it would be impossible to enforce the Antiquities Act of 1906 one hundred percent." He recommended that "no action be taken and the relics remain in their custody until it is decided whether or not a national park will be declared in Wayne County, Utah."[33]

The artifacts remained in the museums run by Pectol and Lee until they apparently loaned their combined collection, including the artifacts to be confiscated by Frazier, to the LDS church's Bureau of Information and Temple Square Mission in Salt Lake City. This occurred sometime before 1939. The Temple Square Mission ran the museum for the church as part of its proselyting efforts, so the shields, robes, and other Pectol artifacts were displayed.[34]

Members of the LDS church found the "High Priest's Vestments" even more fascinating than the shields. Their interest went beyond simple historical curiosity to a spiritual acceptance of the robes. President John H. Taylor of the Temple Square Mission wrote to Bishop Pectol in September 1941 because a Brother Brown wanted to take

Courtesy, Neal Busk.

Ephraim Pectol in his museum in Torrey, Utah. This collection of artifacts has been loaned to several organizations over the years and now resides in the College of Eastern Utah Museum, Utah State University, in Price. The shields have a different story and are now in the possession of the Navajo Nation.

some pictures of your materiel which you have in our case. He particularly wanted to take a picture of the garment, indicating where the marks are. I suggested that he write to you and also suggested that I would speak to the brethren. They felt that it would not be just the best thing to do to permit pictures to be taken of the garment and exhibit [them], even if done so under the good auspices of Brother Brown . . . I am sure you see the wisdom of this, because of the different attitudes that many people would take in regard to it. In addition, it would only emphasize the marks, etc. on the regular garment.[35]

Taylor thought there would be no harm in Brown taking pictures of the shields, however. If these articles of skin clothing were in fact sacred replicas of LDS temple clothing, it is surprising that the church allowed them to be displayed publicly.

Other people saw connections among Masonic ritual, LDS temple ceremonies, and the Indian robes as proof of the validity of LDS doctrine. Pectol opened the discussion when he wrote that "the marks are in the robe . . . if this is truly intended for the purpose it suggests, then the shields I have represent the remainder of the Temple ordinances." In 1947 Elmer McGavin made the connection to Masonry while answering a question about the temple ceremony and its connection to Masonic rites. The robes, he stated, were "undeniable evidence" that the Mormons had not received their temple practices from the Masons: "These skins have been examined by hundreds of people . . . Their genuineness and antiquity cannot be denied. The marks are as distinct and visible as emblems on a Mason's badge or watch fob; yet these skins were certainly marked before 1842, when the Mormons were admitted into Masonry." McGavin told about a skeptical friend who saw the robes and proclaimed, "This was the most valuable evidence ever produced in defense of the Mormon religion."[36]

Others were less convinced. Wallace Stegner cast a suspicious glance at the robes: "The find itself, a deerskin marked with the mystic temple symbols of the Church, is reported to be locked in a strong box in the Church offices in Salt Lake . . . The Church has not seen fit to display it in the Church Museum in Temple Square, [so] it must be either very sacred or very dangerous. One old gentleman who saw it before it was sent to Salt Lake remarked that maybe the temple symbols were on it, if you looked right, but if you looked just the regular way it looked as if the mice had chewed it."[37] While Stegner is correct in asserting that the church thought the robes were very sacred, why he thought the robes were locked away is a mystery. They were publicly displayed at Temple Square from 1939 to 1964, then moved to Capitol Reef.[38] The "High Priest's Vestments" remain with Pectol family members.

OF ARCHAEOLOGY AND MUSEUMS

Archaeologists took up their own professional dialogue, removing the discussion from a religious basis to scientifically measurable description. However, once the descriptive analysis ended and interpretation began, there were varying thoughts among the archaeologists. A brief review of some notable participants provides a glimpse of differing theories. As previously noted, Morss thought the shields were not made by members of the Fremont culture but were most likely fashioned during historic times. Carling Malouf, writing for *American Antiquity* in 1944, included the shields in a list of Utah's archaeological "finds which appear entirely out of place."[39] He thought the shields "may not have as great . . . antiquity as has been claimed" and might be from a post-Puebloan period. H. (Hannah) M. (Marie) Wormington countered this in *A Reappraisal of the Fremont Culture* (1955). Her argument centered around the fact that since the Fremont Indians had many pictographs of large shields, "It seems highly probable . . . that these shields are also of Fremont origin."[40] In 1966, C. Melvin Aikens proposed a possible Plains Indian origin for the Fremont. He pictured them originating in the northwestern Plains, migrating to southern Utah, and embracing the already existing Puebloan cultures. Aikens noted that such an explanation "accounts for . . . northwestern Plains-type shield pictographs . . . [and] the Pectol Shields," along with other apparent anomalies in the Fremont culture.[41]

While the archaeologists bantered back and forth, two of the shields were returned from Temple Square to Wayne County. Charles Kelly, now superintendent of Capitol Reef National Monument, felt that all of Pectol's "artifacts are from the Basketmaker II period of the Fremont River culture" and should be housed in the area from whence they came.[42] The church's Bureau of Information delayed releasing the artifacts until the question of ownership was decided. Pectol insisted that some of Lee's artifacts had been sold or traded to Pectol, but the paperwork was incomplete, so Lee's family disputed the claim. In addition, the federal government demanded that the church give up the artifacts that had been collected on BLM land. In 1951 the Pectol and Lee families agreed to display the artifacts not claimed by the government in Wayne County. The Temple Square Museum was further convinced by letters from Pectol that made it clear that the artifacts had been loaned only temporarily to the church. The Pectol and Lee families then loaned the National Park Service all of Pectol's and Lee's artifacts. The Park Service moved most of the artifacts back to Wayne County in 1953.[43]

One shield and two pieces of the High Priest's Vestments remained in Salt Lake City at the request of Elder Richard L. Evans of the Quorum of the Twelve Apostles. He felt the artifacts should stay at the museum so they could be seen by the "million or more visitors a year" who went through Temple Square.[44] The two shields and most of Pectol's artifacts remained in Torrey instead of Capitol Reef because the park lacked facilities to house them. Instead, they were loaned to the owners of Pectol's old store/museum, Bernard Tracy and Arthur "Doc" Inglesby, who invested $500 in cases for the shields and other artifacts. In 1957 the men requested that the objects be removed in preparation for a new restaurant and hotel being added to the store.[45] The National Park Service temporarily relocated the pieces to a storage facility until 1961, when they were sent to Capitol Reef. The artifacts loaned to the church were soon returned as well, and the park opened a new visitors' center in 1965. Most of the Pectol-Lee collection was then displayed or housed at the park, where Ephraim Pectol had always hoped they would reside.[46]

Placing the shields in Capitol Reef did not quiet the debate over origin; in fact, the discussion actually increased. In 1967 archaeologist Gilbert R. Wenger expressed concern that their presence in the park might misinform the public by implying a Fremont origin:

> We do not feel that these fine specimens should be eliminated [from the exhibit] . . . Even if we eliminate specific reference that the shields are of Fremont origin their association with specimens of the Fremont Culture would infer as much. Preferably, we would rather take a straightforward approach and state in the label something to the effect that "Although these shields were recovered in caves where Fremont items have been found, recent scientific tests suggest they may not be quite as old as the other Fremont materials. Continuing archaeological studies may provide the final answer."[47]

The park's curator took Wenger's advice, labeling the shields accordingly.

A year later the Park Service put the issue of Fremont origin to rest when it received its first set of radiocarbon dates from UCLA. A small piece from the third shield (CARE 12) dated between AD 1650 and 1750.[48] The Fremont culture is generally accepted as having flourished from AD 70 to 1250.[49] In the 1990s the New Zealand Department of Scientific and Industrial Research obtained a second set of radiocarbon dates. The range was much wider and earlier, between AD 1420 and 1640, but still too late for a Fremont origin.[50]

ENTER NATIVE AMERICANS AND NAGPRA

For forty-six years, the shields rested comfortably in their display case at Capitol Reef, receiving an occasional mention in archaeological journals. Then in 1998, enter for the first time the Native American view. Representatives from Zuni Pueblo visited Capitol Reef and saw some small hide-wrapped bundles containing bone, which they considered sensitive grave objects, on display. At their request the items were removed. While the relatively new Native American Graves Protection and Repatriation Act, passed in 1990, was not cited for removal of the items, the spirit of the law was evident.[51] Under this law the federal government recognized the rights of Indian people to their ancestors' cultural items, such as funerary, sacred, and other cultural objects as well as human remains. Every museum and federal agency was required to inventory and notify Native American tribes of any objects that met these criteria. The artifacts were to be repatriated "expeditiously" to a requesting tribe after it demonstrated cultural affiliation with the artifact. The ruling criteria for this determination were to provide a "preponderance of the evidence based upon geographical, kinship, biological, archaeological, anthropological, linguistic, folkloric, oral tradition, historical, or relevant information or expert opinion."[52]

Rather than have the Pectol-Lee collection broken up by repatriation, the Pectol and Lee families asked that the artifacts that had been loaned to the Park Service be returned to them. Two shields stayed on display at the park, and the other remained at the Park Service's Western Archaeological and Conservation Center in Tucson. In 1996 the Park Service returned the remainder of the collection, containing over 200 artifacts, to the Pectol family.[53] They remained in private hands until the family negotiated an agreement with Brigham Young University's Museum of Peoples and Cultures to accept them for temporary display. A family member described the day the artifacts left his house as "one of the happiest days of my life," as he no longer had to worry about their safety.[54] Following the run of the exhibit, the Pectol-Lee collection went to the College of Eastern Utah in Price, where they are currently located.

In 1998 the federal government required all national parks to remove NAGPRA items from display. The two remaining shields joined the third shield in the National Park Service's Western Archaeological and Conservation Center in Tucson.[55] They then became subject to repatriation. The Navajo Nation was the first to submit a claim. By 2002 the Utes in Uintah, the Paiute Tribe of Utah, and the Kaibab Band of Paiutes had also entered a joint repatriation request, as had the Southern Ute and Ute Mountain Ute Tribes in Colorado. The primary argument offered by all claimants, except the Navajo, was rooted in cultural affiliation. The lands where the shields surfaced were traditionally those of the Paiute and Ute people. The Navajos provided a far more detailed explanation of the origin and use of the shields.

In an effort to maintain impartiality while assigning ownership, the government hired four scholars—Lawrence Loendorf, Barton A. Wright, Benson L. Lanford, and Polly Schaafsma—to prepare independent studies of the shields. Based on physical evidence that included materials used in construction and decoration, prehistoric rock art, historic tribal locations, cultural practices, and other considerations, each person was to suggest which tribe he or she thought had made the shields or state that affiliation could not be reasonably established. There was no definitive agreement. Loendorf compared the shields to rock art from the time period of the shields' creation and "tentatively" concluded that two of them were made by Athabascan speakers, meaning Navajo or Apache. The other shield, CARE 191, he believed came from a Puebloan group, possibly Jemez, who were allied with the Navajo during the time the shields were made. This explained how the Navajos obtained it.[56]

Barton Wright compared the Pectol shields to early historic accounts and specimens of Navajo shields. Using this information, he believed the Navajo shields of the time the Pectol shields were made usually had hair on them and frequently an animal design. He declared "in my estimation the Navajo shields do not bear any resemblance to the Pectol Shields . . . The shields that are closest in form resemble the Pueblo type more than the Pectol ones."[57] Benson L. Lanford took a broad view of southern Utah material culture. He looked particularly at painted leather objects from a wide array of cultures and came to the conclusion that the shields were Apache in origin.[58]

Loendorf, Wright, and Lanford submitted their studies in 2001, while rock art specialist Polly Schaafsma submitted her findings in 2002, responding to their methodology. She argued for a Ute origin, declaring that the other studies were flawed and that the shields' discovery on Ute lands identified the real owner. Schaafsma specifically attacked the validity of Navajo oral tradition by saying that Pectol's interpretation "could become the 'basis' for yet another claim, on equal footing with any other story."[59]

JOHN HOLIDAY AND THE NAVAJO INTERPRETATION

What Schaafsma was reacting against was another form of historical record that lies directly at odds with the archaeological emphasis placed on physical, measurable objects. The Navajo Tribe asked John Holiday, a Navajo medicine man and prime witness, and three other tribal members to testify on behalf of its claim.[60] Born in Monument Valley, Utah, around 1919, John grew up in the traditional environment that eventually led to his becoming a Blessing Way singer and a repository of cultural and historical knowledge.[61] On March 8, 2001, the Navajo contingent met with National Park Service officials at the Western Archaeological and Conservation Center. Lee Kreutzer, cultural resources program manager of Capitol Reef and lead investigator for the repatriation claims, held a second meeting with John and two men from the Navajo Nation Historic Preservation Department (NNHPD) in Monument Valley on May 7, 2002.[62] He not only named the individuals who made the shields and told how they got to the burial site, but he also interpreted the meaning of the designs and the powers they held. What follows is a brief summary.

John has knowledge of family members who lived in the vicinity of the No Name (Henry) Mountains, White Face (Boulder) Mountain, and the area southeast of Richfield along the Fremont River. This was prior to the 1860s and the period known to the Navajo as the Fearing Time and the Long Walk, when many were forced into exile at Fort Sumner, New Mexico. This region is not traditionally viewed as Navajo land but rather as Ute territory. The Navajos, who were following a nomadic, herding, hunting-and-gathering lifestyle at this time, were constantly searching for verdant lands. John's grandmother, Woman with Four Horns (named after the type of goats she raised), herded sheep in this area and was able to name other Navajo families living close by.[63]

According to John, the powers of the shields were created spiritually at the beginning of the earth, as were medicine bundles used for healing and protection. The holy people are the ones who control their powers and assisted the first person who made the physical shields in question. These objects are both a representation of nature's invisible powers and a living

Photo by Stan Byrd.

John Holiday, Blessing Way singer from Monument Valley, played a crucial role during the shield repatriation process. His detailed knowledge of family history and explanation of these objects' ceremonial significance led to the determination that they belonged to the Navajo instead of other tribal groups living in the same region.

entity that can control and use those powers on the Navajos' behalf. The shields had been in the possession of eight generations of medicine men before the Fort Sumner experience.[64] Objects of this nature are viewed as alive and so must be "fed" or renewed with songs, prayers, and pollen or sacred stone (ntł'iz) offerings. Transmission of the shields, as with medicine bundles (jish), is made from one medicine man to another, not within a single family.

Prior to the time of the Long Walk, a series of medicine men—some of whom were from the Capitol Reef area—held the responsibility to renew and safeguard the protective shields. Many Goats with White Hair created the shields, making them in the Kaibab Mountains in a thick pine forest with a circular clearing.[65] Custody of the shields went to Man Who Keeps His Mouth Open, then Yellow Forehead, Tall Skinny Man, Man Who Wants to Sit Down, Side Person, Man Who Plays with the Wooden Cards, Man with Metal Teeth, Ropey, and finally to Small Bitter Water.[66]

The shields had different names: Earth Protective Shield, Heaven's Protective Shield, Mountain Protective Shield, and Water's Protective Shield.[67] They were decorated with the likeness of the invisible protective powers held by the natural entity named. For example, the Earth, a living being, has its own shield of protection; by copying its elements, the Navajo can likewise draw upon its protective powers.

To renew the powers held within the shields, the medicine men had to obtain "shake offs," or dust, that transmitted the power from an object or animal that represents the entire object. A few examples clarify the point:

> It [shield/medicine bundle] also acted like a protective shield that medicine men used to enter a cave and shake the sacred dust off a bear's back. They would then take it to Black Rock and shake the sacred dust, then go to Navajo Blanket [syncline east of Mexican Hat, Utah], said to be a snake, and shake off the sacred dust from its back. The collection of this sacred dust is called Sacred to Carry Around, and all medicine men have it with them. They then took the shield to Green Cattail Flat, where they shook the dust off the lightning's back. This lightning was a bird the size of a mourning dove and very bluish in color.[68]

The powers of the shields, once renewed, could not be penetrated by bullets and arrows or evil and witchcraft. They provided protection against all things that can harm a person or a group under its power.

When the US military and its Indian and New Mexican auxiliaries warred against the Navajos to the south, those living near the Henry Mountains remained safe and escaped exile to Fort Sumner: "The Navajo were put in the 'heart' of the shields and were safe. They were not captured. They remained hidden in the Henry Mountains and surrounding area where these sacred shields were and so were never caught . . . They did not go to Fort Sumner because they lived closer to the sacred shields. It is said that these shields were often taken to other parts of our land, throughout the Navajo communities, just as the sacred mountain soil medicine bundle [jish] is carried around."[69]

During this time, however, as the people evaded detection, Ropey and Little Bitter Water Man had control of the shields and wanted to prevent their capture. Little Bitter Water Man hid them and left the area. He became sick and died without telling anyone where the shields were hidden, causing them to be "misplaced."[70] The powers were neglected, their influence waned, and the invasion of Navajo lands and capture of the people resulted in the four-year imprisonment of over 8,000 Navajos. They had lost their protection. With the rediscovery of the shields, an opportunity to renew these powers became possible.

REPATRIATION AND AFTERMATH

Based on an evaluation of all claims submitted by various bands and tribes, Kreutzer recommended that the shields be returned to the Navajo Nation. Her decision took immediate fire but was based in the very heart of the repatriation process and Native American thought, in this case Navajo. Many non-Indians who opposed her findings demanded documentary proof and not just an oral tradition they felt could be manipulated on behalf of the Navajo Nation. Kreutzer pointed out that this view sprang from their cultural heritage, which harked back to the time of the Greeks and now flourishes in a social science tradition that tells only part of the story. She argued: "Because of its intellectual heritage, then, Western culture favors sight over sound and values documentation, particularly textual documentation, over oral information. We grant text a higher authority than speech and we devalue biological memory as a source of knowledge and oral narrative as a means of conveying factual information."[71]

As for the claims of the various tribes, many of them were "non-specific and not linked to a particular oral tradition that they could share with the National Park Service," whereas those of the Navajo Nation were.[72] The others felt the place where the shields had been found was historically their territory and that they had a responsibility to a higher power to reclaim what they believed was theirs. Even though they shared dependence on oral history and mnemonic devices—"external visual symbols such as costumes, masks, totems, design motifs, petroglyphs, and pictographs as memory aids"—as did the Navajo, most of this "information management strategy" was lacking in their claim.[73] Thus Kreutzer awarded possession of the shields to the Navajo, who best fit the criteria outlined in NAGPRA.

Capitol Reef superintendent Albert Hendricks approved the transfer on August 1, 2003.[74] John Holiday and Marklyn Chee of the NNHPD drove to Tucson, retrieved the shields, and brought them to Window

Rock on August 7. Chee felt it was an emotional journey. He drove while Holiday sang and prayed over the shields: "The songs were to revive them and tell them 'You're home'. . . It felt like a good thing to bring them back."[75] Because they are sacred objects, they are not on display and continue to be subject to controversy. Debora Threedy, associate dean of the University of Utah's College of Law, felt the repatriation process demonstrated a major flaw in NAGPRA. She told the *Deseret News* that archaeologists are not necessarily prepared to make a legal determination. In the case of the Pectol shields, "From a scientific point of view, the best you can say about those shields is that their provenance is not known."[76] Other objections to the repatriation focused on the Navajo refusal to display the shields or allow them to be studied by non-Navajo archaeologists. This refusal particularly rankles when some archaeologists feel the provenance is unclear. Chee, interviewed for the same article, reiterated that the shields "are kept in the museum and are not on display. I repeat, not on display . . . They are for ceremonial purposes and they have been reintroduced into ceremonial use."[77]

Others, including some as close as Pectol's grandchildren, have also entered the fray. In a forum held at Brigham Young University on February 7, 2004, grandson Neal Busk declared that "to understand the Pectol collection, one must understand E. P. Pectol." The corollary was that "one cannot understand how the Pectol family feels about the Pectol collection without also understanding him." He went on to say that while the Navajos may have the best claim to the collection, the "best" claim is not necessarily a "sufficient" claim: "It was, and still is, simply that in our judgment, the Navajo claim was not sufficient with far too much credence given to oral tradition with little or no design or historical evidence to back up the oral tradition claim." He felt "the shields could have gone and should have gone to, say, the Utah Museum of Natural History, to be held in common for all tribes if or until a sufficient claim were made as determined by all the Utah tribes. And if a sufficient claim is not possible, should not the shields be ultimately returned to Wayne County where they were found? That would fulfill Ephraim Portman Pectol's dream and the dream of the Pectol family."[78]

The Navajo position remains firm. In 2005 Andrew Curry of *Archaeology* magazine asked Robert Begay, a Navajo archaeologist, what he thought of those who viewed John Holiday's oral history as insufficient proof to warrant repatriation. Begay replied that oral history, under NAGPRA, is as valid as archaeological or scientific evidence: "Strict archaeologists say that according to scientific data our claims aren't valid. We respect that, but we have our traditions too. At some point you have to compromise, and we try to use the NAGPRA process to our advantage."[79] Marklyn Chee of NNHPD agreed, asking, "Who's a better person to teach you what these mean? The people who used them since before written time or scientists whose theories have only been around a while?" Curry, while respecting the right of Native Americans to have input regarding their ancestors' remains, worried that "changing the way human remains are studied—in effect, forbidding any study—could fundamentally alter the way archaeology is done in America."[80]

The odyssey of the Pectol shields began that August night eighty-six years ago and has continued ever since. Initially viewed as proof of the *Book of Mormon*, the shields have seemed out of place in the Capitol Reef area. The shields and "Nephite burial robes" have been used to prove the validity of LDS temple ceremonies, Native American ceremonies, and Masonic rituals. Archaeologists have used the shields to assert a Northern Plains origin for the Fremont culture, to refute such claims, and to suggest trade connections between southern Utah and the Plains. They have been viewed as the reason the Navajos were defeated in the 1860s and spent four agonizing years at Fort Sumner. Until 2003, the shields were the subject of a Native American repatriation battle.

Underlying the controversy is a fundamental issue. Varying perceptions have applied more "color" than is encountered on the physical objects. Even those who pride themselves on their interpretation of factual evidence struggle with finding a definitive answer as to creation and ownership. In the meantime, Navajo medicine men occasionally remove the shields from their containers to renew their powers, feeding them with prayers and songs. Harmony and protection result. Others, not of the same inclination, want an opportunity to study the shields further. Conceivably, this could open the door to lawyers, standing in the wings and ready to apply their perception of who holds proprietary rights to these objects. The odyssey could continue. The crux of this controversy hits at the heart of how we write history, "do" archaeology, and honor religious practices—for "seeing is believing."

NOTES

1. Ephraim Pectol, "The Shields," unpublished, undated manuscript in possession of family member Neal Busk, 1. See also Frank Beckwith, "The High Priest's Vestments," *Improvement Era* (September 1927): 1030.
2. See Dan Vogel, *Indian Origins and the Book of Mormon: Religious Solutions from Columbus to Joseph Smith* (Salt Lake City: Signature Books, 1986).
3. Beckwith, "High Priest's Vestments," 1030.
4. "Archaeological Discovery in Wayne County," *Richfield Reaper,* September 2, 1926, 10.
5. Pectol, "Shields," 1.
6. Ibid.
7. Ibid.
8. Ibid., 3.
9. Ibid.
10. Leona Holt, written description on back of picture of shield cave site, in possession of family members.
11. Lee Ann Kreutzer, "The Pectol/Lee Collection, Capitol Reef National Park, Utah," *Utah Archaeology* 7, no. 1 (1994): 109–110.
12. Pectol, "Shields," 2.
13. Ephraim Pectol, "Wayne County Man Writes of New Wonders," *Richfield Reaper*, October 14, 1926, 4.
14. Beckwith, "High Priest's Vestments."
15. Ibid., 1030.
16. Ibid., 1031.
17. Ibid.
18. Ibid., 1034.
19. "Bishop Pectol Is to Lecture in the First Ward Sunday," *Richfield Reaper*, December 29, 1927, 1.
20. Neal Busk interview with author, October 11, 2007.
21. "Hollywood Stake Slogan Presentation," *Improvement Era* (December 1932): n.p.
22. Noel Morss, *The Ancient Culture of the Fremont River in Utah: Report on the Explorations under the Claflin-Emerson Fund, 1928–1929* (Cambridge, MA: Peabody Museum of American Archaeology and Ethnology, 1931), 69–70.
23. Busk interview with author.
24. Elaine Christensen, *"And I Went Home Rejoicing": The Background, Life, and Posterity of Edward Southwick III* (Provo, UT: J. Grant Stephenson, 1971), 122–125.
25. Bradford J. Frye, *From Barrier to Crossroads: An Administrative History of Capitol Reef National Park, Utah,* vol. 1 (Denver: National Park Service, 1998), 69–71.
26. Busk interview with author.
27. Ibid.
28. Frye, *From Barrier to Crossroads*, 133–144.
29. Charles Kelly, "Biographical Sketch of Ephraim Portman Pectol," unpublished, undated manuscript, Capitol Reef National Park Archives, Capitol Reef, UT, 3–5.
30. Busk interview with author.

31. Shane A. Baker, "In Search of Relics: The History of the Pectol-Lee Collection from Wayne County," in Marti L. Allen and Mauri L. Nelson, eds., *Relics Revisited: New Perspectives on an Early Twentieth-Century Collection* (Provo, UT: Museum of Peoples and Cultures, 2002), 36–37.
32. Busk interview with author.
33. G. G. Frazier to Commissioner General Land Office, Washington, DC, December 9, 1932, Pectol Shield Files, Capitol Reef National Park Archives, Capitol Reef, UT, 1–3.
34. Kreutzer, "Pectol/Lee Collection," 104–105.
35. John H. Taylor to Ephraim P. Pectol, September 4, 1941, Pectol Shield Files, Capitol Reef National Park Archives, Capitol Reef, UT, 1.
36. Elmer Cecil McGavin, *"Mormonism" and Masonry* (Salt Lake City: Stevens and Wallis, 1947), 80–81.
37. Wallace Stegner, *Mormon Country* (New York: Hawthorn Books, 1942), 157–158.
38. Kreutzer, "Pectol/Lee Collection," 111.
39. Carling Malouf, "Thoughts on Utah Archaeology," *American Antiquity* 9, no. 3 (January 1944): 327; http://dx.doi.org/10.2307/275789.
40. H. M. Wormington, *A Reappraisal of the Fremont Culture* (Denver: Denver Museum of Natural History, 1955), 157.
41. C. Melvin Aikens, *Fremont-Promontory-Plains Relationships: Including a Report of Excavations at the Injun Creek and Bear River Number 1 Sites, Northern Utah*, University of Utah Anthropology Papers 82 (Salt Lake City: University of Utah Press, 1966), 11.
42. Charles Kelly, Monthly Narrative Report for December 1953, Pectol Shield Files, Capitol Reef National Park Archives, Capitol Reef, UT.
43. Baker, "In Search of Relics," 38–42.
44. Richard L. Evans to Conrad Le Wirth, May 8, 1953, Pectol Shield Files, Capitol Reef National Park Archives, Capitol Reef, UT.
45. Paul R. Franke to Regional Director, Region Three, August 16, 1957, Pectol Shield Files, Capitol Reef National Park Archives, Capitol Reef, UT.
46. Baker, "In Search of Relics," 42–44.
47. Gilbert R. Wenger to Regional Director, Southwest, January 18, 1967, Pectol Shield Files, Capitol Reef National Park Archives, Capitol Reef, UT, 1.
48. Rainer Berger and W. F. Libby, "UCLA Radiocarbon Dates VII," *Radiocarbon* 10 (1968): 149–160.
49. David B. Madsen, *Exploring the Fremont* (Salt Lake City: University of Utah Press, 1989), 8–13.
50. Lawrence Loendorf, "The Pectol Shields: A Repatriation Study," unpublished manuscript, 2001, Pectol Shield Files, Capitol Reef National Park Archives, Capitol Reef, UT, 7–9.
51. Lee Kreutzer to Neal Busk, December 11, 1998, Pectol Shield Files, Capitol Reef National Park Archives, Capitol Reef, UT.
52. Native American Graves Protection and Repatriation Act as amended (Public Law 101-601, 25 U.S.C. 3001 et seq.), November 16, 1990; www.nps.gov/history/nagpra/mandates/INDEX.HTM.
53. Baker, "In Search of Relics," 44–45.

54. Busk interview with author.
55. Baker, “In Search of Relics,” 45.
56. Loendorf, “Pectol Shields,” 1–2.
57. Barton A. Wright, “Professional Evaluation of Cultural Affiliation of Three Buffalo Hide Shields from Capitol Reef National Park, Utah,” unpublished manuscript, 2001, Pectol Shield Files, Capitol Reef National Park Archives, Capitol Reef, UT, 1–2.
58. Benson L. Lanford, “Tribal Attribution of the Pectol Shields, Capitol Reef National Park, Utah,” unpublished manuscript, 2001, Pectol Shield Files, Capitol Reef National Park Archives, Capitol Reef, UT, 43.
59. Polly Schaafsma, “The Pectol Shields: A Cultural Evaluation,” unpublished manuscript, 2002, Pectol Shield Files, Capitol Reef National Park Archives, Capitol Reef, UT, 35–37.
60. Lee Ann Kreutzer, “Summary of Historical Research and Evaluation of the Repatriation Request Submitted by the Navajo Nation for Capitol Reef Shields,” unpublished manuscript, July 1, 2002, Pectol Shield Files, Capitol Reef National Park Archives, Capitol Reef, UT, 3.
61. See John Holiday and Robert S. McPherson, *A Navajo Legacy: The Life and Teachings of John Holiday* (Norman: University of Oklahoma Press, 2005).
62. John Holiday clarification interview with Lee Ann Kreutzer, May 7, 2002, Pectol Shield Files, Capitol Reef National Park Archives, Capitol Reef, UT.
63. See Holiday and McPherson, *Navajo Legacy*, 176–177, 189–192.
64. Interview with John Holiday and Lee Ann Kreutzer, March 8, 2001, Pectol Shield Files, Capitol Reef National Park Archives, Capitol Reef, UT; also Holiday clarification interview with Kreutzer.
65. Holiday clarification interview with Kreutzer.
66. Ibid.; Holiday and McPherson, *Navajo Legacy*, 189; Kreutzer and Holiday interview.
67. The number of shields and their relation to a medicine bundle, also mentioned by Holiday, becomes somewhat confused in the various oral interviews conducted at different times. In some instances, one gets the impression that there were four separate shields and one got lost; in another instance, there is the impression that all four of the powers were concentrated in one shield that became lost; in Holiday’s interpretation during the Park Service meeting in Tucson, all three of the shields were explained according to traditional Navajo beliefs, the powers of which were found in the three shields. John indicated that the four powers were paired—Earth with Heavens (Sky) and Mountains with Water.
68. Holiday and McPherson, *Navajo Legacy*, 191.
69. Holiday and Kreutzer interview.
70. Holiday clarification interview with Kreutzer.
71. Lee Ann Kreutzer, “Seeing Is Believing and Hearing Is Believing: Thoughts on Oral Tradition and the Pectol Shields,” *Utah Historical Quarterly* 76, no. 4 (Fall 2008): 382.
72. Ibid., 379.
73. Ibid., 381.
74. Repatriation Agreement, August 1, 2003, Pectol Shield Files, Capitol Reef National Park Archives, Capitol Reef, UT.

75. Andrew Curry, “Tribal Challenges: How the Navajo Nation Is Changing the Face of American Archaeology,” *Archaeology* 58, no. 5 (September-October 2005): 66.
76. Joe Bauman, “Indian Artifacts Fuel Discontent,” *Deseret News*, October 10, 2005, B-77; ibid.
78. Neal Busk, “Brigham Young University Symposium Talk, February 7, 2004: A Pectol Family Perspective,” in possession of Neal Busk.
79. Curry, “Tribal Challenges,” 67.
80. Ibid.

8

Of Stars, Goats, and Wind

Navajo Metaphors Then and Now

This second chapter concerning Navajo metaphors returns briefly to the base of those traditional types already discussed, then moves forward to those popular in contemporary culture. Rooted in astute observation and clever thought, they are the latest addition to a proud heritage of creative thinking. Unlike the older type, however, many of which depended on a working knowledge of myths and traditional teachings, these newer ones speak to reservation life today. They provide a view of the world that is both entertaining and unique, exposing an innate sense of humor that has always been a part of Navajo culture. Chief Oren Lyons of the Onondaga Nation of the Iroquois noted during an interview with writer and philosopher Bill Moyer that humor was an essential part of life, especially for those who carry heavy burdens of leadership during unsettled times.[1] *This is also true for the Navajo people, who find happiness and joy in observing*

DOI: 10.7330/9781607322177.c??

> *and then characterizing many of the situations and things encountered in daily life. The result: metaphors that dance through the mind and bring smiles to the lips.*

Laughter, ranging between mirthful chortles and desk-pounding guffaws, escaped out of the room and skipped down the hall. Inside, the half-dozen middle-aged Navajo people sat around a table exchanging words like kids swapping baseball cards—each one anxious to share but keenly interested in what others had to offer. "When the wife leaves, the deer doesn't sit still," "when the sun kills the stars," and "April 15 is when the billy goat lies down" were just a few of the colorful metaphors traded that day. To an outsider they made no sense; for those sitting in the room, they were clever images that describe a situation, a metaphorical thought, or "implicit comparison or analogy" built on the familiar.[2] The deer (husband) does not sit still if his wife leaves but goes in search of a new life; when the sun arises, it does "kill the stars"—a metaphor for morning; and after April 15, the last day to submit taxes, nothing else can be done—the deadline is met, so the frenetic energy of the billy goat ends; he lies down and is difficult to get back on his feet.

There was more to come, but these comparisons characterized important yet changing aspects of Navajo metaphor. Language is far from static; what these adults were sharing around the table derives from a composite linguistic heritage that delights in allusion to past and present thought. They were unconsciously drawing on a colorful bank of memory that showed how older expressions were tied to traditional values and beliefs, rooted in past teachings, and now how more contemporary ones focus on current concerns while maintaining the same keen, often humorous observation that characterized the past. This chapter examines the evolution of Navajo metaphorical thought over the past half century, concluding with the type and direction this practice is taking today.

METAPHOR AND MEANING

Language is an extremely important aspect of Navajo culture. According to traditional teachings, it has been not only a way of expressing ideas but a means through which this world and the ones beneath it were created, both physically and spiritually. Curtis Yanito, a Navajo artist whose father practices ten different ceremonies, explained: "The Navajo

Courtesy, Utah State Historical Society.

The old ways of life are disappearing but still preserved through practices and the language that hangs on metaphorical expression. Just as this young kinaaldá in the past ground corn between two stones outside a male hogan, so do young women today follow in the footsteps of Changing Woman and other holy people.

language is unique because it is so connected to nature. Our words were given to us when everything was made . . . Only pure Navajo words are used in the ceremonies. Navajo words can heal you. Just learning Navajo can heal you. It is nature speaking."[3] He described his father having been hit by a truck, receiving multiple injuries including a broken neck. He was in the hospital in a coma, paralyzed, until the family invited another medicine man to heal him. The prayers began, the needle in the bedside monitor moved "as if lightning had struck it," and the healing process unfolded. Curtis and his brother were shocked: "My father's fingers moved. His toes moved. It was really amazing . . . He [later] walked out of the hospital with a whole body. Even his broken neck healed."[4] The power of words is a major underlying tenet of the Navajo belief system.

In their simplest form, words are thoughts; thoughts precede action; action foments creation. Anthropologist Gary Witherspoon, in *Language and Art in the Navajo Universe,* approaches this complex topic by showing that both creation and control of the world arise through language.[5] While Gladys Reichard discussed how this was philosophically true in Navajo ceremonialism and prayer—the "compulsive word," as she called it, wherein the holy people and those humans who enlist their aide receive divine assistance—the power of language became physically evident through the role Navajo Code Talkers played in the Pacific Theater of World War II. They developed a code, much of which was metaphorical (i.e., "iron fish" for submarine and "bird eggs" for bombs), that baffled Japanese analysts for three years until the end of hostilities.[6] Thus in Navajo thought, language is the basis for this world and survival in it. Metaphors are an important aspect that expresses this relationship.

Anthropologist Keith Basso, a student of Apache metaphor, contends that "in metaphor—perhaps more dramatically than in any other form of symbolic expression—that language and culture come together and display their fundamental inseparability."[7] He came to this realization when studying what the Apaches call "wise words," or metaphorical statements that teach important values by comparing two seemingly unrelated things. The sense of discovery that comes from linking two disparate elements in a novel way provides an enlightening experience that is instructive, enjoyable, and memorable. Basso described aptly the experience my Navajo friends shared during their swapping of metaphors: "It is this act of discovery, coupled with the sometimes puzzling search that precedes it, that can make the interpretation of metaphor an original and personal experience. And it is this same act of discovery—this finding of a meaning that resolves the puzzle—that endows metaphor with the capacity to cause surprise, to structure the perceptions of individuals in unanticipated ways, and to make them 'see' associations they have never seen before."[8] Basso's examples came primarily from elders, who had great facility with the language. Our look at metaphors will also begin with older traditional forms of Navajo thinking, starting with some broader examples of metaphorical thought that eventually lead to the short, pithy statement the Apaches categorized as "wise words."

TRADITIONAL METAPHORS

Two examples from the past—hunger and the first automobile—illustrate how traditional teachings influenced previous development of metaphorical thought. As the holy people established important aspects of Navajo culture, their thinking proceeded through a spiritual then a physical process that led to the creation of the world as we know it. Indeed, in Navajo thought, its "polysemic multivocal" (many meanings and voices) nature increases a structure's significance. An important point is that unlike many symbols in Anglo thinking that only stand for or represent an idea, in Navajo thought many symbols actually become and hold that power they represent. Thus the fire is not just symbolically but actually fed, the fire poker is a real guide and protective agent, and each of the four main posts of a hogan holds powers associated with one of the four sacred mountains.

This type of metaphorical thinking is pervasive throughout traditional Navajo culture. Its language does not just provide a poetic way of viewing the world but also embeds metaphorical imagery into the daily life and thought of the People. While every culture has its unique comparative expressions that amplify its worldview, Navajo culture is especially rich in metaphor. Its stories and teachings are extensive, surpassing many other Native American groups in complexity, while its linguistic syntax emphasizes cultural priorities. Take, for instance, the verb "to go" and how the Navajo language is heavily influenced by this predominant theme. Witherspoon writes of "the astonishing degree to which the Navajo language is dominated by verbs . . . [which] also correspond to the Navajo emphasis on a world in motion . . . I once conservatively estimated that Navajo contained some 356,200 distinct conjugations of the verb 'to go.' These conjugations all apply to the ways in which humans normally 'go.' If we added all the verbs relating 'to move,' as well as 'to go,' such as in walking or running, the number of conjugations would be well into the millions."[9] Not surprisingly, many metaphors revolve around movement.

Many of the older metaphors also allude to events or teachings found in traditional religious stories that provide the basis for specific ceremonies. Other stories may simply reference events in the myth. For example, one central teaching tells how the Twins—Monster Slayer and Born for Water, sons of Changing Woman—went about killing monsters that lived on the earth "in the palm of time" (Creation).[10] This story is the basis for entire ceremonies as well as portions of others. After the Twins killed many destructive monsters, the two holy people decided to allow four—Poverty, Old Age, Lice, and Hunger (or Death)—to survive because each one taught humans some aspect of compassion or appreciation (see chapter 5). At least three of these monsters visited the Navajos during the Livestock Reduction era in the 1930s, when the government removed in some cases as much as half of the herds on which the People depended. Referring to this era, its impact on him and his family, and their response, Jackson Gray Mountain shows how literally the mythological story is expressed through metaphorical prose. He tells how his father lived around Big Mountain—"it was there that his stomach developed beneath him [i.e., he grew up]" and where his family lost their livestock in the 1930s.[11] Excerpts from an interview conducted in 1968 illustrate his personification of qualities encountered during a life defined by teaching tales:

> I was carried by the best of horses. And just when all this good work was becoming secure or when my means of travel were becoming secure, something fell right in the way. And he took up all our horses [and the goats and sheep]. And it came to be John Collier [commissioner of the Bureau of Indian Affairs]—that was his name . . . And so that having taken place, my tail just fell . . . He dropped me into deprivity [*sic*] of meat . . . He swept us all into starvation for meat, into hunger and poverty . . . There is a plant around here that isn't any good—the one that kills horses. And so it was that that's what he was, the one that was named John Collier and so that is what has been stuck in our minds.
>
> The sheep have blossomed again; my children nibble on that. They are going forward on that . . . They work for themselves. They shoot arrows at hunger (meaning work). They also with that shoot arrows at starvation for meat. And it also makes things better for those that hold up the spinning wheel [wool twining spindle—*bee'adizí*] and that's what it's doing it for. It's preparing to fight off hunger. It's also preparing to fight off poverty. It also helps in taking another swallow (meaning obtain food). His performing ceremonies and the women weaving was just enough to keep your heart beating.[12]

The creative application of a traditional story to a specific situation depends on the teachings each individual knows. Since there is a vast array of detailed stories accompanied by different interpretations in Navajo culture, there may be a variety of expressions derived from the same story. Many expressions are not universal. Variations can exist from family to family, as well as between communities on the reservation. While many metaphors simply appear, the product of an individual's thought, there are also times when a very logical pattern may be followed in their creation.

A detailed example is provided by Ryan Hosteen, who tells of a historical event in which a first encounter with something unknown received a name and an explanation as to where it fit in the Navajo worldview. This story, passed down through three generations, illustrates the careful consideration given to identifying and naming a new situation or object and the application of known beliefs to the unknown.[13] It also provides a glimpse into traditional Navajo thought.

Around 1910, two brothers were walking on a trail near the San Juan River in the general vicinity of Beclabito, New Mexico. The previous night's summer rain had swept the sand clean of impressions and refreshed the vegetation. As they moved along they spied two smooth parallel continuous tracks heading either east or west. The impressions zigzagged and twisted around obstacles, appearing to the men to be streaks of lightning that raced along the ground. On second thought, perhaps it was a pair of monster or enemy snakes (*naayéé tł'iish*), since the broader, male track had a crisscross inlaid pattern and the smaller, female track a smoother inlaid pattern. The men followed the impressions, careful not to touch them; but the more they saw, the more they realized they needed help in identifying these mysterious creatures. Other people came to see the trail; a runner went in each direction to see if these creatures could be discovered but returned the next day with no new information other than to say that the tracks seemed endless, adding to their name "Endless Monster Serpents" (Naayéé' doo'ádįįhii). One person felt they were a warning about the Utes who lived not far away and were still viewed as enemies; another thought the holy Lightning People had come to protect the Navajo and been ushered in by the previous rainstorm.

Wanting a definitive answer, the two men sought the assistance of a medicine man named Greasy Mustache (Bidághá 'Ak'ahii), a crystal gazer who saw into the past and future with his stone. This would be the safest way to determine what had made the tracks. When Greasy Mustache arrived, he confirmed the idea of a male and female serpent, warning the people not to touch their tracks. He then set about smoothing the ground with a weaving batten and creating replicas of the four sacred mountains, using dirt from each for his impromptu map. He next made a connecting star-shaped form with ground corn, placed his quartz crystal in the center as he sang, blessed the diagram, and stared into the crystal. An image appeared, but he did not know what it was: "It came sniffing, moving side to side, backing out, and then it moved forward again towards his direction, its tail winding like a snake. Riding it was a pale-skinned ant person with big shining eyes and hair the color of morning sunrise."[14] The image was powered by fire, lightning, and thunder.

Greasy Mustache spoke to the people of events from the Emergence story and drew from its teachings about the story of male and female Big Snake, then talked of life mates:

> This creature is here to show us something new. It is a new way of understanding, a new way of imparting wisdom on another trail of living . . . The male is represented by the left side of the body, the female by the right side. A woman should always travel on the right side of the man. The sexes do not cross each other. They always work together side by side like this trail. A woman should not cross the path of a man on his trail of life's work. When a man is busy about his work, a woman should not be in the way. A woman has her own place and her own work. Together as one, they get things done . . .
>
> The big male serpent's underside is wide. It has four distinct interwoven patterns, like the lightning bolt symbols on a prayer stick. The female is narrow. She also has a distinct pattern on her underside: four straight, narrow, smooth grooves to help her maneuver herself during travels. The imprints came with them from the lower worlds. The serpents, like lightning deities, have pure energy. As five-fingered surface beings [humans], we are easily damaged by contact with their pure light . . .
>
> The serpent couple manifested itself in purity on the northern side of Navajo land to help the Navajo people to re-evaluate themselves in their travels through life. It is teaching us to remember where we came from in order to know where we are going. There is a similarity here with the Road of Life, the trail of longevity. Bless yourself with it so it will be of value to you . . .
>
> Pray so your way of life will be endless. Pray that you will take the least difficult path on your travels. On the road of life there are choices, and each choice leads in a different direction. As we travel, there are hills with rough roads as well as straight and smooth roads. Always stay on the positive pollen pathway.[15]

At first there was a faint but increasing hissing sound, the smell of gas, and a constant sneezing: "Finally the stinky Monster Serpent parted the bushes. Its head and furious face appeared before the crowd. With a fiery glow coming from its huge eyes and a strangely squeaky voice, it loudly declared, 'Akóó, 'akóó [meaning "make way" or "move over"]. The creature slowly crawled out, sniffed, roared, and made terrible noises, even drooling when it divided the bushes. It puffed smoke out of its rear end."[16] The onlookers panicked at their first sight of the Model T Ford, with its brass horn, three-inch narrow and smaller front wheels with slight tread, and its larger back tires with zigzag lightning bolt tread. Because it made a chugging sound, the vehicle soon acquired the name *naachį́į́dii* from *chį́į́h*, meaning "to sniff, or the one that scouts or sniffs around with its nose to the ground." Soon the name was shortened to *chidí*, although Marietta Wetherill recalls Navajos in the early days referring to it as "Get-there-I-guess."[17]

FROM TRADITIONAL TO CONTEMPORARY APPLICATION

Even after the People became familiar with the car, in their view it was still an animate being that had the characteristics of a horse-like creature.[18] In 1991 George Tom from Monument Valley, Utah, declared that "an automobile is more than a horse; it can hear, make noises, and it runs. If it weren't alive, then why does it move? It is alive. It is perfect to look at. But it is similar to a horse as far as its usefulness, and it is blessed just the same way. We pray for either our automobiles or [our] horses."[19] This system of comparison extended to colors. Like horses, cars came in many colors—black, blue, white, red, and yellow. Prayers and blessings extended to both modes of transportation in a similar fashion. Starting with the tip of the tail, moving along its back to the horse's forelegs, then ending with its mouth, the owner blessed his animal through prayer with corn pollen. On a car, one started with the tires, moved forward to the hood, then returned to the tires on the other side.

Today, much of the vocabulary used to describe the parts of a car play upon the Navajo notion that it is an animate being. The headlights are eyes; tires, shoes; battery, heart; engine, head; and gasoline its water. Other words call for greater interpretation. A car window (*chidí bitsés-'*) literally means "car's rock star," or glass, and the windshield wiper (*tsésó yit'oodí*) is "rock star wiper." The name of the rearview mirror (*bii'adéest'į́į́'*) means "the object you look into to see," but the root of the word refers to the crystal used in crystal gazing to divine past or future events. A wrecked car (*chidí bisgą'*) is built around the word that denotes shriveled up or gone dry, as when moisture is removed from a slice of bread.

The names for the internal parts of a car's engine shed additional light on this view of its being animate. A number of those parts have in their names the word *nílch'i*, defined today as "air, breeze, wind, spirit, ghost."[20] In much of the traditional Navajo literature, however, until recently this word also represented the Holy Wind, which served a variety of sacred functions in Navajo thought. For instance, when a child is conceived, four different winds (nílch'i)—Black, White, Yellow, and Blue—enter the infant's body to bring life.[21] The winds combine to form one's spirit that learns of right and wrong and gives the infant personality. The word *'Ii'sizíinii* means "the spirit or one that stands within," while *Ii'sizį Diyinii* is interpreted as "The Holy One [or Ghost] that Stands Within." The spirit that stands within has come to represent the soul inside an individual. Many Navajo stories also portray nílch'i as an external Holy Wind that whispers in a person's ear, warning of trouble and directing the person as to what to do to avoid harm.[22] Recently, as a result of Christian influences, there has been further clarification in religious vocabulary by identifying this spirit as Nílch'i Diyinii ("It is holy; the one possessed of magic power"), making it comparable to the Christian concept of the Holy Ghost.

In naming the parts of the car, the word *nílch'i* is used, not *níyol*, the word for the kind of strong wind one feels blowing on the face. Inside a car's "head" one finds the air filter (*chidí binílch'i yee nídídziihí*—literally, "car's air or wind it breathes by"), an air compressor (*nílch'i bee sik'azí*—the wind that keeps the air cool), a generator (*ajéí néílbézhí*—the thing that boils [recharges] the heart [battery]), the rocker arms (*da'alzhishígíí*—the thing that dances), manifold (*łid bá si'aní*—sits for smoke), and the exhaust pipe (*łid bizooł*—smoke pipe). A car's radiator is called "the home of the bees" (*tsasná bighan*) because of its honeycomb-like indentations. A pickup truck is a "car with its back extending," a convertible is a "car with nothing on top," and a commercial bus (*bii'yajii'áhá*) is "where one sits like a stump" or "sits straight up" because of its seats and the fact that its riders have to remain in that position for hours. An ambulance has a frightening name—"dead people's spirit (ghost) carrier" (*ch'įįdii neiyéhé*), something to avoid in traditional Navajo culture.

The use of the word *nílch'i* has made its way into other modern appliances. In understanding how this Holy Wind communicates, it is not surprising to find it in the name for a television set or movies (*nílch'i*

Courtesy, Ray Hunt family.

Old Man Jack in Dennehotso following a storm. Traditional beliefs about snow teach that young people gain power when they strip and roll around in the first snows of winter. Another practice includes not drinking melted snow from the first few storms. The Navajo characterize snow that falls gently and slowly as a female storm, while a hard-driving blizzard is male.

naalkidí—"air that moves or acts") and an antenna (*níłch'i' halne'é bá yaa'áhí*—"the rod that goes up for the wind's words"). A computer is *béésh na'ałkaahí* ("metal that investigates") or *béésh ntsíkeesí* ("metal that thinks for itself"). The computer's mouse pad is *na'asts'ǫǫsí biyaateeł* ("mouse's sheepskin" [the mouse's sleeping pad]).[23] Other appliances also have animate qualities in their names. A radio is *níłch'i halne'é* ("air that talks"), an iPod is *béésh hataałí* ("metal that sings"), a telephone is *béésh beehane'é* ("metal one talks into") and a tape recorder (*saad bik'inihi'nííłí*) is "that which words are put on." A cell phone is *jaa'ii* ("an object that clings to an ear") but is more normally referred to as "turning or twirling around while holding it to your ear" (*bił njoobałí dóó jaa'jótą'*) or "one with which to spin or twirl around with," since the user is trying to obtain a signal. Another explanation for the turning is that the user is trying to have a private conversation.

KINSHIP AND METAPHOR

Seasons of the year and weather may also be described through metaphor based in keen observation. For instance, spring may be called "breathing air in and out, i.e., deep breathing," since "nature is taking a deep breath . . . [that] takes her all the way through planting, harvesting, winter, and up to next spring."[24] A number of types of snow have descriptive names. "On the branch snow" only sticks to tree branches, telephone poles, fences, and highway signs; thus it does not stay very long, melting in a matter of hours. "Horse tracks snow" is so thin that when a horse walks on it, the hooves expose the bare ground. A third type is called an in-law chaser, a big snowstorm that usually occurs at the beginning of winter and arrives quickly, with dark, ominous clouds. A son-in-law is initially viewed as an outsider to his wife's family, performing many menial chores to prove his value to his conjugal relatives. With the advent of this storm, he has to get outside to ensure that the homestead is prepared—sheep fed and in the corral, water hauled, wood chopped, and camp secured. Navajos joke that this snow encourages the in-law to be industrious even in cold winter weather.[25]

While in-laws play special roles in many cultures, a number of teachings and practices in Navajo tradition define exactly where one stands in relation to the newly adopted family. Sometimes sons-in-law are not well accepted because they are strangers to the family and might be trouble. A new husband is a servant to his in-laws, never sleeps in their home, and immediately responds to their requests. He is in charge of supplying enough chopped wood and hauled water to their camp, all the while avoiding contact with his mother-in-law. For up to ten years he may be in this subservient status, but eventually his in-laws will start asking his advice and he will feel he has won their respect. If he receives a grazing permit from his wife's family, he knows he has been accepted. Maggie Yellowhair gave John Salaybe, a new son-in-law, this advice:

> An in-law must be strong. He must know his priorities. A father's priority is to build a home. You find yourself a tree, a nice cozy place. Get some rags or canvas and make a shade. Go to your in-laws' trash dump and pick up some cans for a cup and coffee maker. Under the tree you can settle and cook your food. This is how you begin. It takes a man with courage to do this. Start in a really humble way. Initiate this kind of living. This condition won't last. Somewhere in

Author photo.

Karen Toledo: "In-laws are owls [associated with bad news] looking to catch a glimpse of anything. Owls have round, staring eyes that never blink. They turn their head and bob up and down so as not to miss a movement and are perfect for hunting. In-laws look for negative things so that your family becomes their prey. That is why we jokingly say that one should 'shield the eyes from the stare of an owl.'"[28]

> the future you will have a nice home with nice things. A man's job is to build a hogan. You can't sleep long hours because you need to do this. The Sun won't wait for you. Don't be lazy. A "real" man has a hoe, shovel, ax, and digging stick. These things are not only useful, but they help you become a man.[26]

For Navajos, an in-law can be helpful by keeping the wind away, and he may protect a family. By saying *naadaaní*, their power helps push the wind aside. When a whirlwind approaches, everybody says "naadaaní, naadaaní, naadaaní," meaning "your son-in-law, your son-in-law, your son-in-law."[27] By saying this, a male destructive wind heading in their direction changes its course and bypasses the group. If a small whirlwind passes over a person, one says a prayer that its effects will not be harmful. These winds bring messages that are not good.

Extensive Navajo metaphors teach of hard work and how one should live. From the beginning of the day to its end, elders taught effectively what it meant to be a Navajo through intense metaphorical language based in observation. Karen Toledo recalled some of her family teachings.[29] A grandmother might start with "I am going to put my finger in your ear" or "grind something in your ear," meaning she wanted to stress a point or lecture the youth. Perhaps a young woman has slept in, so she will be greeted with "the noon sun has beaten you" or "the early day has been taken away." The older woman may joke with the younger "that to sleep through the morning is a sign that an old man is lying on top of you bidding you to keep sleeping." Not surprisingly, a metaphor to signal achievement through a lot of hard work and sweat is "whoo wee—another year has passed successfully like a harvesting grandmother." Jackson Gray Mountain would agree when he counseled, "Corn sprouts and your thoughts are to keep the weeds from overrunning the corn so you lift a hoe. This is the only way you will find good corn."[30]

When a young man "has his arrows come into being" (approaches adulthood—is old enough to have his own arrows), he is warned not to "act like a dog" (irresponsible—male dogs do not care about their litter) or "a bull among cows" (promiscuous) or he will end up with a "good for you it is born" (an illegitimate child) that will be "hopping from place to place and holding on to another person's clothes" (born out of wedlock without a stable home).[31] No matter how well the young father "sharpens a tool" or "really saws" (sings well at an Enemy Way ceremony), he will end up saying "The Coyote I am," meaning he has made mistakes and is learning lessons the hard way. People who are "full of stomach" (greedy) or go "into the ground" (jealous) will have regrets when they "carry it all back" (dịe).[32]

CHANGING METAPHORICAL THOUGHT

Many of these older expressions, or "wise words," and ways of thinking are disappearing as the younger generation's worldview shifts from the sacred teachings of daily life and the mythology previously central to Navajo thought. Basso encountered the problem of language depletion through the loss of elders thirty years ago. As he prepared to depart from the Fort Apache Indian Reservation, having completed his fieldwork, a man approached him and offered, "It's too bad that you didn't try to learn about 'wise words' before. When I was young, old people around here used to make them up all the time. Only a few of them did it and they were the best talkers of all . . . Only the good talkers can make them up like that. They are the ones who *really* speak Apache."[33] Navajos face a similar problem.

Language loss is a huge concern the Navajo Nation is trying valiantly to combat. The tribe has instituted school programs to preserve traditional thought and language and has passed legislation that encourages its use in various aspects of daily life. Still, there are many indications that this uphill battle is being lost in a bombardment of twenty-first-century media and lifestyle choices. John E. Salaybe Jr., a medicine man and frequent contributor to *Leading the Way*, a contemporary Navajo publication concerning traditional Navajo practices, bemoans the fact that children are losing facility in the tongue of the People. He notes that thirty-five-year-old adults are "good markers for the well-being of a language" and that when young people below this age are not speaking it, the language is considered to be dying out.[34] Salaybe goes on to say that in the 1930s, 90 percent of Navajo children were fluent in the language, but with the increasing emphasis placed on school attendance and immersion in the dominant society's worldview, this facility has increasingly faded. In 2006, when he tested 240 students at Dilkon Community School in Arizona, he found that only "10 percent knew simple Navajo words. Only 3 percent of the students could speak Navajo in whole sentences, and the rest knew nothing."[35]

Perhaps they have lost what Marietta Wetherill had gained in the early 1900s when a Navajo man complimented her on her linguistic ability: "Her tongue is thin enough to speak the tongue of the Diné."[36]

Jackson Gray Mountain put it a different way. Speaking of today's youth, he said: "From here the things that we talked to them about, they fail to meet up to its standards . . . They always talk back and the words they use aren't the words of life. Someone who questions and asks about some words of life, he is the one who will advance."[37] Yet some young people are sensitive to the problem. Karen Toledo, who bridges both worlds, believes that "at ceremonial gatherings, being an English only chatterbox [i.e., "frog"—a person who is always talking] is not encouraged in the Diné culture. Being a Navajo chatterbox is acceptable. Speaking the Diné language helps the Holy Ones hear."[38]

The problem does not lie only in the loss of language. Many elders regret the slipping away of cultural values and teachings discussed in chapter 5. Eighty-year-old Ada Benally characterized the problem this way:

"We have tried to carry on their [elders'] teachings but our children won't listen. They are trampling all over us. Our children want things their way. They want to live as they wish."[39] Many others express similar anxiety: "A child might be well-educated yet dwell in all the wrongdoings. The younger ones will follow their example and fail too."[40] Isabel Lee said of today's youth, "They are addicted to television, causing them to be deaf to what we try to teach them. It's like that all over. If we live completely like the white man, I wonder how we will continue to exist . . . Because we have become deaf, we do not listen or obey; we are wearing pants, wearing the wrong clothes; we have completely re-dressed ourselves in the white men's culture."[41] Benally bewails that few young people wear the traditional hairstyle and are losing their language; women wear pants and put on eye makeup, while most seem to lack discipline: "All these things are the doing of the white man. The present generation is practicing this. For most of the older generation, we still abide by and keep sacred the teachings of our elders, whereas our children do not believe in it."[42]

The old ways of instructing are gone. Compare and contrast today's school system and family education methods to what eighty-year-old John Norton encountered growing up in the first quarter of the twentieth century:

> The old teachings of our elders were very strict. They would point their finger straight into your eyes and say, "Those pupils of yours are there for you to see with; that nose of yours is for you to smell with; the openings on the side of your head are for you to listen and hear with. Therefore, do not do what is forbidden! Leave things alone."
>
> No one talked back to their elders and no one told jokes about them. They were very strict when they taught us things, and these teachings were not soft. At first we got a very stern talk about something, but it ended with a friendly tone like this: "My child, my baby. You are learning from this. You will live by it. By doing this or getting me something, you are learning the important part of your life which you can use in your future. One day you will talk to your grandchildren this way as I am talking to you. All trails lead to one place, and one day you will end up there."[43]

Members of today's middle-aged generation, well on their way to taking the place of the elders of yesteryear, are part of that large cultural shift. They are in a distinct transition from a generation of grandparents raised in the old practices of the livestock industry as found in the

Navajo elders have always held a place of respect in traditional culture. Years of hard life have given them wisdom and foresight to guide those who are younger if they are willing to learn. But in a day of ease and comfort encased in a permissive society, the elders' teachings are viewed as strict and "not soft," so they may fall on deaf ears.

first third of the twentieth century. Their parents were taught by these elders but attended the white man's school and primarily lived a life on the reservation that was far more settled and oriented toward many of the aspects found in the dominant culture—school, healthcare, wage employment, and the introduction of mainstream media. As a second generation removed from the stereotypical traditional lifestyle of the 1920s and 1930s, the third generation struggles even more with accepting the traditions and speaking the language.

The internal conflict this creates was shared by a friend who wishes to remain anonymous but who I will call Jane. She tells of her experience growing up during this time of change and the turmoil she felt in her life.[44] As a young Navajo woman born and raised in Monument Valley, she came from a family whose grandmother and, to a lesser extent, mother practiced the old ways. She echoes from the other side of the canyon, that is, from the perspective of a youth going through this transition, what these elders said. As a young girl in the 1960s she saw movie stars on television with their hair down "for no purpose." She tried it herself and received chastisement for offending the holy people. She compromised: "The idea of sitting half-naked in a ceremony got me to braid my hair." At one point she returned to the hair bun, but peer tension overpowered her: "I will be one of them [those not following the old teachings] again because I am ashamed to wear my hair in a knot. Each day I am forced by outside pressure to change myself to fit a white man's world. I feel I do not know what my culture has to offer me."

Her uncle asked her to carry the prayer stick as part of the Enemy Way ceremony, but she again felt embarrassed. Her mother stressed that it was an honor to do so, but Jane was "crushed": "The worst part about it was that the girls I was going to school with were there and they giggled at me, just like Coyote who ridiculed tradition. I felt like running from the place with sacred ointments on me, but somehow I did not do that." At the same time, fights between young men broke out, contrary to the purpose of the ceremony: "The older people said that we should not have our own blood running down our bodies because we were warring against the spirit of our enemies." The elders explained that this is why so many Navajo people die in auto accidents and other violent ways.

Just as in the Coyote tales, Jane saw competition and excess all about her—in the miniskirts, music, and general lifestyle popular at that time. Laziness instead of hard work, sleeping in until seven in the morning as opposed to arising before sunrise, and increased alcoholism and unemployment were part of the fallout from changing lifestyles: "At the crack of dawn holy people come from the east to my home to bless it with favorable things or hardships and illness. When they are coming through I might be asleep. They would say, 'If she wants that, send her the sickness.' If I were awake, they would say I am their child . . . I now see what it is like on the reservation. Only a few people are awake by dawn and the rest are like me. It is the downfall of the Navajo people."

Jane recalled the story of when one of the four sacred mountains went wild. Sometime during the time of creation, one of the female mountains began acting strangely—wearing her hair down and then cutting it, shortening her dress, being rude to relatives, and generally engaging in excessive and inappropriate behavior. The holy beings prepared a smoke of mountain tobacco and administered it to her, quieting her "craziness." They prophesied that in the future humans would act the same way, but now a pattern for healing had been established. Today, mountain smoke medicine is given to young men and women who engage in excessive and bizarre behavior: "Whenever a person goes somewhat crazy or if one's mind is lost or if one wanders off unknowingly but had once walked about normally, there is a ceremony. Just as with the mountains in the past [medicine men and the holy people] settle them down. Mountain tobacco is given to that person. He or she will then become better."[45] Jane concluded her story by saying, "I know I am trying to convert myself to another culture which looks easy but it is not. This is why I am in between my own culture and that of the white man."

METAPHORS FOR TODAY

With the diminishing cultural basis from which traditional metaphors were derived and the acceptance of white culture, it is not surprising that a different set of metaphors is emerging. Historically, the Navajo language has shown great flexibility to incorporate new elements as they appear. This, coupled with incisive observation, has led to a new set of metaphors that provide the same "act of discovery," or twist, found in the old style of speech that now describes the modern world of today's People. Some of these metaphors are widespread, others perhaps less well-known, but they all come from recorded Navajo speech.

Clayton Long, director of the San Juan School District's Bilingual Program in Utah, offers a number of insightful examples.[46] For instance, a politician is "he made an ear for money," linking the practice of lobbying and financial dealings with identifying a lamb by a particular cut or mark in its ear for ownership—similar to the English use of something that is "earmarked" in a budget. That same person may be a "coyote" because he does not hold back but jumps into things without a careful plan. It is hoped that he is not "nighttime" (clueless) or "runs up to the front with it" (an outspoken person who is always talking) but rather that he "walks in the path of the sun" (goes in the right direction) and "his word makes this move" (he makes things happen). Sometimes he may fall prey to a "buzzard" (a woman who flirts with a married man) and become an "ear" (someone who does not listen to his wife or the other woman's husband). If he acts like a "billy goat" (gets into things he shouldn't, which can include being sexually active) and a "snake" (sneaky), he may end up with "the one who stands by a house (or leans against a wall)" (a prostitute). He becomes like "an old horse that saw the green pasture" (an old man who finds a young woman to pursue—nothing will stop him). Next he will turn to a "wide bottle" (liquor sold in narrow bottles shaped like a flask), "go out boating" (get drunk), then "fall over like a rope" (pass out from drinking). To earn money he will spend time at "Downward-you-throw-it" (a casino, from pulling the handle of a slot machine). Before he knows it, his name will appear in "Gossiping Paper" (the *Navajo Times*—a newspaper that reports on reservation issues, is investigative in nature, and publishes letters to the editor).

Shopping also has its own vocabulary. While Anglos may call it a "flea market," to Navajos it is "you-have-the-bed-bugs-again" or "takes-all-day" or "husbands-avoid-it," while a mall is "quickly-walking-through." To purchase something one uses "rubbing back and forth" (swiping a credit card). Carla Phillips, a Navajo student of metaphors, explains that credit cards, debit cards, and food stamps are all categorized as "invisible money" (*béeso doo yit'íinii*): "After a while a person could lose his or her balance printed on the receipt. For that reason, an elder finds it difficult to understand how money is contained within that little card, for it has no pockets. The money is considered invisible."[47] While shopping, one may encounter "The-Ones-who-talk-much-and-fast [also 'with much sense']" (French tourists), "Metal Hats" (Germans, from wearing military helmets), "Red Shirts" (Russians, associated with communism), and other whites—all of whom are characterized as "ants" because they are always busy building and working.

At this point, the reader is ready to try his or her hand at unexplained modern Navajo metaphors. While no self-respecting Navajo speaker would cram them into a fictitious story this way, what follows is an opportunity to "discover" with a sense of enjoyment the colorful language of contemporary Navajo. There is a mix of some of the more traditional metaphors with slang. An answer key follows.

> A few days after John and Mary had *driving the horses in,* they decided to go to *Where the Knees Go Up in the Air* to get something to eat. They were in a hurry, so they went to the *stick your hand in.* John was tired of eating *in-law stares with this* and *slap around bread,* so he wanted something cooked on *lazy ash.* Whatever it was, he was going to smother it in *cat's blood* and *baby poop.* Mary, on the other hand, wanted an *apple with a tail* and a *green purse* with lots of eye *pupils* but absolutely no *where the eyes go blind.* Perhaps a large *sucking up the soup* would go nicely with her chowder. Add a little *salt's buddy*, and it should taste just right. After eating, they decided to go to *chicken* and ride on *with me it turns and brings me into the sky.* John was happy as he drove down the road, so he really began *sharpening his tool.*

Here is a key to what you just read:

Driving the horses in (łį́į́' neelkaad) = wedding (also may be 'iigeh). This act of chasing the horses into the bride's camp began an exchange that occurred at the beginning of a traditional wedding ceremony.[48]

Where the Knees Go Up in the Air = MacDonald's Restaurant. The golden arches look like the knees under the table as one eats.

Stick your hand in = drive-through window.

In-law stares with this = Ramen or Cup o' Noodles soup, used when a wife is too lazy to cook or is in too much of a hurry. The in-law finds this hard to believe and thinks the food offered should be better.

Slap around bread = flat tortilla bread made by slapping it between two hands.

Lazy (or crazy) ash = charcoal that does not burn in a natural way, goes out in a half hour, or takes an hour-and-a-half to cook the food.

Cat's blood = ketchup because the words sound similar and because of its red color.

Baby poop = mustard, since a baby on a milk diet has yellow-colored stool.

Apple with a tail = pear.

Green purse = lettuce because of its folds and "pockets."

Pupils = black olives that look like the pupil of an eye.
Where the eyes go blind = mushrooms in a tossed salad because on the reservation there is a wild mushroom that, when animals eat it, can cause them to go blind and die.
Sucking up the soup = dinner roll eaten with soup and used as a sop.
Salt's buddy = pepper.
Chicken = Fourth of July rodeo.
With me it turns and brings me into the sky = Ferris wheel.
Sharpening his tool = energetically singing, as in an Enemy Way ceremony.

The Navajo language is versatile, able to adapt to the latest situation as long as it continues to be used. Its evolving base of metaphors shifts to incorporate ideas in a changing worldview, employed through intense observation mixed with a sense of humor. For the listener, whether hearing metaphors from the past or the present, a sense of "discovery" adds to the delight of a conversation as speaker and listener share the give-and-take of clever interaction.

In summary: (1) Navajo language holds power, explains the essence of an object, and was part of that object's creation. (2) Metaphors and metaphorical thought are an incisive means to understand a culture's worldview. (3) Many traditional Navajo metaphors were rooted in the sacred teachings and mythology of the past and, by alluding to events from those stories, provided "wise words" to live by. (4) Immersion in the dominant worldview through education and activity has encouraged loss of Navajo language and cultural teachings, thus shifting the understanding from which metaphors derived. (5) Contemporary Navajo metaphor is still dependent on keen observation that incorporates many aspects of daily life not found in the older culture. (6) Still, a sense of "discovery" as listener and speaker "'see' [and share] associations they have never seen before" results when communicating with metaphors. (7) For this culturally determined practice to persist, Navajo language with its accompanying perception must continue. The younger generation cannot wait until there is no longer an elder to "put a finger in their ear." Navajo speakers must act now to preserve the language, lest in the future they end up saying "Baadáádiikai—We have wandered or walked away from it."

NOTES

1 Oren Lyons with Bill Moyer, *The Faithkeeper* (Cooper Station, NY: Mystic Fire Video, 1991).

2. "Metaphor," *American Heritage Dictionary*, 2nd ed. (Boston: Houghton Mifflin, 1985), 790.

3. Curtis Yanito, "It's All about Language," *Leading the Way* 8, no. 1 (January 2010): 12.

4. Ibid., 12–13.

5. Gary Witherspoon, *Language and Art in the Navajo Universe* (Ann Arbor: University of Michigan Press, 1977).

6. See Gladys A. Reichard, *Prayer: The Compulsive Word*, American Ethnological Society Monograph 7 (Seattle: University of Washington Press, 1944); Doris A. Paul, *The Navajo Code Talkers* (Bryn Mawr, PA: Dorrance, 1973); Kenji Kawano, *Warriors: Navajo Code Talkers* (Flagstaff, AZ: Northland, 1990); Leo Platero, "How Navajos Make Words," *San Juan Record*, June 13, 2007, 16.

7. Keith H. Basso, *Western Apache Language and Culture: Essays in Linguistic Anthropology* (Tucson: University of Arizona Press, 1990), 79.

8. Ibid., 57–58.

9. Witherspoon, *Language and Art*, 48–49.

10. For different versions of this story, see Berard Haile, *Upward Moving and Emergence Way: The Gishin Biye' Version* (Lincoln: University of Nebraska Press, 1981); Paul G. Zolbrod, *Diné bahane': The Navajo Creation Story* (Albuquerque: University of New Mexico Press, 1984); Aileen O'Bryan, *Navaho Indian Myths* (New York: Dover, 1956).

11. Jackson Gray Mountain interview with Gary Shumway, June 14, 1968, Doris Duke #474, Doris Duke Oral History Project, American West Center, University of Utah, Salt Lake City, 2.

12. Ibid., 11–14.

13. Ryan Hosteen, "Giving the Unknown a Name," *Leading the Way* 6, nos. 4–5 (April–May 2008): 14–16, 21–23.

14. Ibid., 14.

15. Ibid., 14–15.

16. Ibid., 15.

17. Kathryn Gabriel, ed., *Marietta Wetherill: Life with the Navajos in Chaco Canyon* (Albuquerque: University of New Mexico Press, 1992), 109.

18. For a lengthy discussion of the Navajos' perspective of the introduction of the car into their culture, see Robert S. McPherson, "The Chidi and Flying Metal Come to the Navajos," in *Navajo Land, Navajo Culture: The Utah Experience in the Twentieth Century* (Norman: University of Oklahoma Press, 2001), 84–101.

19. George Tom interview with author, August 7, 1991.

20. Robert W. Young and William Morgan Sr., *The Navajo Language: A Grammar and Colloquial Dictionary*, 4th ed. (Albuquerque: University of New Mexico Press, 1987), 643.

21. John E. Salaybe Jr. and Kathleen Manolescu, "The Creation of an Individual," *Leading the Way* 6, no. 4 (April 2008): 3.

22. For an excellent discussion of nílch'i, see James K. McNeley, *Holy Wind in Navajo Philosophy* (Tucson: University of Arizona Press, 1981).

23. Ted Kee, "New Navajo Words," *Leading the Way* 2, no. 8 (August 2008): 12.
24. John E. Salaybe Jr. and Kathleen Manolescu, "Spring: A Time of Reawakening," *Leading the Way* 9, no. 4 (April 2011): 2.
25. Rhoda Kascoli, "Navajo February Snows," n.d., used with permission, in possession of author.
26. John E. Salaybe Jr. and Kathleen Manolescu, "Being a Husband," *Leading the Way* 4, no. 6 (June 2006): 3.
27. A person should not walk into a small whirlwind or dust devil because it will affect his breathing. These winds are believed to be the spirits of people who have died and have returned. Some of them may not be good. The same is true with tornadoes, but because Navajos know the songs and prayers that can control them, these winds will not harm the People. Herbert Toledo, "Remembering My Dad: Hastiin Ts'ósí," *Leading the Way* 6, no. 3 (March 2008): 21.
28. Karen Toledo, paper on metaphors, January 11, 2008, used with permission, in possession of author.
29. Ibid.
30. Gray Mountain interview with Shumway, 5.
31. Charlie Mitchell, "A Navaho's Historical Reminiscences," in Edward Sapir, ed., *Navajo Texts* (Iowa City: University of Iowa Press, 1942), 341.
32. Carla Phillips, paper, April 29, 2003, used with permission, in possession of author.
33. Basso, *Western Apache Language and Culture*, 79.
34. John E. Salaybe Jr., "Keeping Navajo Alive," *Leading the Way* 8, no. 2 (February 2010): 20; Isabel Lee interview with author, February 13, 1991.
35. Salaybe, "Keeping Navajo Alive," 20.
36. Gabriel, *Marietta Wetherill*, 13.
37. Gray Mountain interview with Shumway, 21.
38. Toledo, paper on metaphors.
39. Ada Benally interview with author, February 6, 1991.
40. Susie Yazzie interview with author, August 6, 1991.
41. Isabel Lee interview with author, February 13, 1991.
42. Ada Benally interview with author.
43. John Norton interview with author, January 16, 1991.
44. Student paper, "Prophecies of What It Will Be Like," March 2, 1990, used with permission.
45. Mary Blueyes interview with author, February 9, 1994.
46. Clayton Long interview with author, January 18, 2008.
47. Phillips paper.
48. Tom Chee, "Navajo Language: The Heart and Soul of Navajo Culture," *Leading the Way* 9, no. 2 (February 2011): 2.

9

Gambling on the Future

Navajo Elders, Jiní, and Prophetic Warnings

I have spent the past thirty-plus years conversing with Navajo elders, and I can safely say that one topic is uppermost in their thoughts—what will happen to future generations. The fear is that when the old people pass away, so will much of traditional culture—the language, religion, social relations, and a host of other elements that make Navajo teachings unique and important, literally, a gift from the gods. Who will be there to provide guidance? How will the "new Navajo" dress, act, speak, and, most important, raise the next generation? To have a sense of what the future will be like, the People turn to the past.

This final chapter discusses the end of the world by looking at its beginning. In keeping with a cyclical view of history as explained in the myths, one can understand what the end of the world will be like. Some examples come from the destruction of the worlds beneath this one, others from the Anaasází and

DOI: 10.7330/9781607322177.c09

> *their Great Gambler, and still others from prophesied signposts embedded in today's society. They all provide guidance along the way that warns with caution. Yet fascination with today's American culture is a strong magnet whose force is difficult to overcome. Only the future will tell if the teachings from the past had it right enough to counter these attractive forces.*

One of the greatest concerns for Navajo elders today is the loss of cultural values. Youth in particular receive censure for not practicing many of the traditional teachings that carried the elders through tough times—the loss of livestock in the 1930s, participation in World War II, entry into the wage economy of the 1950s, mining during the Cold War in the 1950s and 1960s, and the start of bewildering technological changes in the 1970s that reached full force by the beginning of the twenty-first century. Constant as a pole star, traditional values guided the elders, shaping their understanding of the world as handed down by parents and grandparents. Rooted in the sacred stories that defined the origin of ceremonies, the mythic past not only explained what happened at the time of creation, "in the palm of time," but also taught how current events were to be understood and what the future holds.[1] The basis for the Navajo worldview has always been encased in a religious framework that yielded a practical yet philosophical interpretation of the world and its events.

Jiní often precedes and concludes the sharing of traditional teachings. A literal translation of this word is "it is said," "one says," or "by word of mouth."[2] In some cases it can also mean hearsay, but it usually carries a stronger, more forceful connotation, suggesting that the speaker did not witness the event or story about to be told but that it is true and needs to be considered. Where the term *hearsay* in English suggests that its veracity is questionable, jiní carries no such feeling. The story is true and relevant. Thus the teachings of Navajo elders, entwined in the past, hold relevance today, even though the teller was not present when the event occurred or will take place in the future.

A note about historicity before "rubbing [various] teachings in the ear." A question often arises about how old or traditional certain teachings are. The material gathered for this chapter comes primarily from elders (average age seventy at the time) interviewed in the early 1990s. They spoke of hearing their grandmothers and grandfathers tell of things that were to happen in the future. This would mean those elders (two to three generations from present) were born around the beginning of the twentieth century, when much of Navajo culture was still intact before inroads from the dominant culture were adopted.

As shown in previous chapters, religious stories and metaphors are central in understanding Navajo thought—whether speaking of the past, present, or, in this case, the future. Unlike the solely linear approach to time expressed in Anglo culture, Navajos conceptualize time in what anthropologist Douglas R. Givens calls a "complex linear temporal dimension."[3] In its simplest form, this means there is a combination of shorter linear periods interspersed with small cycles, both of which are encased in a larger cyclical series of episodes. Thus Navajo thinking, in a very real sense, teaches that "history repeats itself" in such a way that the patterns established in the past will appear again in the future. One should learn from these patterns, or else similar results are inevitable.

This large-scale cyclical pattern is seen in events surrounding the three or four mythological worlds beneath this one, the Glittering World that earth surface or five-fingered people now inhabit. While there are various versions with differing details, the general theme inhabitants encounter in each of these worlds is one of a new beginning, growth, and development, followed by disobedience, strife, decay, and destruction. Emergence of those remaining into a different sphere, and a new beginning follows. While within each of these worlds are improvements and a greater sophistication in life, the fundamental issues that tear at the fabric of the "society" composed of insects, animals, and pre-human forms remains constant—greed, pride, fighting, and death are at their roots. When the holy people assisted the Diné into this world and received their human form, they also obtained instruction as to how to live and avoid the issues that had plagued the inhabitants of previous worlds. At the same time, there were no guarantees. A new cycle of growth and development started that could fall into the same traps encountered previously. Thus today's elders who are knowledgeable in lessons from the past look at contemporary patterns and events to warn the People of what to avoid in the future.

GREAT GAMBLER: THE TEACHINGS

One of the premier myths that teaches of that future is about the Great Gambler and his life in Chaco Canyon, New Mexico. Two of

Courtesy, San Juan County Historical Commission, Blanding, UT.

Hastiin Tso was a powerful medicine man in Monument Valley who played an influential role in both ceremonial and community events. Today, many elders bemoan the loss of people like him who understood the depth of Navajo thought and tradition. With the passing of each generation comes a significant loss of the old ways.

the most complete accounts concerning this individual are provided by Washington Matthews (1897) and Sandoval with Aileen O'Bryan (1927), which are also two of the oldest versions.[4] Both provide complete stories but have slight variations, as would be expected in an oral tradition. There is no reason to question the authenticity of either of these narratives or others introduced as supplementary information found in contemporary oral interviews. The story is central to Navajo mythology in discussing today's society and provides a wealth of understanding when interpreting current or future events.

Jiní, there was a proud and haughty man known as the Great Gambler. Nááhwíiłbįįh (variously translated as "One Who Wins You as a Prize," "He Who Wins Men," "He Always Wins") was the offspring of a poor woman and Sun Bearer (Jóhonaa'éí). His father created and groomed him to win turquoise and beads from wealthy Anaasází living in the vicinity of Chaco Canyon.[5] The young man grew tall and handsome, learned all the songs and games associated with gambling, and became unbeatable in contests of chance. He truly had a winning way. Jóhonaa'éí sent him forth with two turquoise earrings "the shape and size of a [silver] dollar," which he used as bait to get the betting started.[6] He lured the Anaasází in, first winning their crops (livelihood), then their possessions, and then the people as his slaves. The Great Gambler even won the chief and his wife, as well as the large turquoise Jóhonaa'éí desired. But he coveted all that he owned, refused to give a small part to Sun Bearer, and proudly challenged him with "you will be next. I will gamble with you. Come on."[7]

Irate, the father vowed revenge. He went to a different group of Anaasází, the Mirage People, and took a second wife with whom he raised another son identical to the first. Later, Sun Bearer charged the young man to defeat the Great Gambler in the eight (some versions say nine) games of chance, then to bring the large turquoise to him. With the help of animals, the holy people, and the Holy Wind (Níłch'i), the young man approached the Gambler and challenged him to his different contests. In each instance the powerful ruler lost, and as the stakes of winner-take-all increased, the Great Gambler's confidence decreased until he finally forfeited everything, including his life. Rather than kill his brother, the young man placed him on a Bow of Darkness and shot him into the sky. As he soared into the heavens the Gambler yelled "adios" and vowed to return later to recapture that which belonged to him.[8] The young man rendered to his father the desired turquoise and freed all the enslaved people, letting them go to lands of their choice.

This précis of a story Elder Tom Ration insists takes two to three nights to prepare and requires the same amount of time to relate ("Telling about the Cliff Dwellers or the Ancient Ones takes a lot of time") is filled with comparative elements for the present.[9] What appears to be a common motif that runs through many Navajo stories—poor boy with supernatural help overpowers a potent evil person, recognizes the source of his success, and gives the holy people the things requested—becomes a map for today's concerns. Underlying the tale is a series of specific points the elders align with current events and problems. Indeed, much of what holds true for the Great Gambler is expanded on a broader front to encompass the Anaasází later in their history, as well as today's youth.

First, the Gambler. A review of the details in both the O'Bryan (O) and Matthews (M) versions emphasizes two destructive combinations—sex and jealousy, and betting with pride. Women in the tale are enslaved and become sex objects. The Gambler had won "a great many wives" as well as that of the Anaasází chief; the captured men built houses for them, as well as the Gambler's mansion known today as Pueblo Alto[10] (O). It is interesting that archaeologists first believed Pueblo Bonito and other dwellings in Chaco constituted North America's first apartment complex. Now it is believed to have been more of a ruling ceremonial center and at the nexus of a trade network with high-status goods that ranged throughout the San Juan Basin and beyond.[11] Whatever it was, the Great Gambler is closely identified with it, and there is no doubt that strong social and political forces were at work to direct the building. Whether free or enslaved, coerced or voluntary, the site speaks of power and control.

When the young man—the brother we will name Twin—approached Pueblo Alto, he met the Gambler's head wife, "one of the prettiest women in the whole land" (M), and slept with her by the spring where she went for water. Although she supposed at first that it was her husband, she soon learned her error but committed adultery anyway. "The young man did this to 'split the mind' of the Gambler" (O, p. 55). As soon as the wife returned home, Gambler knew she had been with another man. When Twin entered the home, Gambler recognized him as the culprit, jealousy colored his thoughts, and he resorted immediately to gambling to "have him in my power" (O). Two beautiful women of divine parentage who had accompanied Twin became his stake for all of Gambler's wives and servants (O and M).

Now it was time to bet. In the past, Gambler had won the people incrementally. When he came to Chaco Canyon, he first obtained property until no one had anything, forcing them to start betting their lives. Soon he had their lives as well and began drawing Anaasází from neighboring pueblos, near and far. Their relatives came to win back their loved ones and were ensnared; then "the children of these men and women came to try to win back their parents, but they succeeded only in adding themselves to the number of the Gambler's slaves" (M, p. 82). Next, the leaders from various pueblos tried to win their people's freedom and became entrapped; finally, "people from other pueblos came in such numbers to play and lose that they could keep count no longer" (ibid.). This time, however, the Great Gambler staked all he had against the Twin.

For many Navajo people the eight contests have counterparts in the sports and entertainment of today. For instance, one game was like dice, where either seven (O) or thirteen (M) sticks had their two sides painted either white or black (O) or red (M). When tossed in the air, all white won for one side, all black (or red) for the other. Many elders see this as comparable to gambling in casinos. There was a game like golf, where a curved shinny stick hits a ball into a hole. Another game featured a curved stick shaped like a rainbow; like flipping coins, the side it landed on determined who won. A shooting game required runners to throw a spear through a rolling hoop; another was like soccer or football, where runners had to kick a stick across four lines drawn on a track. Twin kicked it a fourth time and "over the house it flew" (O). He also had to interpret pictures drawn by the Gambler, specifying what each represented or held within. As in the television programs *Deal or No Deal*, *Concentration*, or *One versus One Hundred*, Twin matched his knowledge against questions of interpretation and chance. Another game was one of speed and strength, where the two men raced to two sticks, with the first to pull his stick out of the ground winning.

The final game was a foot race four times around a circular track. By the time the Gambler reached this point, he was dejected and desperate. Twin, in contrast, assisted by the holy people and animals, was ready to finish the contest. Holy Wind warned Twin as he ran that Gambler would try to kill him, but every time the brother shot an arrow, Wind told Twin when and how to duck. He then returned the violence: "When the Gambler passed him the young man took aim and shot him in the leg, just below the knee. The next time he shot him halfway up the body. The third arrow he shot between the shoulders. The fourth arrow he sent behind the head . . . The young man circled around the Gambler and ran on ahead," winning the race (O, p. 61). Gambling led to violence. Following the race the Gambler cried, "I lose. I lose all, even my life. My life is yours," then threw himself on the ground broken-hearted.[12] Matthews's version shows a less penitent loser, "saying bitter things, bemoaning his fate, and cursing and threatening his enemies. 'I will kill you all with lightning. I will send war and disease among you. May the cold freeze you! May the fire burn you! May the waters drown you!'"[13]

All that was left was to get rid of him. Instead of killing the Gambler, Twin shot him into the sky, muttering and cursing as he went (M). He called out "long ago I died in the center of the earth"; a little farther, "my spirit will want to return there"; and finally, "adios."[14] He went to the moon and received a new people, the Mexicans, with all types of livestock—sheep, donkeys, horses, goats, and wealth—before returning to the earth with them as their god.[15]

GREAT GAMBLER AND ANAASÁZÍ: CONTEMPORARY APPLICATION

Louisa Wetherill shares a different version of the Gambler.[16] He was not only fortunate in games of chance but also introduced a "blue gum" (wire lettuce [*Stephanomeria pauciflora*]; its root contains a narcotic gum) that proved addictive to both his subjects and himself.[17] "The people went from bad to worse. The men gambled all the time. They did not take care of their corn fields nor did they perform any of their religious ceremonies."[18] Following the drugs was sexual license, when Gambler took Sun Bearer's wife without permission. Starvation, drought, and death ensued. Many of the old men who knew the ceremonies died, healers forgot medicinal practices, and old knowledge was lost forever. The people killed the Great Gambler, swearing to never follow his practices again.[19]

Another version told by Tom Ration connects many of the Gambler's doings to today. As the people prepared to shoot him into the sky, he

In Navajo thought, Chaco Canyon is synonymous with the Great Gambler, his abuse of power, and his promise to return to recoup his losses. No one typifies more the teachings of what happens when the holy people are ignored, allowing greed, pride, and corruption to reign.

warned that he would return and be above them (suggesting to Ration airplanes and that Gambler "must have been a white man"). Gambler threatened, "In the future there will be round objects which the people will play games with to win. They will be a reminder of me." Ration reasoned:

> We know that today many pieces of game equipment are round—like baseballs, volleyballs, basketballs, and golf balls. People play with them to win. They all are part of the white man's games that have been introduced to us . . . Whatever is round belongs to him. He also said that the lightning flash would be his power, and also the wind. He added, "When I return, everything that is round will roll beneath you with the wind. We will travel on the rolling rainbow arc." Today that is all very obvious. We travel on the highways with yellow and white stripes. A highway reminds us of the rainbow as it curves. The round objects under us are the wheels of whatever we travel in—trucks, automobiles, trains, bicycles and other things; and we travel with the wind. The lightning, I also know, has to do with electric

> current. People have lights in their homes and business places, along with all kinds of electrical devices . . . Taking these things together, One-Who-Wins-You must have been a white man. We Navajos also call the radio "Wind that Talks." It is a white man's invention.[20]

John Holiday, a Blessing Way singer, tells a different version. Sleeping Ute Mountain in the corner of southwestern Colorado is the body of the Great Gambler. He lies there, having been defeated by a holy being who challenged him to a game of chance. Gambler lost everything—the land and its people—and then was shot into the earth: "As he was descending, the people heard him speak in English, the white man's language . . . 'I will come back. I will be back to beat you at the game. I will win back your language, your mind, your sacred songs, and prayers.' And that has happened. Today, the white men are here, and he [Gambler] has all that he said he would win back."[21] This is also the reason the Ute Mountain Ute Casino is located in Towaoc at the base of Sleeping Ute Mountain. Playing cards are said to "belong" to the Great Gambler.[22]

The fact that these negative beliefs about games of chance and the Great Gambler were not isolated, meaningless stories was proven in 1994 and again in 1997. Twice the Navajo Nation Council put forth a referendum to see if the People would accept a casino on reservation land. In 1994, local newspapers left no doubt: "Navajos Say a Big 'No' to Gaming."[23] The article explained that a staggering 5,000 majority in votes overwhelmed the initiative out of fear that acceptance would "open the door to organized crime" and that many members would "become addicted to gaming like many now are addicted to alcohol." This in spite of the estimated 1,600 jobs the casino would bring to the reservation and the fact that the "Navajo Is Poorest of [the] Major Indian Tribes."[24]

Three years later, *Navajo Times* headlines prophetically warned against the second attempt: "No Gambling on Navajo Myths."[25] The article—based on interviews with a half dozen medicine men—reported that they wanted to avoid any situation reminiscent of the Great Gambler, citing his addictive behavior, greed, and immoral attitude. Wilson Aronilth said, "I was told that if you own sacred items such as a medicine bundle, prayer feathers, and corn pollen, and you gamble, you will pay negative consequences for it . . . My grandmother told me it can make you go blind so that is why I don't go to casinos."[26] Johnson Denison, another healer and dean of instruction at Diné College, after relating elements of the Great Gambler story, warned, "There are many Navajo mythologies about gambling and it's always been part of Navajo culture, but it is associated with control and can make you go crazy."[27] Alfred Yazzie referred to the fulfillment of the Gambler's promise: "When the language becomes one, our people will become confused and become enemies to each other . . . Today, a majority of the Navajo people does not speak Navajo or understand the traditional Navajo culture."[28]

In spite of this resistance from traditionalists, casinos on the reservation became a reality. On October 16, 2001, the Navajo Nation Council passed a gaming ordinance that President Kelsey Begaye did not veto, launching plans for its first casino in Tóhajiileehí (formerly Cañoncito).[29] As of 2010 the tribe was "Betting on Casinos, Tribe Going Full-Bore on Gaming Development," announcing that over the next two years it would be building five new facilities across the reservation.[30] If Fire Rock, the first Navajo casino to unlock its doors on November 19, 2008, is any indicator, these other gaming sites will also be successful. A year after opening, it claimed more than 51,000 members in its Players Club, 70 percent of whom were Navajo; a year later 95 percent of its customer base was identified as Navajo.[31] There is little doubt that there are now many "Great Gamblers."

Moving beyond the Great Gambler to the Anaasází as a group, the same message unfolds. They were a highly gifted people, blessed by the holy beings with talents that far surpassed those of normal humans. They became haughty and proud and were destroyed. This general theme has been discussed elsewhere, but a few points bear repeating.[32] First, the Anaasází are pictured as having a large population, "as numerous as red ants," and as owning large farms, fine houses, and many game animals.[33] New inventions allowed them to plant more and larger fields, giving rise to population increase. Control, abuse, and power characterized their creative but insensitive lives. Spiritual impoverishment followed.

The Anaasází proudly displayed their beautiful woven baskets and fired pottery covered with holy symbols, repeated often without regard for their sacredness. What had been potent images of healing were now commonplace. A type of design craze followed in which profane symbols were mixed with those of religious importance and placed on clothes, bowls, baskets, pots, blankets, rocks, and stone axes. The designs became more complicated and beautiful each day. Insulted and angry, the holy people withheld rain and sent huge tornadoes with swirling fireballs that swept through the canyons and killed those in their path.[34] Another version tells how the designs on the pottery and baskets were reversed, spiraling in a counterclockwise direction, suggesting witchcraft. The Anaasází also copied forms of lightning, rainbows, and the wind—causing the gods to send the great wind that removed the air and killed the people as they slept or sat in their homes.[35]

Some Navajos suggest that the Anaasází learned to travel through supernatural means but then abused the power: "They learned to fly . . . that is why their houses are in the cliffs . . . [but] the holy beings had their feelings hurt by it . . . [and] said it was not good and killed them off."[36] A more detailed account says that the Anaasází were a highly gifted people who obtained their knowledge through prayer. They asked the gods to allow them to travel by lightning, which was granted. After a while they started killing each other with it, which is why their dwellings are often burned: "To use it [lightning] they had to go by high standards, and when these were broken they paid a price."[37] The gods removed the air and killed many as they knelt and begged for forgiveness. Today, Anaasází are found buried in that position.

Disrespect for the sacred, inventiveness, competition, and greed are qualities shunned in traditional Navajo society but accepted—in some cases encouraged—in white America. Many elders suggest that Anglos and nontraditional Navajos are walking the same path to destruction followed by the Anaasází. Fred Yazzie made this comparison:

> Just like now, the Anglos are designing many things. They are making big guns and poison gas. Whatever will harm humans, they are designing. What happened then [with the Anaasází] I am relating to what is happening now . . . When they designed on their pottery, they reversed the drawings, yet people did not believe they were overly inventive. And that can lead to self-destruction. Now the Anglos are going up to the moon and space. Whatever obstacle is in their way, they will not allow it to stop them. Some are killed doing this and others return from their quest. Do these people believe in the holy beings or God? . . . The Anaasází built with ease [*doo bił nahontł'ah da*] houses in the cliffs. Their mind probably did all this, and this was like a big competition between them. They started to fly and then got jealous of each other.[38]

GOING "CRAZY"

As society becomes more complex, the teachings of the elders are forgotten, and a general downward spiral approaches a climax, life as we know it will be destroyed. The end of the world will unfold as predicted. What are the signs of the times? After reviewing dozens of explanations about what it will be like, a number of conclusions can be drawn. First is the uniformity of what is being said. In almost every instance, the elders interviewed stated that it was their grandmothers and grandfathers, or in some instances their great-grandmothers and great-grandfathers, who had talked to them about the end of the world. This suggests that these teachings were discussed very early in the twentieth century, before many of the changes encountered today occurred. Uniformity also existed in the signs or events that connote the change. Many of the interviews cited are from southeastern Utah—from Navajo Mountain to Aneth and from Monument Valley to Blanding—covering a large geographic area. The teachings are widespread and accepted. A third point is that the person sharing the information, without hesitation, linked the end of the world with what happened to the Anaasází and often mentioned the Great Gambler. What follows is a condensation of what they believe to be important proof that the end of the world is near.

A general characterization of this time is that things will go "crazy," an oft-used term. Hear the elders. Jiní, "There is a jumbled mess in the midst of our people that has gotten out of hand. Our young men have gone crazy; our young women have gone crazy. They are into many things they are not supposed to be in[to]. They are even marrying into their own clan . . . We are consuming things that are dangerous and smoking them. These are driving us crazy. It gets us where we are not responsible for our actions. There is no thinking going on. Our brains are messed up. Our bodies are messed up and feel numb."[39] Ada Black agreed: "When wine and beer became available, our thoughts got all messed up. Everything is going crazy because of it, and it is even used during the Enemy Way ceremony . . . Now we are in the midst of this craziness. If we could stop the drinking for a year, the people would come back to their senses. There would be no stealing, no spouse abuse, and no fighting among the people . . . [but] we cannot handle the pressure as it surrounds us."[40] Cecil Parrish concurred: "Now we have gone crazy, just as it has been said of the Anaasází. This is happening to us, too."[41] Again, shades of the Great

Gambler: "Before the game started, Gambler got together some weeds and let all the people smell of them. They all went a little bit crazy. They didn't have the mind that they had had and they wanted to play all the more . . . Gambler threw his ball first but it didn't go through the hole, for the people had made him crazy too."[42] For the Navajo, substance abuse and chaos go hand in hand.

All of this was foreseen and predicted, based on twelve generations. The first dozen generations would be "clearly noticed [defined—perhaps in a genealogical sense through clan relations], but after that, everything will be out of order and unclear, confused . . . Back in 1940 my grandfather said eight generations had passed, and we have four more. After the four have passed, everything will change—a new or different beginning will occur."[43]

Another teaching about the end of the world is that the Navajos and Apaches in the south will come together to join the Athabaskan-speaking people in the north. Elders teach that there are ancestral people who came from the same tribe but separated long ago. Navajos call those who live in Canada, Alaska, and Siberia the Diné Náhodlóinie (Those Who Exist Elsewhere). The people in those areas call themselves the Beday Diné, which translates as the Winter People.[44] Jim Dandy visited these Athabaskan speakers and found many linguistic and cultural beliefs similar to those of the Navajo. He mentioned:

> Our ancestors always said that someday we would gather with all of our own people again, who speak the same language. I am not clear as to whether they will come here to the Southwest or we [will] go to the north. There are some that are now moving onto the Navajo Reservation, while some Navajos are living in the Yukon. At the same time, there are Navajos in Monument Valley who say we should never join with them. We will have to see what happens in the future.[45]

Before the end, however, this gathering will take place.

LANGUAGE LOSS

Language loss is another indicator of approaching cataclysmic change. John Holiday referred to the "white man's god"—meaning the Great Gambler—speaking four times, saying "I shall return someday to win back your language, mind, plans, songs, and prayers—everything."

John continued: "He returned, and today most of our people are speaking the white man's language. Even the smallest child speaks English . . . The Navajos are holy, but if they outgrow their prayers, songs, language, and wisdom, it will be the end."[46] Francis T. Nez and Kathleen Manolescu shared another story of language loss connected with the end of the world:

> There was a certain spiritual being that appeared. He came around from out of the blue. At that time everyone had one language. Everyone understood one another well. This spiritual being spoke all different kinds of languages. Then the different tribes began to speak their own language: Japanese, Mongolian, Diné, English, and so on. When the people saw this spiritual being again, everyone spoke different languages. The spiritual being stood there and smiled, "After the human was made, First Woman and First Man, they soon descended off into different colors, different languages. When all humans speak one language again, it's the end." We know this time is coming near because everyone in the world is learning English today.[47]

This is a major grievance with the elders, although it had long been prophesied. Ada Black's maternal grandmother warned that there would come a time when the "language of the enemy [Anglo] will be the only one spoken, and it will be that time when the harmony of living will pass away and chaos will come to exist."[48] She cautioned not to let the children lose their language, but they are. Velta Luther explained that it is the parents' fault. Many are full-blooded Navajos, yet they talk to their children in English. The children, in turn, "push their native language to the side. They all talk English now."[49] Jim Dandy feels as though "almost everybody seems to speak it [English] now. Most of the elders, who did not go to school, still just know Navajo. Once they pass away that could end fluent speakers, bringing us to the last days simply because younger people, for the most part, are not learning it. This is a huge loss in understanding."[50]

One direct result of language loss is that the ceremonies, with all their associated teachings, will be gone. Velta continued: "Now the younger generations [are] not teaching themselves the ceremonies. None. They are just out there doing something else, even though the father is right there with the medicine bundle . . . The ceremonies are dying with these elders."[51] Kayo Holiday feels that abandoning the Navajo language is wrong, the culture is jeopardized, and it is "time for the world to go

Courtesy, Milton Snow Collection, Navajo Nation Museum, Window Rock, AZ.

Elders fear language loss will lead to cultural loss and the end of traditional practices. Although the Navajo Nation has taken many steps to ensure language survival, many Navajos still do not speak their language.

crazy."[52] Over fifty years ago, medicine man Frank Mitchell warned that the youth were already disobedient to such an extent that there will be "no great hope for the future."[53] For medicine man Buck Navajo, it is too late: "All of the people are in school. There are no true Navajos now. The teachings of our elders are going."[54]

EDUCATION AND TODAY'S SOCIETY

When the end comes, it will happen in the "blink of an eye," just as it did for the Anaasází.[55] The same forces that destroyed them will destroy us. Wind is the most prominent of these forces. Just as the Anaasází "invented a way to fly . . . wanted to duplicate the tornado and air, and made new inventions with air, so has the white man [who] is like the holy people. They do not hesitate to invent things or fear to try the impossible. They were given 'the gift' to succeed and accomplish everything."[56]

Today's education has brought about these changes, but it has gone too far. While the Anaasází put their sacred designs on pottery, controlled electricity, and learned to fly, white society has taken the Holy Wind and made airplanes, learned how to duplicate the human body, and funneled electricity into homes.[57] They are inventing something new every day using these powers: "We travel fast on it [electricity]. Airplanes are made out of electricity. It also goes into our homes. We eat what was cooked on it. It is used for everything and so that very name will kill us all. Jiní, there was liquid fire. It is here. Any one of those can do us in."[58] This is what is taught in schools—how to do these things. Education is taking the children to "un-foretold levels. Whatever was said not to do, they are doing it. So it comes back to us . . . We try to tell them not to do these things—the only way is pleading with them—but they do not listen to us. We did not teach our children what we were taught."[59] Consequently, "Their minds will be small—they won't think like we used to."[60]

Navajo modesty in dress is another practice under assault. Girls and women should not wear pants; this item of clothing belongs to men. Susie Yazzie sees the problem as symptomatic of a series of issues:

> When females change their skirts to pants and cut their hair, they are living the white man's way and become a bonus to that society—the women become a prize to them. They are considered captured [*yish-nááh*]. If this continues, we will outgrow our religion. We will lose our beliefs and respect. Things will worsen when a woman starts wearing men's hats and living a man's character and lifestyle. We will lose all respect for our clans; we won't know who we are. When the "end" is near, our crops will fail to grow, our youth will be lost.[61]

Stella Cly echoed the concern that when a woman acts and dresses like a man, "it's hard to tell the difference now."[62] How can the holy people distinguish between the two?

Jim Dandy recalls the teachings of his father and mother, who warned that the end of the world would come when Navajo clothing became immodest. His mother was embarrassed by the way girls began to dress, especially when wearing pants. She taught his sisters not to put them on and that she would rather see them wear skirts down to their ankles, so as not to expose their knees or any part of their legs:

> Mother believed that was best, but when the last days are here people are not going to care. They will go topless and it will not bother them. Father always said, "We're going to go back. Television is not going to be good because what you see there is not what you're trying to teach." Even though children are taught not to get involved in drinking, television advertises all kinds of things to children, saying it is okay to drink and how to do it. Dad always said, "They're going to put the Navajo people in pictures and advertisements one of these days and have us dressed in that way, teaching the wrong things."[63]

Hair, as part of dress, is also crucially important. More than just following a stylish fashion, the hair knot (*tsiiyéél*) symbolizes a covenant with the holy people and a number of blessings that derive from it: "All men and women used to wear their hair in a knot, but today most of them have cut or shaved their hair. We were forbidden to cut our hair because that bonded us to the heavenly beings—particularly the rain. We have long hair as a symbol of rain. If one cuts their hair it will no longer rain; there will be a cloudless sky. That might be the cause of our rainless weather these days."[64] Another said, "[Our children's children] are doing crazy things with their hair. Jiní, it is the dark clouds. No wonder it does not rain. When you cut your hair, you are cutting the dark clouds off you, jiní. This is why it is very sacred and powerful."[65] "When they all cut their hair off, the end will come to what we know."[66]

Sexual promiscuity and abortion are other indicators of the end of the world. Life is given to a baby as soon as it is conceived, so that child is alive and should not be harmed. Dandy's grandfather warned: "Grandson, I just want you to know that a sign of the end is when people do what they're not supposed to do. You are killing that child; it's murder. You kill that child when it starts to grow, it's still murder."[67] In traditional culture there is a ceremony called Ajiłee, meaning Excess or Deer Way, that helps when people overindulge in sexual passion, drinking, or other harmful activities.[68] The ceremony corrects the problem and returns the person to harmony. Deer smoke (*bįįh nát'oh*) is another means to create proper balance.[69] In either case, these ceremonies produce harmony in an individual's thinking and put him or her back on the right path: "These are all part of the teachings that the elders have given to warn about the end of the world. It is fast approaching."[70]

Other signs of the times are only touched upon briefly here. Some of these include a horse bearing twins, corn seeds failing to grow, babies born with teeth and white hair, racial intermarriage becoming prevalent, four-legged animals conversing with humans, insects swarming the land, and drought drying the ground.[71] Women in tribal leadership positions cause problems because this is actually a man's domain. Kayo Holiday's great-grandfather taught that "whenever a woman shall become a leader that will be the end. Our clanship will disappear. We will all be mixed . . . It is like that in Window Rock, the leaders have multiplied [another sign—too many]; even women are leaders, like council women."[72]

ENVIRONMENTAL SIGNS OF THE TIMES

Four metals were used to kill the monsters that once inhabited the earth. At the end of their destruction, the Twins—Monster Slayer and Born for Water—surrendered these powerful weapons received from Sun Bearer. He, in turn, sent these tools to the four directions, where they were buried. The four Metal People—Dark Walking Metal, Blue Walking Metal, Yellow Walking Metal, and Crystal Walking Metal—went into the mountains but said they would return when the end was near. Susie Yazzie believes "uranium minerals, chemicals, and rocks which produce atomic bombs will destroy the entire world. The 'Metal People' will come back by way of the uranium rock and its related forms to destroy our earth."[73]

John Holiday explained that the reason so many wildfires rage out of control in the mountains is because of the destruction of mountain soil bundles that uncaring people have desecrated: "We rarely heard about these fires before this happened, but ever since our people started throwing away or burning their prayer and mountain soil bundles, nothing has been the same. They have brought suffering and unhappiness to our people."[74] Frank Mitchell found other indicators in nature. Rocks in a nearby canyon began to split, just as they did before World War II, indicating another global war—possibly with nuclear weapons—in the future. New plants, birds, and animals he had never seen before began living near his home. Frank commented: "I do not believe evil beings will take over at the end like the priests say. These new plants and animals will."[75]

Weather is yet another sign of the times. One indicator is when the San Juan River dries four times. As of 1992, it had dried twice.[76] At the time of creation, Mother Earth and Father Sky refused to work together. Instead they battled each other, saying, "I'm the holy being; I'm the one that rules." Consequently, there was no rain.[77] The same thing is happening now, just as it did with the Anaasází, who faced a similar situation when the gods punished them for bad behavior. Jim Dandy believes, "There are a lot of things that are going to happen to us. Wind is warning people, especially those on the East Coast but also in other places where there have never before been problems with winds like tornadoes. Even on the reservation there are strong male winds that have not been there before, bears and other holy animals moving on[to] Navajo lands, and destruction of livestock. A final sign is when an Indian person travels to the moon. These are the types of things that are supposed to happen at the end of the world."[78]

The time for performing ceremonies affects changes in weather, another indicator of approaching problems. For example, the Yé'ii bicheii ceremonies, which should be held no sooner than mid-October, are starting earlier and earlier each year. The people are worried about this: "Why did they do that? It's not time for winter yet. It will cause the frost to come early." They fear that those who farm will lose their crops to freezing temperatures brought in prematurely: "You have caused the cold to come. Now it's going to be winter." Other people start telling Coyote stories too soon or sing Coyote story songs, which are other ways to cause frost. To tell these stories before there is frost is to risk offending the animals and insects the stories are about. The Yé'ii bicheii ceremony ushers in the cold and helps a lot of people at the same time.[79]

Mid-October is the earliest any of these activities should be held. If cold or snow comes at the normal time, then it is correct to hold these ceremonies. But now, people are holding Enemy Way ceremonies, which are only performed in the summer, later and later in the year. This ceremony should never be held after the Yé'ii bicheii ceremonies have started, but it is happening. That is why there is a mixing of the seasons, with warm winters and cold summers. By mid- to late October, seasonal change has ended, freezing has taken place, the harvest is in, and people say, "Put all

Author photo.

In spite of dire predictions for the future, as long as the Navajo people remain wedded to the land, recite their prayers, respect the holy people, and remember their ancestors' ways, life will be abundant. Tradition serves as the pole star around which existence rotates yet remains constant, fixed for the future.

your medicine bundles away and start the Yé'ii bicheii ceremony." They are afraid and complaining about what is going on now and feel the climate has changed quite a bit. This is what has caused the changes, so now a lot of thundering takes place after the ceremonies, and male lightning strikes in the winter.

Dandy believes the Navajo people should be following their traditional schedule of seasonal preparations, just as the animals do. People should get their corn out of the field and ready to dry, then gather and prepare ingredients for kneel-down bread so it is available for the year. Hunting takes place in the fall, and the meat is preserved. By doing this they would be saving and preparing, just like the coyote prepares for winter. But they are not willing to follow those patterns, so the seasons are getting confused; people are worrying about it, especially those who farm, because the frost is going to hit them all at once. Navajos say holy people are going to go to the medicine men and tell them what to do to correct the situation. Many feel the time has come for this to happen, but it is going to be hard.

On May 3, 1996, that is exactly what happened. Two holy people visited two women—sixty-one-year-old Sarah Begay and her ninety-six-year-old mother, Irene Yazzie—at Rocky Ridge, Arizona. Sarah described the event: "The next thing I knew there was a loud boom overhead and then a whistle. It sounded like someone was talking outside so I went out to see what was going on and saw two white-haired, older Navajo men . . . I got scared and started to go back into the house when one of them said: 'Don't be afraid, we are here to help you. You already know what we're here for.'"[80] The men explained that the holy people were concerned because they no longer received offerings of corn pollen, ntł'iz, and prayers and that the people were not following traditional practices. Drought resulted. After delivering their warning they disappeared, leaving behind four footprints outlined in white corn pollen.

Anthropologist Maureen Trudelle Schwarz interviewed a number of elders who provided an outline of subsequent events. Many Navajos took this incident seriously. By May 20 over 6,000 people had visited the site, Navajo Nation president Albert Hale had declared it a permanent shrine, and a number of hand tremblers confirmed through divination that the sighting was genuine and the warning must be heeded.[81] Schwarz cited one man as stating, "We were told long ago that the gods would return when we began fighting amongst ourselves, stopped talking to one another, and bad things were happening."[82]

Navajo Nation speaker Kelsey Begaye, who later became president (1999–2003), declared that June 20 would be the initial Navajo Nation Unity Day, filled with prayer and harmony. The following day the nine-month drought broke, with a rainstorm that heralded future showers in the coming weeks. Begaye identified the core of the problems confronting Navajo culture: "The majority of our children are not speaking their Navajo language; they are not being taught their cultural and traditional values; the foundation of family values are [*sic*] not being emphasized to them; and we are straying from our spiritual strength and values. We must begin our journey back to being a strong Nation, we must start now."[83] Sustaining this direction of change is difficult, given the strong influences of the dominant culture; but based on mythological and historical patterns, it encourages Navajos to return to the roots that have served them well in the past.

END OF THE WORLD

If the pattern established in previous worlds is fulfilled, the People will know that it is because of all the warnings not heeded. What will the end of this cyclical pattern be like? John Holiday described it as a "changeover" similar to what happened to the Anaasází. The destruction will be complete, the ground "overturned," the means of livelihood destroyed, the medicine men put in the mountains for safekeeping, with the cleansing of the unrepentant taking place "as quickly as lightning."[84] Yet parts of this changeover are occurring now. The seasons first established at the beginning of this world are shortening, as seen when summer becomes more like winter and winter like summer. Eventually, they will "pass over each other and change places."[85] This changeover will signal the end of this life and a new beginning, which will occur without warning. Prior to this, the medicine men will be removed to the four sacred mountains, where they will be protected and prepared for their return with a renewed power of the Blessing Way ceremony.

A similar change will take place in raising children. Elders say that in the beginning people used to live for 100 years as a normal span of life. That situation has diminished over time, and now young people are growing older at an ever-increasingly younger age. Young girls well below the age of puberty—eleven, eight, then six—will have babies that are born at an increasingly older age: "The changeover will be complete when a child is born with gray hair and aged like an elder, as with old men and women . . . This is the crossover of human life, just as it will happen to the seasons."[86]

Thus the end will arrive.

Within the myriad examples that warn of future problems, one finds general explanations as to what will occur and why. While there are many different interpretations, the general pattern is clear. The mythology surrounding the previous worlds provides a grand-scale scenario that identifies the ending of each of them as a result of conditions comparable to what is encountered in this world. A cyclical pattern illustrated from the past by the Anaasází gives a concrete example of what happens when traditional teachings provided by the holy people are ignored. On an individual basis, the Great Gambler is the ultimate illustration of a person gone astray. But that was the past. Today's elders see similar ideas and problems emerging. Contemporary examples push the thesis forward: to ignore the sacred and traditional is to invite disaster. The past is a prototype for the future wherein a cyclical pattern downward spirals to the conclusion: a finale brought on by abuse of the sacred, pride, inventiveness, and loss of culture and tradition. From an outsider's view:

> Through abuse of the things and relationships that were created, the Navajo can affect this cosmic tide, to the effect of their shortening the period to be lived in this world. So due to the pulsating movement that is occurring during and through this period of time a certain circularity can be seen; the beginning and the end of this world exhibit the same forms, after which a similar cycle . . . is to commence.[87]

One-hundred-two-year-old medicine woman Rose Mitchell provides an equally concise insider's perspective for the younger generation on how to avoid approaching doom: "You need to learn things like your language, your ceremonies, how to be a good person, how to live according to the Blessing Way. You need to understand that, use the Blessing Way in your own life, and follow it as a guide to keep yourself and your family strong and to face hardships as they come along."[88] Other elders agree. Jiní.

NOTES

1. Navajo elders, speaking of a mythic past when the world was "soft," use the phrase *in the palm of time*. Encapsulated in these words are the feelings that this mystical period was something remembered, important, sacred. It was a time when important things happened: the gods formed patterns and "stretched" the world so it was habitable for man.
2. Robert W. Young and William Morgan Sr., *The Navajo Language: A Grammar and Colloquial Dictionary*, 4th ed. (Albuquerque: University of New Mexico Press, 1987), 489.
3. See Douglas R. Givens, *An Analysis of Navajo Temporality* (Lanham, MD: University Press of America, 1979).
4. Washington Matthews, *Navajo Legends* (Salt Lake City: University of Utah Press, 1994 [1897]), 81–87; Aileen O'Bryan, *Navaho Indian Myths* (New York: Dover, 1993), 48–62.
5. The Anaasází (*anaa'*: war, alien, enemy; *sází*: ancestor), a Navajo term glossed as "ancestral or alien enemies," inhabited the Four Corners region from 200 BC to AD 1300. The Navajo view them as a gifted people who eventually denied the blessings and powers given them by the holy beings and so were cursed, punished, and destroyed for taking the sacred and making it profane. Robert S. McPherson, *Sacred Land, Sacred View: Navajo Perceptions of the Four Corners Region,* Charles Redd Center for Western Studies Monograph 19 (Provo, UT: Brigham Young University Press, 1992).

6. O'Bryan, *Navajo Indian Myths,* 49.
7. Ibid., 50.
8. Ibid., 62. In Matthews's version the Gambler's words were said to be inaudible, but he would return later as leader of the Mexicans.
9. Tom Ration interview, cited in Broderick H. Johnson, ed., *Stories of Traditional Navajo Life and Culture by Twenty-Two Navajo Men and Women* (Tsaile, AZ: Navajo Community College Press, 1977), 316.
10. Neil Judd, *The Material Culture of Pueblo Bonito*, Smithsonian Miscellaneous Collection 124 (Washington, DC: Smithsonian Institution Press, 1954), 351.
11. See Kendrick Frazier, *People of Chaco: A Canyon and Its Culture* (New York: W. W. Norton, 1986); Kathryn Gabriel, *Roads to Center Place: A Cultural Atlas of Chaco Canyon and the Anasazi* (Boulder, CO: Johnson Books, 1991).
12. O'Bryan, *Navajo Indian Myths,* 61.
13. Matthews, *Navajo Legends,* 86.
14. O'Bryan, *Navajo Indian Myths,* 61–62.
15. Matthews, *Navajo Legends,* 86–87.
16. Lulu [Louisa] Wetherill, Wade Wetherill, and Byron Cummings, "A Navaho Folk Tale of Pueblo Bonito," *Art and Archaeology* 14, no. 3 (September 1922): 132—136.
17. Leland C. Wyman and Stuart K. Harris, *The Ethnobotany of the Kayenta Navaho* (Albuquerque: University of New Mexico Press, 1951), 50.
18. Lulu [Louisa] Wetherill, Wade Wetherill, and Byron Cummings, "The Story of Blue Feather," in Mary G. Boyer, ed., *Arizona in Literature* (Glendale, CA: Arthur H. Clark, 1934), 524.
19. Ibid., 525.
20. Ration interview, cited in Johnson, *Stories of Traditional Navajo Life*, 318.
21. John Holiday and Robert S. McPherson, *A Navajo Legacy: The Life and Teachings of John Holiday* (Norman: University of Oklahoma Press, 2005), 366–367.
22. Isabel Lee interview with author, February 13, 1991.
23. "Navajos Say a Big 'No' to Gaming," *Indian Trader* [Gallup, NM], December 22, 1994, 22.
24. "Navajo Is Poorest of Major Indian Tribes," *Indian Trader*, December 16, 1994, 16.
25. Roberta John, "No Gambling on Navajo Myths," *Navajo Times* [Window Rock, AZ], August 14, 1997, 1.
26. Ibid.
27. Ibid.
28. Ibid.
29. Peter Iverson, *Diné: A History of the Navajos* (Albuquerque: University of New Mexico Press, 2002), 281–282.
30. Bill Donovan, "Betting on Casinos, Tribe Going Full-Bore on Gaming Development," *Navajo Times*, March 4, 2010, A-1.
31. Ibid., A-3; Bill Donovan, "A 1st Good Year for Fire Rock," *Navajo Times*, November 5, 2009, A-1.
32. See McPherson, *Sacred Land, Sacred View*, 87–94.
33. Berard Haile, *Upward Moving and Emergence Way: The Gishin Biyé Version* (Lincoln: University of Nebraska Press, 1981), 217.

34. Rose Atene interview with Chris Atene, February 21, 1983.
35. Irene Silentman, "Canyon de Chelly, a Navajo View," *Exploration* (1986): 52–53.
36. Ada Black and Harvey Black interview with Bertha Parrish, June 18, 1987, San Juan County Historical Society, Blanding, UT.
37. Daniel Shirley interview with author, June 24, 1987.
38. Fred Yazzie interview with author, November 5, 1987.
39. Fred Yazzie interview with author, August 6, 1991.
40. Ada Black interview with author, October 11, 1991.
41. Cecil Parrish interview with author, October 10, 1991.
42. Gretchen Chapin, "A Navajo Myth from Chaco Canyon," *New Mexico Anthropologist* 4, no. 4 (October–December 1940): 65.
43. Susie Yazzie interviews with author, August 6, 1991, and November 10, 2000.
44. For a recent study that looks at linguistic relations between northern and southern Athabaskan speakers, see Edward J. Vajda, "Dene-Yeniseic in Past and Future Perspective," http://www.adn.com/2010/07/05/1354714/new-language-research-supports.html.
45. Jim Dandy interview with author, September 26, 2007.
46. Holiday and McPherson, *Navajo Legacy*, 288.
47. Francis T. Nez Sr. and Kathleen Manolescu, "Fire: The Heart of Life," *Leading the Way* 2, no. 10 (October 2004): 17.
48. Ada Black interview with author.
49. Velta Luther interview with author, April 8, 1992.
50. Dandy interview with author.
51. Luther interview with author.
52. Kayo Holiday interview with author, October 11, 1991.
53. Charlotte J. Frisbie and David P. McAllester, eds., *Navajo Blessingway Singer: The Autobiography of Frank Mitchell, 1881–1967* (Tucson: University of Arizona Press, 1978), 311.
54. Buck Navajo interview with author, December 16, 1991.
55. Sally Manygoats interview with author, April 8, 1992.
56. Susie Yazzie interview with author, August 6, 1991; Floyd Laughter interview with author, April 9, 1992.
57. Ada Black interview with author; Buck Navajo interview with author; Ada Benally interview with author, February 6, 1991; John Knot Begay interview with author, May 7, 1991.
58. Fred Yazzie interview with author, August 6, 1991.
59. Ibid.
60. Susie Yazzie interview with author, August 6, 1991.
61. Ibid.
62. Stella Cly interview with author, August 7, 1991.
63. Dandy interview with author.
64. Ibid.
65. Ada Black interview with author.
66. Charlie Blueyes and Mary Blueyes interview with author, n.d., 1992.
67. Dandy interview with author.
68. See Karl Luckert, *A Navajo Bringing-Home Ceremony: The Claus Chee Sonny Version of Deerway Ajilee* (Flagstaff: Museum of Northern Arizona Press, 1978).

69. Both deer tobacco and mountain tobacco can have a calming effect on an individual: "When you face hardship in life, you can pick up tobacco to renew your thinking. This applies to such conditions as lost mental capacities, losing the will to live, mourning, and indecisiveness. When things are in this state, your heart and mind have no empty space. Tobacco creates space for good things to enter. It lets air permeate throughout your heart and mind. It helps make the transition to reality as it allows good things to enter your heart and mind"; John E. Salaybe Jr. and Kathleen Manolescu, "Rededicating Family Life: The Tobacco Songs," *Leading the Way* 5, no. 1 (January 2007): 21. Erwyn Curley adds: "The tobacco is a token or key to opening up my heart to the Great Spirit. This smoke helps me contact him . . . The first smoke we blow to Mother Earth. The second smoke we blow to Father Sky, the Great Spirit. The third smoke we blow to the fire, our grandparents and their teachings. The fourth smoke we blow on ourselves"; Curley, "Pride and Strength with Humility," *Leading the Way* 4, no. 11 (November 2006): 4.
70. Dandy interview with author.
71. Isabel Lee interview with author, February 13, 1991; Ada Benally interview with author; Fred Yazzie interview with author, August 6, 1991; Parrish interview with author; Navajo interview with author.
72. Kayo Holiday interview with author.
73. Susie Yazzie interview with author, November 10, 2000; Fred Yazzie interview with author, August 6, 1991.
74. Holiday and McPherson, *Navajo Legacy*, 287.
75. Frisbie and McAllester, *Navajo Blessingway Singer*, 314.
76. Charlie Blueyes and Mary Blueyes interview with author.
77. "As it was said, one day Mother Earth wanted to be the boss. She said 'It's me. I'm it.' The people from above said 'No, it's me. I'm the boss. You're down there, I'm up here. Everything grows from me.' Mother Earth and the Thunder People got mad at one another. Mother Earth said, 'Heck with you. Just because you're a man, you think you're all it. You're not.' The people upstairs then stopped everything. There was no rain, nothing. We know this to be true because of the dry period in history. The Anasazi and some Mexican tribes disappeared. A lot of people died. Mother Earth finally made peace. 'Let's work together'"; Nez and Manolescu, "Fire," 16.
78. Dandy interview with author.
79. Ibid.
80. Sarah Begay cited in Maureen Trudelle Schwarz, *Navajo Lifeways: Contemporary Issues, Ancient Knowledge* (Norman: University of Oklahoma Press, 2001), 70.
81. Ibid., 73.
82. Ibid., 76.
83. Kelsey Begaye cited in ibid., 97–98.
84. Holiday and McPherson, *Navajo Legacy*, 285.
85. Ibid.
86. Ibid., 285–286.
87. Rik Pinxten, Ingrid Van Dooren, and Frank Harvey, *The Anthropology of Space* (Philadelphia: University of Pennsylvania Press, 1983), 19.

88. Rose Mitchell with editor Charlotte J. Frisbie, *Tall Woman: The Life Story of Rose Mitchell, a Navajo Woman, ca. 1874–1977* (Albuquerque: University of New Mexico Press, 2001), 293.

Bibliography

GOVERNMENT DOCUMENTS AND ARCHIVES

J. Lee Correll Collection, Navajo Nation, Window Rock, Arizona.

James McLaughlin Papers. Assumption Abbey Archives, Microfilm #5, on file in the Denver Public Library, Denver, Colorado.

Milton Snow Collection, Navajo Nation Museum, Window Rock, AZ.

Native American Graves Protection and Repatriation Act as amended. Public Law 101-601; 25 U.S.C. 3001 et seq. November 16, 1990. www.nps.gov/history/nagpra/MANDATES/INDEX.HTM.

Pectol Shield Files, Capitol Reef National Park Archives, Capitol Reef, Utah.

Report on Employment of United States Soldiers in Arresting By-a-lil-le and Other Navajo Indians. 60th Cong., 1st sess., May 25, 1908.

US Bureau of Indian Affairs. Letters Received by Office of Indian Affairs, New Mexico Superintendency, 1884–1919, National Archives, Washington, DC.

US Congress, Senate. *Testimony Regarding Trouble on Navajo Reservation.* 60th Cong., 2nd sess., 1909.

INTERVIEWS

Atene, Rose. Interview with Chris Atene, February 21, 1983.

Atkinson, Karenita. Discussion with author, August 24, 1998.

Bailey, Sally Draper. Interview with Aubrey Williams, January 29, 1961. Doris Duke Collection #740, Special Collections, University of Utah Library, Salt Lake City, UT.

Begay, Fernandez. Interview with author, February 2, 1994.

Begay, Florence. Interview with author, April 29, 1988, and January 30, 1991.

Begay, John. Interview with author, May 7, 1991.

Begay, John Joe. Interview with author, September 18, 1990.

Begay, John Knot. Interview with author, May 7, 1991.

Begay, Rose. Interview with Bertha Parrish, June 17, 1987. San Juan County Historical Society, Blanding, UT.

Benally, Ada. Interview with author, February 6, 1991, and February 2, 1994.

Benally, Baxter. Discussion with author, February 9, 1994, and September 24, 2007.

Benally, Dan. Interview with author, February 2, 1994.

Benally, James. Discussion with author, November 19, 2007.

Benally, Slim. Interview with author, July 8, 1988.
Bitsinnie, Gladys. Interview with author, March 26, 1993.
Black, Ada. Interview with author, October 11, 1991, and February 2, 1994.
Black, Ada. Interview with Bertha Parrish, June 18, 1987. San Juan County Historical Society, Blanding, UT.
Black, Ada, and Harvey Black. Interview with Bertha Parrish, June 18, 1987.
Black, Mae. Interview with Janet Wilcox, July 15, 1987. San Juan County Historical Society, Blanding, UT.
Black, Sam. Interview with author, December 18, 1993.
Blueyes, Charlie. Interview with author, June 7, 1988, and August 28, 1988.
Blueyes, Charlie, and Mary Blueyes. Interview with author, n.d., 1992.
Blueyes, Mary. Interview with author, July 25, 1988, March 20, 1992, and February 9, 1994.
Busk, Neal. Interview with author, October 11, 2007.
Butt, Pearl. Interview with Jody Bailey, July 2, 1987. San Juan County Historical Society, Blanding, UT.
Canyon, Betty. Interview with author, September 10, 1991.
Chief, Emma. Interview with Samuel Moon, August 7, 1975. Southeastern Utah Project, Utah State Historical Society and California State University Oral History Program, Fullerton, CA.
Cly, Guy. Interview with author, August 7, 1991.
Cly, Stella. Interview with author, August 7, 1991.
Cly, Ted. Interview with Samuel Moon, September 28, 1973. Southeastern Utah Project, Utah State Historical Society and California State University Oral History Program, Fullerton, CA.
Dandy, Jim. Discussion with author, September 24, 2007, and October 29, 2007.
Dandy, Jim. Interview with author, September 26, 2007, and October 8, 2007.
Francis, Jenny. Interview with author, March 23, 1993.
Frost, Seraphine. Interview with Deniane Gutke, July 6, 1987. San Juan County Historical Society, Blanding, UT.
Grandson, Nellie. Interview with author, December 16, 1993.
Graymountain, Gilmore. Interview with author, April 7, 1992.
Gray Mountain, Jackson. Interview with Gary Shumway, June 14, 1968, Doris Duke #474. Doris Duke Oral History Project, American West Center, University of Utah, Salt Lake City, UT.
Haycock, Bud. Interview with author, October 10, 1991.
Holiday, Joanne Oshley. Interview with author, May 8, 1996.
Holiday, John. Interview with author, September 9, 1991, and April 15, 2005.
Holiday, Kayo. Interview with author, October 11, 1991.
Holiday, Keith. Interview with author, April 9, 1992.
Holiday, Marilyn. Interview with author, April 9, 1992.
Holiday, Marilyn. Discussion with author, June 20, 1993.
Holiday, Marilyn. Discussion with author, September 23, 2007.
Holiday, Shone. Interview with author, September 10, 1991.
Holiday, Shone. Interview with Samuel Moon, July 21, 1975. Southeastern Utah Project, Utah State Historical Society and California State University Oral History Program, Fullerton, CA.

Holiday, Tallis. Interview with author, November 3, 1987, and September 10, 1991.
Howard, Maimie. Interview with author, July 19 and August 2, 1988.
Hunt, Ray. Interview with Janet Wilcox, July 20, 1987. San Juan County Historical Society, Blanding, UT.
Jay, Mary. Interview with author, February 27, 1991.
Jones, S. P. Interview with author, December 20, 1985.
Ketchum, Wanda. Interview with author, September 11, 1993.
Laughter, Floyd. Interview with author, April 9, 1992.
Lee, Isabel. Interview with author, February 13, 1991.
Lee, Sally. Interview with author, February 13, 1991.
Liebler, H. Baxter. Interview with Daniel B. Kelly, June 27, 1972. Southeastern Utah Project, Utah State Historical Society and California State University Oral History Program, Fullerton, CA.
Liebler, Joan. Interview with author, March 4, 1994.
Long, Clayton. Interview with author, January 18, 2008.
Luther, Velta. Interview with author, April 8, 1992.
Lyman, Margie. Interview with Helen Shumway, April 11, 1986. San Juan County Historical Society, Blanding, UT.
Manygoats, Joe. Interview with author, December 16 and December 18, 1991.
Manygoats, Sally. Interview with author, April 8, 1992.
Mose, Don. Interview with author, June 7, 2011.
Musselman, Rusty. Interview with author, July 6, 1987. San Juan County Historical Society, Blanding, UT.
Navajo, Buck. Interview with author, December 16, 1991.
Nez, Martha. Interview with author, August 2 and August 10, 1988.
Norton, Florence. Interview with author, March 6, 1991.
Norton, John. Interview with author, January 16, 1991.
Oliver, Harvey. Interview with author, May 14, 1991.
Oshley, Navajo. Interview with Winston Hurst and Wesley Oshley, January 5, 1978.
Parrish, Cecil. Interview with author, October 10, 1991.
Phillips, Pearl. Interview with Bertha Parrish, June 17, 1987. San Juan County Historical Society, Blanding, UT.
Pickett, Catherine. Interview with author, May 14, 1994.
Redd, Ray. Interview with Jody Bailey, July 16, 1987. San Juan County Historical Society, Blanding, UT.
Sakizzie, Ella. Interview with author, May 14, 1991.
Sampson, Mary Rose, and John P. Sampson. Interview with author, February 9, 1994.
Shirley, Daniel. Interview with author, June 24, 1987.
Shorty, Jessie. Interview with author, February 9, 1994.
Shorty, John. Interview with author, February 2 and 9, 1994.
Silas, Jane Byalily. Interview with author, February 27, 1991.
Tallis, Britt. Interview with author, December 6, 1993.
Tom, George. Interview with author, August 7, 1991.
Walters, Harry. Personal communication with author, January 28, 2012.
Weston, Margaret. Interview with author, February 13, 1991.
White, Ruth. Discussion with author, March 14, 1994.
Whitehorse, Ben. Interview with author, January 30, 1991.

Yazzie, Fred. Interview with author, November 5, 1987, and August 6, 1991.
Yazzie, Suzie. Interview with author, August 6, 1991, and November 10, 2000.

BOOKS AND ARTICLES

Acrey, Bill. *Navajo History: The Land and the People*. Shiprock, NM: Department of Curriculum Materials Development, Central Consolidated School District No. 22, 1988.

Aikens, C. Melvin. *Fremont-Promontory-Plains Relationships: Including a Report of Excavations at the Injun Creek and Bear River Number 1 Sites, Northern Utah.* University of Utah Anthropology Papers 82. Salt Lake City: University of Utah Press, 1966.

Basso, Keith H. *Western Apache Language and Culture: Essays in Linguistic Anthropology*. Tucson: University of Arizona Press, 1990.

Bahr, Howard M., ed. *The Navajo as Seen by the Franciscans, 1898–1921: A Sourcebook*. Lanham, MD: The Scarecrow Press, 2004.

Bailey, Garrick, and Roberta Glenn Bailey. *A History of the Navajos: The Reservation Years*. Santa Fe, NM: School of American Research Press, 1986.

Baker, Shane A. "In Search of Relics: The History of the Pectol-Lee Collection from Wayne County." In Marti L. Allen and Mauri L. Nelson, eds., *Relics Revisited: New Perspectives on an Early Twentieth-Century Collection*, 21–54. Provo, UT: Museum of Peoples and Cultures, 2002.

Beckwith, Frank. "The High Priest's Vestments." *Improvement Era,* September 1927, 1029–37.

Benally, Malcolm D. *Bitter Water: Diné Histories of the Navajo-Hopi Land Dispute*. Tucson: University of Arizona Press, 2011.

Berger, Rainer, and W. F. Libby. "UCLA Radiocarbon Dates VII." *Radiocarbon* 10 (1968): 149–60.

Brady, Margaret K. *Some Kind of Power: Navajo Children's Skinwalker Narratives*. Salt Lake City: University of Utah Press, 1984.

Bulow, Ernest L. *Navajo Taboos*. Gallup, NM: Southwesterner Books, 1982.

Chapin, Gretchen. "A Navajo Myth from Chaco Canyon." *New Mexico Anthropologist* 4, no. 4 (October–December 1940): 63–6.

Chee, Tom. "Navajo Language: The Heart and Soul of Navajo Culture." *Leading the Way* 9, no. 2 (February 2011): 2–3.

Christensen, Elaine. *"And I Went Home Rejoicing": The Background, Life, and Posterity of Edward Southwick III.* Provo, UT: J. Grant Stephenson, 1971.

Clark, H. Jackson. *The Owl in Monument Canyon.* Salt Lake City: University of Utah Press, 1993.

Clark, LaVerne Harrell. *They Sang for Horses: The Impact of the Horse on Navajo and Apache Folklore*. Tucson: University of Arizona Press, 1966.

Clark, Mary Ann. "The Hair Tie and the Kinaalda." *Leading the Way* 7, no. 4 (April 2009): 1, 18–20.

Correll, J. Lee. *Bai-a-lil-le: Medicine Man or Witch?* Biographical Series 3. Window Rock, AZ: Navajo Historical Publications, 1970.

Crosby, Alfred W. *America's Forgotten Pandemic: The Influenza of 1918*. New York: Cambridge University Press, 1989.

Curley, Erwyn. "Pride and Strength with Humility." *Leading the Way* 4, no. 11 (November 2006): 2–4.

Curry, Andrew. "Tribal Challenges: How the Navajo Nation Is Changing the Face of American Archaeology." *Archaeology* 58, no. 5 (September/October 2005): 57–67.

Dyk, Walter. *A Navaho Autobiography*. New York: Viking Fund Publication in Anthropology, 1947.

Dyk, Walter. *Son of Old Man Hat*. Lincoln: University of Nebraska Press, 1938.

Dyk, Walter, and Ruth Dyk. *Left Handed: A Navajo Autobiography*. New York: Columbia University Press, 1980.

Eliade, Mircea. *The Sacred and the Profane: The Nature of Religion*. New York: Harcourt, Brace and World, 1957.

Evans, Will. *Along Navajo Trails: Recollections of a Trader*. Logan: Utah State University Press, 2005.

Farella, John R. *The Main Stalk: A Synthesis of Navajo Philosophy*. Tucson: University of Arizona Press, 1984.

Faunce, Hilda. *Desert Wife*. Lincoln: University of Nebraska Press, 1928.

Franciscan Fathers. *An Ethnologic Dictionary of the Navajo Language*. Saint Michaels, AZ: Saint Michaels Press, 1910.

Frazier, Kendrick. *People of Chaco: A Canyon and Its Culture*. New York: W. W. Norton, 1986.

Frisbie, Charlotte J., and David P. McAllester, eds. *Navajo Blessingway Singer: The Autobiography of Frank Mitchell, 1881–1967*. Tucson: University of Arizona Press, 1978.

Frye, Bradford J. *From Barrier to Crossroads: An Administrative History of Capitol Reef National Park, Utah*. vol. 1. Denver: National Park Service, 1998.

Gabriel, Kathryn, ed. *Marietta Wetherill: Life with the Navajos in Chaco Canyon*. Albuquerque: University of New Mexico Press, 1992.

Gabriel, Kathryn. *Roads to Center Place: A Cultural Atlas of Chaco Canyon and the Anasazi*. Boulder, CO: Johnson Books, 1991.

Gillmor, Frances, and Louisa Wade Wetherill. *Traders to the Navahos*. Albuquerque: University of New Mexico Press, 1953.

Givens, Douglas R. *An Analysis of Navajo Temporality*. Lanham, MD: University Press of America, 1979.

Hadley, Linda. *Hózhǫǫjí Hane' (Blessingway)*. Rough Rock, AZ: Rough Rock Demonstration School, 1986.

Haile, Berard. "Soul Concepts of the Navaho." In *Annali Lateranensi* 7: 59–94. Vatican City: Vatican Polyglot Press, 1943.

Haile, Berard. *Starlore among the Navaho*. Santa Fe, NM: Museum of Navajo Ceremonial Art, 1947.

Haile, Berard. *Upward Moving and Emergence Way: The Gishin Biye' Version*. Lincoln: University of Nebraska Press, 1981.

Hausman, Gerald. *The Gift of the Gila Monster: Navajo Ceremonial Tales*. New York: Touchstone Books, 1993.

Hill, W. W. *Navaho Agricultural and Hunting Methods*. New Haven, CT: Yale University Press, 1938.

Hill, W. W. *Navaho Warfare*. Yale University Publications in Anthropology 5. New Haven, CT: Yale University Press, 1936.

Holiday, John, and Robert S. McPherson. *A Navajo Legacy: The Life and Teachings of John Holiday*. Norman: University of Oklahoma Press, 2005.

Hosteen, Ryan. "Giving the Unknown a Name." *Leading the Way* 6, nos. 4–5 (April–May 2008): 14–16, 21–23.

Iverson, Peter. *Diné: A History of the Navajos*. Albuquerque: University of New Mexico Press, 2002.

Johnson, Broderick H., ed. *Stories of Traditional Navajo Life and Culture by Twenty-two Navajo Men and Women*. Tsaile, AZ: Navajo Community College Press, 1977.

Judd, Neil. *The Material Culture of Pueblo Bonito*. Smithsonian Miscellaneous Collection 124. Washington, DC: Smithsonian Institution Press, 1954.

Kawano, Kenji. *Warriors: Navajo Code Talkers*. Flagstaff, AZ: Northland, 1990.

Kee, Ted. "New Navajo Words." *Leading the Way* 2, no. 8 (August 2008): 12.

Kluckhohn, Clyde. *Navaho Witchcraft*. Boston: Beacon, 1944.

Kluckhohn, Clyde, and Dorothea Leighton. *The Navaho*. Cambridge, MA: Harvard University Press, 1946.

Kluckhohn, Clyde., W. W. Hill, and Lucy Wales Kluckhohn. *Navaho Material Culture*. Cambridge, MA: Harvard University Press, 1971.

Kreutzer, Lee Ann. "The Pectol/Lee Collection, Capitol Reef National Park, Utah." *Utah Archaeology* 7, no. 1 (1994): 104–16.

Kreutzer, Lee Ann. "Seeing Is Believing and Hearing Is Believing: Thoughts on Oral Tradition and the Pectol Shields." *Utah Historical Quarterly* 76, no. 4 (Fall 2008): 377–84.

Leupp, Francis E. "'Law or No Law' in Indian Administration." *The Outlook* (January 30, 1909): 261–3.

Levy, Jerrold E. *In the Beginning: The Navajo Genesis*. Los Angeles: University of California Press, 1998.

Liebler, H. Baxter. *Boil My Heart for Me*. Salt Lake City: University of Utah Press, 1994.

Liebler, H. Baxter. "Christian Concepts and Navaho Words." *Utah Humanities Review* 2, no. 2 (April 1948): 169–75.

Liebler, H. Baxter. *Moccasin Tracks*. New York: Blackshaw, 1939.

Liebler, H. Baxter. "The Social and Cultural Patterns of the Navajo Indian." *Utah Historical Quarterly* 30, no. 4 (Fall 1962): 298–325.

Locke, Raymond F. *The Book of the Navajo*. Los Angeles: Mankind Press, 1976.

Luckert, Karl. *A Navajo Bringing-Home Ceremony: The Claus Chee Sonny Version of Deerway Ajilee*. Flagstaff: Museum of Northern Arizona Press, 1978.

Lyons, Oren, with Bill Moyer. *The Faithkeeper.* Cooper Station, NY: Mystic Fire Video, 1991.

Madsen, David B. *Exploring the Fremont*. Salt Lake City: University of Utah Press, 1989.

Malouf, Carling. "Thoughts on Utah Archaeology." *American Antiquity* 9, no. 3 (January 1944): 319–28. http://dx.doi.org/10.2307/275789.

Matthews, Washington. *Navaho Legends*. Salt Lake City: University of Utah Press, 1994 [1897].

Matthews, Washington. "A Part of the Navajos' Mythology." *American Antiquarian* 5: 207–24. Chicago, 1883. Special Collections, Harold B. Lee Library, Brigham Young University, Provo, UT.

McGavin, E. Cecil. *"Mormonism" and Masonry*. Salt Lake City: Stevens & Wallis, 1947.

McNeil, William H. *Plagues and People*. Garden City, NY: Doubleday Press, 1976.

McNeley, James K. *Holy Wind in Navajo Philosophy*. Tucson: University of Arizona Press, 1981.

McNitt, Frank. *The Indian Traders*. Norman: University of Oklahoma Press, 1962.

McPherson, Robert S. *The Journey of Navajo Oshley: An Autobiography and Life History*. Logan: Utah State University Press, 2000.

McPherson, Robert S. *Navajo Land, Navajo Culture: The Utah Experience in the Twentieth Century*. Norman: University of Oklahoma Press, 2001.

McPherson, Robert S. *Sacred Land, Sacred View: Navajo Perception of the Four Corners Region*. Charles Redd Center for Western Studies Monograph 19. Provo: Brigham Young University Press, 1992.

McPherson, Robert S. "Navajos, Mormons, and Henry L. Mitchell." *Utah Historical Quarterly* 55, no. 1 (Winter 1987): 50–65.

McPherson, Robert S. "Howard R. Antes and the Navajo Faith Mission: Evangelist of Southeastern Utah." *Utah Historical Quarterly* 65, no. 1 (Winter 1997): 4–24.

Mitchell, Charlie. "A Navaho's Historical Reminiscences." In *Navajo Texts*, ed. Edward Sapir, 336–97. Iowa City: University of Iowa Press, 1942.

Mitchell, Rose, with Charlotte J. Frisbie, ed. *Tall Woman: The Life Story of Rose Mitchell, a Navajo Woman, ca. 1874–1977*. Albuquerque: University of New Mexico Press, 2001.

Moon, Samuel. *Tall Sheep: Harry Goulding, Monument Valley Trader*. Norman: University of Oklahoma Press, 1992.

Morgan, William. *Human Wolves among the Navajo*. Yale University Publications in Anthropology 11. New Haven, CT: Yale University Press, 1936.

Morgan, William. "Navaho Treatment of Sickness: Diagnosticians." *American Anthropologist* 33, no. 3 (Summer 1931): 390–402. http://dx.doi.org/10.1525/aa.1931.33.3.02a00050.

Morss, Noel. *The Ancient Culture of the Fremont River in Utah: Report on the Explorations under the Claflin-Emerson Fund, 1928–1929*. Cambridge, MA: Peabody Museum of American Archaeology and Ethnology, 1931.

Mose, Don. *Honeeshgish: A Navajo Legend*. Blanding, UT: San Juan School District Media Center, 2006.

Navajo, Buck. "Navajo Basket Teachings." *Leading the Way* 4, no. 9 (September 2006): 4–5.

Newcomb, Franc Johnson. *Hosteen Klah: Navaho Medicine Man and Sand Painter*. Norman: University of Oklahoma Press, 1964.

Newcomb, Franc Johnson. *Navaho Folk Tales*. Albuquerque: University of New Mexico Press, 1967.

Newcomb, Franc Johnson. *Navaho Neighbors*. Norman: University of Oklahoma Press, 1966.

Newcomb, Franc Johnson, Stanley Fishler, and Mary C. Wheelwright. *A Study of Navajo Symbolism*. Papers of the Peabody Museum 32, no. 3. Cambridge, MA: Harvard University Press, 1956.

Nez, Francis T., Sr., and Kathleen Manolescu. "Fire: The Heart of Life." *Leading the Way* 2, no. 10 (October 2004): 1, 16–17.

O'Bryan, Aileen. *The Diné: Origin Myths of the Navaho Indians*. Bureau of American Ethnology Bulletin 163. Washington, DC: Smithsonian Institution, 1956. Reprinted as *Navaho Indian Myths* (New York: Dover, 1956).

Parman, Donald L. "The 'Big Stick' in Indian Affairs: The Bai-a-lil-le Incident in 1909." *Arizona and the West* 20 (Fall 1978): 343–60.

Paul, Doris A. *The Navajo Code Talkers*. Bryn Mawr, PA: Dorrance, 1973.

Persico, Joseph E. "The Great Swine Flu Epidemic of 1918." *American Heritage* 27 (June 1976): 28–31, 80–86.

Pinxten, Rik, Ingrid Van Dooren, and Frank Harvey. *The Anthropology of Space*. Philadelphia: University of Pennsylvania Press, 1983.

Reagan, Albert B. "The Influenza and the Navajo." *Proceedings of the Indiana Academy of Science* 29, 243–47. Fort Wayne, IN: Fort Wayne Printing Company, 1921.

Red House Clansman. "The One with Magic Power." In *Navajo Historical Selections,* ed. Robert W. Young and William Morgan. Navajo Historical Series #3. Lawrence, KS: Bureau of Indian Affairs, 1954.

Reichard, Gladys A. *Navaho Religion: A Study of Symbolism*. Princeton, NJ: Princeton University Press, 1950.

Reichard, Gladys A. *Prayer: The Compulsive Word*. American Ethnological Society Monograph 7. Seattle: University of Washington Press, 1944.

Richardson, Gladwell. *Navajo Trader*. Tucson: University of Arizona Press, 1986.

Roberts, Willow. *Stokes Carson: Twentieth Century Trading on the Navajo Reservation*. Albuquerque: University of New Mexico Press, 1987.

Russell, Scott C. "The Navajo and the 1918 Pandemic." In C. F. Merlos and R. J. Miller, eds., *Health and Disease in the Prehistoric Southwest,* 380–90. Tempe: Arizona State University Press, 1985.

Saint-Exupéry, Antoine de. *Wind, Sand, and Stars*. New York: Harcourt, Brace, 1940.

Salaybe, John E., Jr. "Keeping Navajo Alive." *Leading the Way* 8, no. 2 (February 2010): 20.

Salaybe, John E., Jr., and Kathleen Manolescu. "The Beginning of Marriage and Family: Corn Story Teachings." *Leading the Way* 6, no. 11 (November 2008): 4–5.

Salaybe, John E., Jr., and Kathleen Manolescu. "Being a Husband." *Leading the Way* 4, no. 6 (June 2006): 2–4.

Salaybe, John E., Jr., and Kathleen Manolescu. "The Creation of an Individual." *Leading the Way* 6, no. 4 (April 2008): 3.

Salaybe, John E., Jr., and Kathleen Manolescu. "Rededicating Family Life: The Tobacco Songs." *Leading the Way* 5, no. 1 (January 2007): 19–21.

Salaybe, John E., Jr., and Kathleen Manolescu. "Spring: A Time of Reawakening." *Leading the Way* 9, no. 4 (April 2011): 2–5.

Schwarz, Maureen Trudelle. *Molded in the Image of Changing Woman: Navajo Views on the Human Body and Personhood*. Tucson: University of Arizona Press, 1997.

Schwarz, Maureen Trudelle. *Navajo Lifeways: Contemporary Issues, Ancient Knowledge*. Norman: University of Oklahoma Press, 2001.

Silentman, Irene. "Canyon de Chelly, A Navajo View." *Exploration* (1986): 52–53.

Simpson, Georgiana Kennedy. *Navajo Ceremonial Baskets: Sacred Symbols, Sacred Space*. Summertown, TN: Native Voices, 2003.

Stegner, Wallace. *Mormon Country*. New York: Hawthorn Books, 1942.

Talmadge, Marian Huxall, and Iris Pavey Gilmore. "Padre of the San Juan." *Desert Magazine* 11, no. 10 (August 1948): 5–9.

Tierney, Gail D. "Botany and Witchcraft." *El Palacio* 80, no. 2 (Summer 1974): 44–50. Medline:11615066.

Toledo, Herbert. "Remembering My Dad: Hastiin Ts'ósí." *Leading the Way* 6, no. 3 (March 2008): 20–22.

Turk, Toni. *Rooted in San Juan: A Genealogical Study of Burials in San Juan County, Utah, 1879–1995*. Salt Lake City: Publishers Press, 1995.

Vajda, Edward J. "Dene-Yeniseic in Past and Future Perspective." http://www.adn.com/2010/07/05/1354714/new-language-research-supports.html.

Van Valkenburgh, Richard. "Wolf Men of the Navajo." *Desert Magazine* 11, no. 3 (January 1948): 4–8.

Vogel, Dan. *Indian Origins and the Book of Mormon: Religious Solutions from Columbus to Joseph Smith*. Salt Lake City, UT: Signature Books, 1986.

Walking Thunder. *Walking Thunder: Diné Medicine Woman*. Ed. Bradford Keeney. Philadelphia: Ringing Rocks, 2001.

Wetherill, Lulu [Louisa], Wade Wetherill, and Byron Cummings. "A Navaho Folk Tale of Pueblo Bonito." *Art and Archaeology* 14, no. 3 (September 1922): 132–36.

Wetherill, Lulu [Louisa], Wade Wetherill, and Byron Cummings. "The Story of Blue Feather." In Mary G. Boyer, ed., *Arizona in Literature*, 522–25. Glendale, CA: Arthur H. Clark, 1934.

Wheelwright, Mary C. *The Myth and Prayers of the Great Star Chant and the Myth of the Coyote Chant*. Santa Fe, NM: Museum of Navajo Ceremonial Art, 1956.

Wheelwright, Mary C. *Myth of Natóhe Bakáji Hatrál*. Santa Fe, NM: Museum of Navajo Ceremonial Art, 1958.

Wheelwright, Mary C. *Myth of Willa-Chee-Ji Degínnh-Keygo Hatrál*. Santa Fe, NM: Museum of Navajo Ceremonial Art, 1958.

Wheelwright, Mary C., ed. *Navajo Creation Myth: The Story of the Emergence*, by Hasteen Klah. Santa Fe, NM: Museum of Navajo Ceremonial Art, 1942.

Wilson, Dave. "Family Fire Poker Teachings." *Leading the Way* 9, no. 7 (July 2011): 10–2.

Witherspoon, Gary. *Language and Art in the Navajo Universe*. Ann Arbor: University of Michigan Press, 1977.

Wormington, H. M. *A Reappraisal of the Fremont Culture*. Denver: Denver Museum of Natural History, 1955.

Wyman, Leland C. *The Mountainway of the Navajo*. Tucson: University of Arizona Press, 1975.

Wyman, Leland C. "Navaho Diagnosticians." *American Anthropologist* 38, no. 2 (April–June 1936): 236–46. http://dx.doi.org/10.1525/aa.1936.38.2.02a00050.

Wyman, Leland C. "Origin Legends of Navaho Divinatory Rites." *Journal of American Folklore* 49, no. 191–92 (January–June 1936): 134–42. http://dx.doi.org/10.2307/535487.

Wyman, Leland C., and Stuart K. Harris. *The Ethnobotany of the Kayenta Navaho*. Albuquerque: University of New Mexico Press, 1951.

Yanito, Curtis. "It's All about Language." *Leading the Way* 8, no. 1 (January 2010): 1, 12–15.

Yellowhair, Maggie. "Why Weavers Leave an Opening." *Leading the Way* 6, no. 5 (May 2008): 20–1.

Young, Robert W., and William Morgan, Sr. *The Navajo Language: A Grammar and Colloquial Dictionary*. 4th ed. Albuquerque: University of New Mexico Press, 1987.

Zolbrod, Paul G. *Diné bahane': The Navajo Creation Story*. Albuquerque: University of New Mexico Press, 1984.

MANUSCRIPTS

Griffin-Pierce, Trudy. "Power through Order: Ethnoastronomy in Navajo Sandpaintings of the Heavens." PhD dissertation, University of Arizona, Tucson, 1987.

Jones, Kumen. "The Writings of Kumen Jones." Manuscript. Special Collections, Harold B. Lee Library, Brigham Young University, Provo, UT.

Kascoli, Rhoda. "Navajo February Snows." Unpublished paper, n.d. Used with permission, in possession of author.

Lyman, Albert R. "History of San Juan County, 1879–1917." Manuscript, Special Collections, Harold B. Lee Library, Brigham Young University, Provo, UT.

Pectol, Ephraim. "The Shields." Manuscript. In possession of family member Neal Busk.

Phillips, Carla. Paper, April 29, 2003. Used with permission, in possession of author.

Toledo, Karen. Paper on metaphors, January 11, 2008. Used with permission, in possession of author.

NEWSPAPERS

Deseret News [Salt Lake City], 2005

Farmington [NM] *Enterprise*, 1907

Farmington [NM] *Times,* 1916

Grand Valley Times [Moab, UT], 1918–1919

Indian Trader [Gallup, NM], 1994

Mancos [CO] *Times Tribune*, 1918–1919

Navajo Times [Window Rock, AZ], 1997–1998, 2009–2010

Richfield [UT] *Reaper,* 1926–1927

San Juan [UT] *Record,* 1972, 2007

Index

Page numbers in italics indicate illustrations.